FAMILY TREE OF SETH GOVINDRAM SEKSARIA

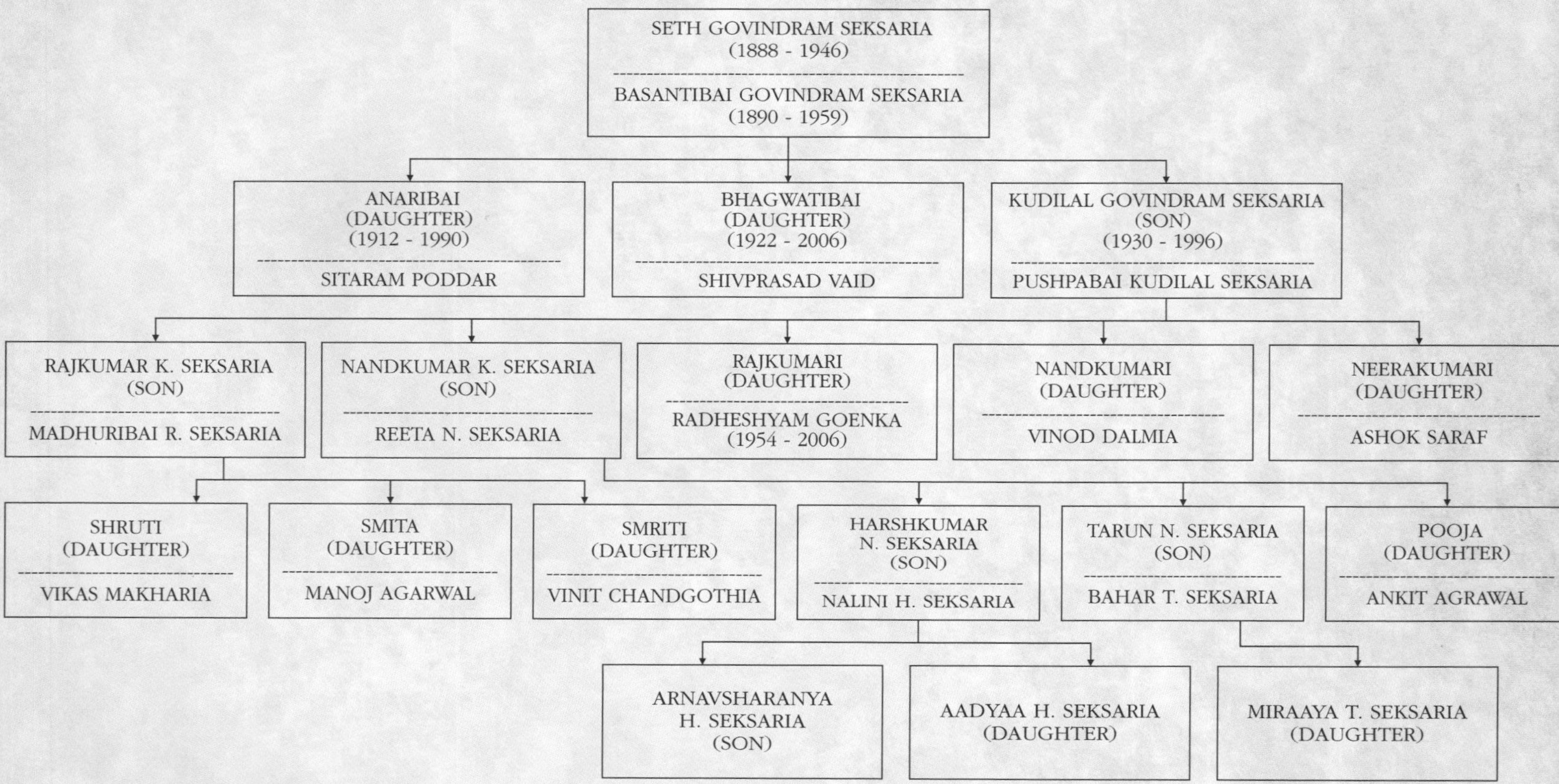

GOVINDRAM SEKSARIA

GOVINDRAM SEKSARIA

THE UNTOLD SAGA OF AN EMPIRE-BUILDER

MINHAZ MERCHANT

AMARYLLIS

AMARYLLIS
An imprint of Manjul Publishing House Pvt. Ltd.
• 7/32, Ansari Road, Daryaganj, New Delhi 110 002
Website: www.manjulindia.com
Registered Office:
• 10, Nishat Colony, Bhopal 462 003 – India

ISBN 978-93-88241-88-5

This edition first published in 2019

Printed and bound in India by Thomson Press (India) Ltd.

Contents

Author's Note

Not many Indians receive obituaries in *The New York Times*. Govindram Seksaria did. He kept a low profile throughout his life. But that didn't prevent international newspapers from paying fulsome tribute to him when he passed away on 22nd May, 1946, just fifteen months before India won Independence.

The New York Times wrote on 23rd May, 1946: 'Govindram Gordhandas Seksaria, a leading cotton market figure, industrialist, philanthropist and member of the New York Cotton Exchange, died today of a heart attack a few minutes after he had given a considerable sum to charity. He was associated with all the important Chambers of Commerce in India. Mr. Seksaria had been a member of the New York Cotton Exchange since 1934.'

Seksaria was a remarkable individual for several reasons. First, he was unlettered and yet dealt with India's most distinguished men on equal terms. Second, he mastered the art and science of risk management. His trading philosophy was strikingly similar to what hedge fund managers routinely practice today. In that sense he was decades ahead of his time. Third, he displayed extraordinary generosity and humility throughout his life to family, business associates, employees and simply to those in need.

He was a quiet but firm supporter of the freedom struggle led by Mahatma Gandhi. He donated copious sums to the cause as well as engaged in a wide range of philanthropy, especially, education and healthcare.

Seksaria, like Dhirubhai Ambani (who was 13 years old when Seksaria died in 1946), was one of a kind. He broke the mould, took risks, integrated his operations and was fearless.

He never travelled abroad, rarely socialised and led a spartan life. Beneath the calm visage though lay a sharp mind. He could memorise his trades and constantly surprised colleagues with his insight into global markets.

He was a pioneer too in girls' education, demonstrating a modernity that again was decades ahead of the prevailing customs in both the Marwari community and the country as a whole.

When Seksaria died in 1946, his only son Kudilal was just 16 years old. He never had a chance to spend much time with his father. Kudilal Seksaria himself passed away in 1996 and obviously his personal recollections about his father were related to me by his son Nandkumar. What emerges is a man of wisdom and kindness. The night before he passed away, Seksaria called his son to his bedside. He told Kudilal that his wealth should be divided equally among his brothers, Kudilal's uncles; his two daughters, Kudilal's sisters, should be taken good care of and the family trusts should be well looked after.

Above all, what distinguished the remarkable life and work of one of the wealthiest but least known businessmen of pre-Independent India was his modesty. Seksaria gave no interviews, spoke rarely in public and donated to charities without asking for recognition or honours.

Seksaria was a peer of some of India's greatest pre-Independence business families, ranging from the Bajajs to the Birlas. National leaders like Mahatma Gandhi, Pandit Jawaharlal

Nehru and Sardar Vallabhbhai Patel visited him. Mahatma Gandhi also acknowledged his generous contributions to the freedom movement.

In every sense of the word, Govindram Seksaria's life was truly extraordinary. It needs to be told.

Acknowledgements

In a work of this kind, team effort is essential. The book would not have been possible without the extraordinary determination and vision of Nandkumar Seksaria. Very little information was available on his grandfather Govindram Seksaria. Over the years, the Seksaria family had built an archive of written material on Govindramji and interviews with those who knew him or had heard interesting anecdotes and stories about him.

Since Govindramji died in 1946 and gave no published interviews during his lifetime, the nuggets of archival information on him added up to only a sketchy account of his life and work. But it soon became obvious that even in those nuggets lay a hidden wealth of stories. Articles in *The New York Times* and *The Wall Street Journal* spoke of him with a mixture of awe and bewilderment: here was a man who knew no English, nor even Hindi, but traded globally, amassed an enormous fortune, was respected by his peers like Jamnalal Bajaj and donated generously to the freedom movement led by Mahatma Gandhi.

Govindramji lived and worked in British-occupied India. The era was seminal: two World Wars, the Great Depression and India's struggle for independence. When I began working on the project, the information available on Govindramji was nebulous. We received early help from Nirati Agarwal and Aditi Mehta who put together literally thousands of pages of archival material of the period in which Seksaria lived before Independence. Sadly, just a few kernels on Govindramji emerged.

Mirra Savara, who had earlier done preliminary work on the project, led the initial research effort. The indefatigable Kaizeen Jehangir and the meticulous Freyan Patel delved deeper into the research material.

In London, Professor Allaine Cerwonka, dean of Social Sciences at the University of East London and her colleague, Professor Anna Loutfi, analysed Govindramji's work, business strategy and legacy with great acuity.

Without this team of extraordinary researchers, analysts and academics, this book would not have been written.

Several others provided valuable information. I am grateful to Professor Banwari (Ben) Kedia of the University of Memphis who helped locate articles on Govindramji in *The New York Times*; the late Mangtulal Seksaria for his keen inputs; commodities magnate Suresh Kotak, whose counsel helped me understand Govindramji's unique modus operandi; Dr. Sharad Kumar, dean, DSIMS, Mumbai, who helped translate relevant portions of Hindi transcripts into English; Suvigya Sharma for his fine cover portrait of Govindramji and Aditya Malkani of Think Education. A special thanks too to the Royal Udaipur archives, the Jamnalal Bajaj archives and the Udaipur archives for sharing historically important information as well as to those several individuals with whom I conducted interviews during the course of researching and writing this book.

Govindramji's great-grandson Harsh Seksaria was the pivot around whom the project revolved. He was methodical and industrious and kept matters on an even keel. To him I owe a great debt of gratitude for reading the manuscript several times, making valuable suggestions and adding insights that have made the book what it is.

I'd like to especially thank Govindramji's grandson Nandkumar Seksaria for his wise insights and for being generous with his time. He encouraged the research team and myself to probe ever deeper into what made Govindramji the man he was: trader, speculator, industrialist and above all, a kind and generous soul.

I acknowledge with gratitude the help of my colleague Vatsala de Sousa who provided invaluable context and character to the manuscript. Finally, without the diligence of Rukshana Kumar this book would not have been completed.

I'm grateful to my wife Kahini for her constant encouragement during the writing of the book and to my sister Perveez for vetting the manuscript and offering suggestions and advice.

A final thanks to Manoj Kulkarni, the editor of Amaryllis Publishing House and Vikas Rakheja, its managing director, for their impeccable professionalism during the production of this book.

This has been one of the most complex projects I've undertaken. It has also been one of the most intellectually stimulating because of the outstanding team of people I worked with including both the research team and the Seksaria family. It has been a privilege to be associated with them.

Chapter One

From the Cradle of Rajputana

In the cool Paris autumn of October 1888, the Dutch post-impressionist master, Vincent Van Gogh, paced up and down in his brother Theo's apartment, engrossed in deep thought. He had gifted his iconic series of paintings, *Two Sunflowers,* to Paul Gauguin, the celebrated French artist.

Several thousand miles away in the arid plains of north-west India, the dry late-October air heralded an early winter. In an old haveli built by Baldeodas Seksaria in the village of Nawalgarh, a child was born to his son Gordhandas and wife Manibai on 19th October, 1888. His name: Govindram.

More than a century later another of Van Gogh's works, *L'Allée des Alyscamps,* painted in 1888, would be sold at an auction in New York by Sotheby's for $66.30 million (Rs. 455 crore). Govindram Seksaria would meanwhile go on to become one of India's wealthiest businessmen with trading operations stretching in an arc from New York to Liverpool to Bombay. This is his untold story.

Nawalgarh lies in the heart of Jhunjhunu. Part of the former princely state of Jaipur in Rajputana, Jhunjhunu would produce some of India's most remarkable business leaders. The patronage of Thakur Nawal Singh transformed this nondescript region, populated by a few thousand families, into a centre of trade and commerce. 'Traditional industries in the region were tie-and-dye, lac bangle-making and artistic shoe-making. The town symbolises the intersection of the timeless with time; it is the confluence of tradition and modernity.'[1]

Govindram lived in a joint family with his father's brothers, their wives and children. Traditionally, joint families held joint businesses. Govindram's father Gordhandas and his brothers Ramchandra, Gangadhar and Onkarmal were small cloth merchants. They owned a shop for which they had to purchase materials from Sikar that was located 15 miles from where they lived. Railways had not yet been built. The only means of travel was on camel back or bullock carts, making it a difficult and arduous journey. Once the elders of the family passed away, it was the young cousins who took over the small business.[2]

Staying in a joint family inculcated strong core values in Govindram, values that later in life ensured both his near and distant family would always be well taken care of. Savitribai Nathani, Govindram's niece and younger brother Ramnath's daughter, reminisces: 'I have heard that *Tauji's* mother on her deathbed blessed him and said that you will become a successful man one day but promise me you will take care of your siblings. Govindramji had three brothers, Bholaramji, Ramnathji and Makhanlalji and three sisters, Jimabai, Banarsibai and Majibai. Of the three brothers, Ramnathji expired before Govindramji who was the eldest among the seven children. Our family had a small cloth business and a relatively modest income.'

The future held hope. But no one in the family could have imagined quite the extraordinary future that awaited Govindram.

---

[1]*History of Nawalgarh.*

[2]Ibid.

Young Govindram spent his formative years in the cloistered environment of dusty Nawalgarh. At the turn of the century, India was immersed in poverty. Literacy was barely 10 per cent. Indian business was restricted to a few large companies favoured by the British and small Indian firms that traded with one another. The more enterprising businessmen among them travelled to Africa and Aden to find work or make tidy fortunes.

As the new century dawned, Govindram Seksaria, not yet 12, was—in the time-honoured tradition of Marwaris—already alert to the business environment around him. What did he see when he looked around him? In 1900, the world must have appeared intimidating to a 12 year-old boy from a village in Rajputana, as Rajasthan was then known. Meanwhile Jawaharlal Nehru, born a year after Govindram, was an 11 year-old boy being groomed by his wealthy lawyer-father Motilal for a career at the bar following a 'proper' English education at Harrow and Cambridge.

Two more different young men could scarcely be imagined. Jawaharlal, mildly effete, sheltered in the palatial Anand Bhawan, was absorbing the cultural plurality and vibrancy of the 1900s Allahabad. Govindram, bright-eyed and imbued with a curious mind, lived a world apart in an old haveli in Nawalgarh. Their paths would cross forty years later, each then at the pinnacle of his career.

As I wrote in my biography of Nehru's grandson, Rajiv Gandhi, 'Jawaharlal had a secluded childhood. An only child for eleven years (when his first sister was born), he grew up quickly, too quickly perhaps, in the exclusive company of adults. He had an English tutor, a young man named F.T. Brooks, a protégé of Annie Besant, the theosophist. He attempted to induct spiritual values in young Jawaharlal only to be rebuffed by Motilal. The elder Nehru was, till his son and political circumstances converted him many years later, much attached to Western rationalism; he looked down on anything that smacked even slightly of Oriental mysticism.'

'Motilal had admiration for the British and all things British and brought Jawaharlal up to be a proper young Englishman. He sent him to Harrow and then to Cambridge. It was, ironically, in these institutions that Jawaharlal's fierce opposition to British rule was born. The proper English gentleman Motilal wished to create did, in fact, become English in speech, habit and manner. However, in political ideology he became passionately Indian, almost as if he was reacting to his inapposite British upbringing.'

'When Jawaharlal returned to India, he returned not to join his father as an enthusiastic and privileged subject of the British Empire who wished to perpetuate it indefinitely but as a passionate nationalist committed to its ouster. Over the next few years, Jawaharlal Nehru, now a married man in his twenties, changed rapidly from a Cambridge-returned dilettante dressed in formal Western clothes to a fiery freedom fighter, adopting Indian dress, speech and the ideals of his new mentor, Mahatma Gandhi. His goal: self-rule.'

Despite being one of India's wealthiest businessmen, Govindram had lived a quiet, frugal life. Raised in a family of limited means, he had defied the odds to straddle the worlds of trading, industry, education and philanthropy. Though reticent to acknowledge leaders from outside the Western Anglosphere, global newspapers were drawn to note his passing. *The New York Times*, usually parsimonious in praise, noted in its fulsome obituary on 23rd May, 1946: 'Govindram Gordhandas Seksaria, a leading cotton market figure, industrialist and philanthropist and member of the New York Cotton Exchange, died today of a heart attack. Mr. Seksaria had been a member of the New York Cotton Exchange since 1934.'

According to the family, Govindram donated Rs. 50 lakh to charity shortly before his death. Newspaper reports place his total gifts to charitable causes during his lifetime at around Rs. 2 crore which would be equivalent to several hundred times that figure at today's prices more than 70 years later.

What was the secret of Seksaria's extraordinary success? In a word: integration. Just as, fifty years later, Dhirubhai Ambani would build Reliance Industries into a global enterprise through backward integration, Govindram Seksaria built his diverse business group through forward integration. Seksaria's strategy of forward integration involved a wide range of commodities that could be both traded and manufactured. The commodity Seksaria initially selected for trading was cotton. This expanded in the 1920s through the 1930s to include cotton seed oil, vegetable oil, sugar, bullion and grains. They on the surface may seem like random commodities on an arbitrary list of useful goods but in fact, reflected careful and strategic thinking.

The manufacture of commodities, moreover, was cost-effective in terms of materials, labour, power and resources. Production was not adversely affected by tariffs enforced by the British. Colonial regulations, many of them stifling, compelled Indian industrialists to calculate minimal returns upon which to build and expand domestic production.

Such levels of diversification across trade, speculation and industry were unique in the global capitalist milieu of the West at the time. But in Seksaria's case, it reflected business acuity born of years of family networks and insider knowledge as well as a penchant for risk-taking in seemingly adverse conditions. In order to place Seksaria's achievements in the context of his era, the key lies in understanding his ability to leverage profits from speculation to build a large industrial enterprise.

Dhirubhai Ambani's strategy five decades later was backward integration: from textile manufacturing in the 1970s to speciality chemicals in the 1980s to petrochemicals in the 1990s to oil refining in the 2000s and finally to gas exploration in the 2010s.

Govindram Seksaria's forward integration began with speculation in commodities, followed by trading and then using profits from both to establish manufacturing units across the country. He deployed as raw material the same commodities – especially, cotton – that he traded in. This allowed him to speculate fearlessly in large quantities. He could give deliveries from his mills when needed or take deliveries to feed his mills when required. Counter-traders could not match this key advantage.

Nandkumar Seksaria was born six years after his grandfather Govindram died. His informal manner conceals a sharp, insightful mind. How does he assess Govindram's strategy of forward integration? 'Apart from cotton and bullion, my grandfather was trading in food grains and pulses as well. He had *pedhis* all over the country. And again we see the typical strategy of forward integration. He was doing this in vegetables and pulses. He had quite a few oil mills and cotton ginning plants across the country, including a cotton seed oil extraction plant in Hyderabad-Sindh. Around the 1930s, he had started making big money and had become a crorepati. Forward integration was the key.'

Shekhawati is a region in Rajasthan that falls under the modern districts of Sikar and Jhunjhunu, often dubbed the 'open air art gallery of India.' The region earned its name from the famous frescoes that adorn the walls of its many havelis. Nawalgarh lies close to the centre of the Shekhawati region. It had a population of 63,948, according to the 2011 census.[3] Nawalgarh is divided into 30 wards for which elections are held every five years. The literacy rate there is 74.44 per cent, higher than the state average of 66.11 per cent. In Nawalgarh, male literacy rate is 86.46 per cent while the female literacy rate is 61.67 per cent.

After the death of Shekhawati ruler, Shardul Singh, sometime between 1740 and 1750 (the dates vary, though most sources say 1742), his kingdom was divided into five equal parts. Each was ruled by one of his surviving sons. Collectively, these newly demarcated kingdoms were referred to as 'Panchpana'. The fifth son, Nawal Singh, established the *thikana* of Nawalgarh. Founded at the site of the village Rohili, Nawal Singh had already established a fort at this location in 1737.

[3]http://www.census2011.co.in/data/town/800484-nawalgarh-rajasthan.html.

Following the death of Nawal Singh in 1780, his eldest son Narsinghdas became the titular head. Narsinghdas ruled for 10 years and died in 1790. Subsequently, the ancestral property was divided amongst his four sons. The tradition of division of ancestral property continued with subsequent rulers as well. From 1828 to 1923 Nawalgarh remained divided into four *panas*. Only after the death of Thakur Kalyan Singh in 1926, did Thakur Roop Singh become the ruler of three *panas* of Nawalgarh Thikana.[4]

Govindram, aged 15, accompanied his father to Bombay in 1903. A few uneventful months later, the family returned to Nawalgarh. Soon after their return home, young Govindram lost his father in 1905. Within a short period, tragically, he lost his mother as well. Govindram had married Basantibai at the age of eleven in Nawalgarh. He became an orphan at sixteen and got the responsibility of taking care of his young wife and his six siblings.

When Govindram got married, his bride was given just one gold *kada*. The girl's mother said to her father: 'What kind of match have you chosen? Our daughter has just got one gold *kada*.' The father replied: 'That's okay, they are nice people.' Later on, when Seksaria earned considerable wealth, he told his mother-in-law jokingly: 'Look, are you happy now? Your daughter is glittering in gold!'

Govindram shifted base to Mumbai from Nawalgarh in 1905. His nephew, Mangtulal Seksaria says, Govindram, not yet 17, came to Bombay alone at first, soon after the *shraddha* ceremony for his parents. His wife followed him later. According to his daughter-in-law Pushpabai, Basantibai used to say that Govindram had to sell some of her gold ornaments to complete the rituals when his parents passed away. She also used to say that Govindram and Basantibai used to live in a building near the plot where Nemani building stands today at Hughes Road,

[4]https://shekhawativirasatabhiyan.wordpress.com/latest/page/3/

Mumbai. Construction of Nemani building was proceeding at the time, around 1920. The couple's first child, a daughter, Anaribai, would have been eight years old then; their second child, a daughter, Bhagwatibai, would be born soon thereafter, in 1922 in Nawalgarh.

At first Govindram stayed in Bombay's Matti Galli at a *Basa* from where his business was also conducted. He lived there with his cousin Kanhaiyalal, shifting residences before moving to a house in Khattar Galli at Kalbadevi in 1927, then one of the city's nerve centres. Pushpabai recalls her mother-in-law, Basantibai telling her that the Khattar Galli house was bought for Rs. 57,000 and whatever rent came from the building was used by her to take care of the family's household expenses.

The tough, unforgiving, arid environment of Rajputana moulded the character of Marwaris. By the time Govindram moved to Bombay, Marwaris as a community were already gaining prominence in trading.

According to the book, *A History of Modern South Asia: Politics, States, Diasporas* by Ian Talbot, 'Speculation on prices of grain and cotton, as well as rain bargains—wagers on when the first day of the rains would arrive—was, however, more common among Marwari migrants from Bikaner, where there was an indigenous speculative tradition, than among those from Jodhpur.' *In Entrepreneurship and Industry in India,* Rajat Ray theorises the reason why migrants from the Shekhawati region particularly took to speculation and surmises that the exact reason is uncertain. According to him, the most common form of speculation would be in the form of rain bargains.

Teji-mandi transactions were also well-known and practised. The opium business was conducted by Marwaris in the Malwa region. Unsurprisingly, the earliest speculation took place in this commodity. 'Speculation was, however, considered disreputable even by the established Shekhawati firms and the very fact that the Shekhawati Marwaris were often late-comers to the big cities may partially explain their option for this route,' writes Ray.

Although, not much is known about Govindram's early life in Bombay, an article in the spiritual magazine *Kalyan* relates an anecdote on his brief employment with a Marwari *dharamshala*. As a result of his inability to read and write, Govindram could work there only for a day. For his wages he received 8 annas from the owner and another 8 annas to help him make ends meet. The manager showed much kindness to young Govindram. Years later, as he prospered, Govindram repaid the kindness with a generous donation to the *dharamshala*.

The *Kalyan* article provides a vivid account of the incident: 'Young Seksaria took that one rupee and left. After some years Seksaria became a big and successful speculator. One day a young man came to him seeking help for a charitable organisation. He told Seksaria the name of the organisation. Seksaria immediately gave Rs. 1 lakh to that young man! The man happily went to his father and told him how a seth gave him a donation of Rs. 1 lakh. His father said, "this is a really noble thing that he has done. We must felicitate him with a felicitation letter. Tomorrow we will go to him."

'The next day father and son went to that seth. The seth kept looking at the old man. The father said 'due to old age now I am unable to look after the organisation. My son is handling the noble cause. You have donated Rs. 1 lakh. I am really happy and wanted to see you personally. We wish to publicly felicitate you for such a great donation. Also, can you address the gathering? Please give your speech in writing so that it can be printed.'

Seksaria told the old man that he does not think so much is required to be done for such a small thing. 'Since you have come personally I would like to donate Rs. 1 lakh more, which you can use as per your wish.' Saying this Seksaria immediately opened the safe and gave Rs. 1 lakh in cash to the old man. He said 'This is not an obligation. I am just clearing an old debt.' The old man didn't understand. He said, 'I don't understand what you mean.'

'Many years ago,' Seksaria explained, 'I came to the city for the first time. I worked for one day at your organisation. I was illiterate hence, I was removed from the job by you. But as a remuneration of one day you gave me eight annas. In return for that eight annas, I had given Rs. 1 lakh. After removing me from the job, you called me back and out of pity you gave me eight annas more as a donation. In return of that donation, now I am giving Rs. 1 lakh more.' Hearing this, the father's eyes became moist and he said, 'Sethji, you have actually given a very big return.'

Seksaria replied, 'Here also you are mistaken. The value of money depends upon one's situation and mind. For a poor person, eight annas is his entire wealth and for a super-rich man even one lakh rupees is like eight annas. With the grace of God and your blessings I have earned well. Hence, I am just settling my account. As far as giving a speech is concerned, I don't know how to read or write.'

The old man asked again: 'Then can we install a nameplate with your name engraved on it?'

Seksaria said, 'No, please don't do that. I will get into trouble. Income-tax officers will make my life miserable. I prefer to spend my money for my country's well-being instead of paying tax to the British government.'

Times at the turn of the century were tough. Shortages abounded. Poor monsoons and rural distress created grinding poverty across India. The author and historian Claude Markovits writes that 'by 1900, although, an agricultural crisis had been largely overcome, agricultural production tended to slacken. However, the *Swadeshi* movement helped promote and diversify industrial development. In 1907, the Tata Iron and Steel Company was founded amidst patriotic fervour despite hostility from the British colonial government. It would serve as a benchmark for the growth of indigenous manufacturing industry.'

Apart from business, Marwaris have a long history of being politically engaged. Prominent community members had acted as advisors to the princely state rulers of Rajputana. Marwari youth were beginning to participate in the incipient freedom movement. Still a teenager, Govindram was busy earning a living. Yet, already his business and political instincts were sharp. Quietly, he absorbed events unfolding around him. He would soon be swept into their vortex.

Geopolitics was to play a key role in Govindram's business career. It is important, therefore, to frame his life and work in the context of events in the early 1900s. These developments laid the ground for the opportunities that would present themselves decades later – opportunities Govindram would seize with both hands.

Britain had long employed a policy of quelling revolts in its colonies by introducing social reforms. Yet Britain's economic problems at home had forced the Conservative party government during its decade in power to slow down these reforms. In 1900, 30 per cent of Britain's population lived below the poverty line. There were great inequalities between the rich and poor. It was estimated that while a working class family lived on 18 shillings a week, a middle-class family lived on 10 pounds a week. For the wealthy, the figure ran into multiples of this. The situation would only improve in 1906 when a Liberal party government in London introduced wide-ranging economic and social reforms.

During the 1880s and 1890s, Britain pursued a policy of avoiding political alliances that involved major military commitments. This policy, known as 'Splendid Isolation' not entirely unlike today's Brexit, was primarily associated with Prime Minister Lord Salisbury. Though, the British army was relatively small, the Royal Navy was the largest in the world. When Germany began to build up its own navy, Britain regarded it as a hostile act, leading to a breakdown in relations between the two countries. France had been Britain's traditional rival, especially in colonial expansion. Both imperial powers now grew increasingly suspicious of Russia extending its influence in the Balkans.

The Boer Wars (1899-1902) compelled Britain to abandon its

self-imposed isolation. On 11th October, 1899, the second Boer (*the Dutch and Afrikaans term for farmers*) War broke out after Britain rejected the so-called Transvaal ultimatum. In the first Boer War thousands of Voortrekkers (people of Dutch extraction) had established two independent republics in the Transvaal and Orange County in the interior of South Africa. The Transvaal ultimatum had demanded that all disputes between the British and the Boers be settled by arbitration; that British troops on the borders be withdrawn and that troops bound for South Africa by ship not disembark.

In the course of the war, the British army was reinforced by volunteer contingents from Canada, Australia, New Zealand, the Cape Colony and Natal. In 1902, Britain formed an alliance with Japan, mainly directed against Russia. In 1904, it settled its colonial differences with France and the *entente cordiale* was established. Eventually in 1907, Britain grudgingly became part of an alliance with Russia and France known as the Triple Entente.

Meanwhile, even as Govindram and his young family were finding their bearings in colonial Bombay, the demand for self-rule had gripped colonised people across the world. The movement towards independence had begun a few years earlier and would rapidly gather pace. In January 1901, after several constitutional conventions, the six states of Australia (New South Wales, Tasmania, South Australia, Western Australia, Victoria and Queensland) federated, creating the Commonwealth of Australia. The country moved from being a collection of colonies to a dominion of the British Empire.

In 1902, Cuba gained independence from the United States. In 1905, Ireland demanded self-rule from Britain. Norway achieved full independence with the Norwegian Parliament declaring that its union with Sweden stood dissolved. In 1908, the Young Turk Revolution of the Ottoman Empire, which in essence was the overthrow of Sultan Abdul Hamid II's autocratic power and the introduction of parliamentary government, seized the world's attention. The new regime though, was soon discredited by a declaration of independence by Bulgaria in October 1908, the annexation of Bosnia and Herzegovina by Austria and the annexation of Crete by Greece.

All these events would alter the way the world conducted business, trade and politics. It was possibly the most riveting period in contemporary history with far-reaching consequences. India would not prove immune to the waves of change lapping at its shores. And Govindram Seksaria, like his peers—the Birlas, Tatas, Bajajs and Walchands—would soon leverage the extraordinary opportunities that lay ahead in a turbulent century.

In a special report looking back at the world economy, *The Economist*[5] analysed the shift in the balance of power from the West to the East. The report showed how China and India would dominate the world economy in 2030 just as Europe and America had dominated it between 1850 and 2000.

The economist-historian Angus Maddison provided a series of compelling statistics to demonstrate India's advanced production in, for example, cotton as early as during the 1800s. Indian cotton producers had been forced by the British colonial government to increase output prior to Independence to feed textile mills in Lancashire. According to Maddison, India exported 1,02,000 metric tonnes of cotton in 1850; 2,50,000 tonnes in 1863; 3,26,000 tonnes in 1905; 4,56,000 tonnes in 1915 and peaking at 7,38,000 tonnes in 1930. After independence in 1947, cotton exports fell to 2,11,000 tonnes. Home production was retained for domestic consumption at Independence rather than exported to Lancashire at low fixed prices.

Of all the events in the first decade of the twentieth century, none had quite the impact on business, trade and politics as the Russo-Japanese War. The conflict broke out in February 1904 and

[5] 3rd October, 2015.

ended in September 1905. It brought traditional enemies—the Russian Empire and the Empire of Japan to the battlefield. Japan had always deeply resented Russia's expansionist policy. It now fought over rival imperial ambitions in Manchuria and Korea.

The brief war would roil global markets, giving 16 year old Govindram, about to begin his career an early insight into how conflicts could open up profitable arbitrage and trading opportunities.

During the Sino-Japanese War (1894-95), Russia along with Germany and France had formed the 'Triple Intervention' which forced Japan to give up its claims on ports in South Manchuria and the Liaodong Peninsula despite its victory over China. After this, Russia entered the region, taking control of the strategically placed warm water port of Port Arthur. Though, Japan sought to settle the dispute through a negotiated agreement, Russia's Tsar Nicholas II seriously underestimated his Asian foe's capability and willingness to go to war. What followed were a series of small clashes between the two nations.

In 1904, Japan launched an attack on the Russian fleet at Port Arthur. Following this, a formal declaration of war was received in Moscow. This surprise attack earned Japan an early victory. For the next year, Russia and Japan clashed in Korea and the Sea of Japan. The Japanese scored significant victories, but the number of casualties was high on both sides. Most of the Russian Baltic fleet had been destroyed by May 1905. The heavy financial toll of the war and the increasing number of fatalities led the two countries to seek an end to the fighting.

For most of the short war, the Japanese were on the offensive. They used massed military assaults against defensive positions. The complete victory of the Japanese military stunned the world. It transformed the balance of power in Asia and established Japan as a regional power. It was the first time an Asian country had defeated a European nation on the battlefield.

United States President, Theodore Roosevelt helped negotiate a peace treaty between the representatives of the two warring nations. They met at Portsmouth, New Hampshire, in 1905.

Negotiations took place in August and the final agreement was signed in September 1905. The Treaty of Portsmouth formally ended the Russo-Japanese War. The treaty ceded Port Arthur to Japan, affirmed the Japanese presence in South Manchuria and Korea and also ceded the southern half of the island of Sakhalin to Japan.

The Japanese victory had far-reaching consequences. It increased self-confidence among nationalists in colonised Asian countries from India and Indonesia to Malaya and the Philippines. India's 290 million people—18 per cent of the world's population at the time—were elated. As Jawaharlal Nehru said years later, 'Japan's victory lessened the feeling of inferiority from which most of us suffered. A great European power had been defeated. Thus, Asia could still defeat Europe as it had done in the past.'

Seksaria was then still an impressionable teenager. However, he carefully studied market movements during the years Russia and Japan went to war. His observations on how war affects markets, creating both challenges and opportunities, would prepare him for profitable speculation a decade later, during and after the First World War.

Apart from a cessation of trading between nations at war, the overall impact of conflict on commodities often leads to recession in many industries. The cotton trade was especially affected during the Russo-Japanese War. In their excellent account of the war, David Wolff and others[6] write: 'Although war supplies were in greater demand, the Russo-Japanese War plunged all other sectors of industry into recession, as all finance was directed towards the war. This inevitably cast a dark shadow over traditional businesses in Kyoto, where there was little heavy

[6]*The Russo-Japanese War in Global Perspective: World War Zero*, Volume 2, edited by David Wolff, Steve Marks, Bruce Menning, David Schimmelpenninck van der Oye, John Steinberg and Shinji Yokote:

industry. Suffering from the repercussions of this effect, the sales revenue in Kyoto fell. Among the major businesses in Kyoto, the largest was the textile industry which accounted for 86.7 per cent of office premises and 86.2 per cent of total employees. Most produced silk and were located in the Nishijin and Tango districts. Demand for luxurious silk products dwindled, adding to the already strained circumstances and inflicting significant damage on Kyoto's economy.'

'The newspaper *Heimin Shinbun* (24th April, 1904) described how the recession afflicted weaving regions other than Nishijin. In Nagoya, the export of white cotton to Korea stopped, cotton blankets suffered a 20 per cent price reduction and weavers were badly off with no accommodation loans from banks. In Isezaki, Kiryu and Ashikaga, there were many jobless weavers due to shutdowns or decreasing production. In Nagahama, the price of *Chirimen* crepe fabric was down by 10 per cent, yet there was no dealing.'

The first decade of the twentieth century would prove pivotal for India's incipient business houses in more ways than one. The world was changing rapidly. India and its restless business pioneers stood on the cusp of a new era. Govindram had by now absorbed an important lesson: knowledgeable traders could earn large returns if they acted decisively in uncertain times. It was a dictum that would serve him well throughout his career.

By 1910, Britain had slipped into relative decline compared to Germany and the United States. The US had already surpassed Britain as the world's largest economy; Germany was rapidly catching up. Though, Britain continued to be the banking and shipbuilding capital of the world, its economy was now growing slowly. Economists attribute this sluggish growth to Britain's failure to modernise its factories. In 1910, German steel production was twice that of Britain. American coal output had raced ahead of Britain's. Demand rose among British lawmakers for increased tariffs to stem the tide, leading to a split in the Conservative party. This paved the way for the Liberal party's victory in the next general election.

Aware of Britain's declining power in the global steel industry, British colonial authorities allowed the Tatas to set up an iron and steel company. Work began on construction of a plant in Jamshedpur in 1908. Production commenced in February 1912. The British promised to buy surplus steel from the Tatas. Tata Iron and Steel company would become a leading metals producer worldwide. But as importantly, it emerged as a symbol of Indian technological and entrepreneurial skill, inspiring an entire generation of pre-Independence businessmen.

Govindram was just 23 years old when the first steel ingot was rolled out at Tata Iron and Steel in February 1912. But his clear, observant mind was ticking over: great opportunities in trading and industry beckoned. He was determined to grasp them.

The growth of Indian firms in banking, insurance and industry would now be propelled by the *Swadeshi* movement. Govindram was already immersed in trading. Nehru, then 22, had returned from England with a degree in natural science from Cambridge University and a law degree from London's Inner Temple. A callow young man with a sharp intellect and the liquid eyes of a dreamer, Jawaharlal was greatly influenced by Fabian socialist ideas. Different as their backgrounds were, Govindram would, 30 years later, emerge as one of the most generous donors to the Congress party that Nehru then led with Mahatma Gandhi, Sardar Vallabhbhai Patel, Maulana Abul Kalam Azad and other freedom fighters.

Of the three Imperial Durbars held in India during the British Raj to mark the succession of an Emperor or Empress, the only one attended by a reigning sovereign was in 1911. In 1877, a durbar had been held to proclaim Queen Victoria as Empress of India. In 1903, the country celebrated the succession of King Edward VII and Queen Alexandra. But it was only in December 1911, a few months after his coronation in Britain that George V accompanied by wife Mary undertook a tour of India. The royal couple began their visit in Bombay after touring the Middle-East. The durbars were initiated in the hope of securing the loyalty of Maharajas and Nawabs as well as the Indian people. Their Majesties landed at Apollo Bunder. Thousands of Indians gathered on its rampart to see the first reigning British monarch visit India.

Though deeply engrossed in business, young Govindram's natural curiosity about the man who ruled his country from thousands of miles away would have impelled him to follow the royal couple's journey through the press as they travelled from Bombay to the Delhi Durbar and then on to Nepal for a hunting expedition. His inherent sense of nationalism would have been aroused by Sayajirao Gaekwad of Baroda who appeared 'in the simplest of simple dress,' and then turned his back on the royal couple—a mild form of political resistance that was reported in febrile tones in the British press.

Govindram's innate simplicity would have been appalled too at the exorbitant sum of money allocated for the royal trip (over 6,00,000 pounds sterling). King George's 85-acre camp spared no expense in the creation of a temporary city with hundreds of tents for the accommodation of the royal party's guests and servants, dining areas, reception tents, arenas for sporting events and military reviews, communication centres for the press, extensive gardens in which English roses bloomed, health facilities and pathways.

The Calcutta Durbar in 1911 was especially significant: King George V announced the reversal of Lord Curzon's 1905 partition of Bengal. He also transferred the capital from Calcutta to Delhi to avoid increasing militancy and *Swadeshi* boycotts in Bengal. The Red Fort became the royal seat where the King and Queen revived the custom of darshan, appearing on the fort's balcony in full regalia and robes. Nearly 1,00,000 people passed to view their royal highnesses.

Within three decades, as freedom from British colonial rule approached, Govindram, in his 50s and at the peak of his career, would himself be welcomed by the Royalty of Udaipur, Jaipur and the Holkars of Indore.

Chapter Two

The Lessons of War And Peace

The First World War broke out in 1914. Commodity prices rose and fell. Govindram studied the turbulent market closely. By the end of the war he had become something of an expert in cotton speculation. In recognition, the government gave him membership of the Cotton Contracts Board in 1919. Govindram was just 30 years old.

Europe had not fought a major war for nearly a century. The effects of peace could be seen in the technological progress and cultural vibrancy across the continent just before the onset of the First World War. No one could have imagined the destruction and devastation that lay ahead. The Great War, as it was known, killed more people, involved more countries and cost more money than any other previous conflict in history. It is estimated that 14 million people died, of whom over five million were civilians from 28 countries. As many as seven million men were left permanently disabled. Around $186 billion in direct costs and another $151 billion in indirect costs at 1918 prices were spent in the war years. The legacy of bitterness the conflict bequeathed would spark the Second World War two decades later.

Govindram absorbed many lessons speculating amidst market swings during the war years. His trading activities were poised to expand significantly. Never before had technology been harnessed to such destructive ends. The nature of modern warfare changed forever. Carrier pigeons and horses that armies relied on at the start of the conflict soon gave way to tanks, submarines, airplanes equipped with bombs, machine guns and poison gas.

Politically, the war ushered in the death of empires and the birth of new nations. National boundaries were redrawn. Four major monarchies collapsed. In 1917, the Russian Revolution lifted the Bolsheviks to power. The Russian Empire was replaced by a socialist government led by Vladimir Lenin. In Europe, new states like Estonia, Finland, Latvia and Lithuania emerged: they had formerly been part of the Russian Empire. In defeated and weary Germany, the left-leaning Weimar Republic would stay in power till the 1930s when Adolf Hitler became chancellor. The Austro-Hungarian Empire broke up into several independent states that included Poland, Czechoslovakia, Yugoslavia, Hungary and Austria. While parts of the former Ottoman empire in the Middle-East were placed under the mandate of France and Britain after 1918, the rump would morph into the Republic of Turkey.

Ten thousand miles away in India, Govindram watched these developments intently. Well entrenched in business, he had made, lost and remade large sums of money speculating on cotton and bullion during the First World War and its aftermath. Buoyed by success and quickly learning lessons from failure, Govindram was on his way to becoming a respected young trader.

Indian business though was still in its infancy. Apart from the Tatas, few Indian business houses had established large enterprises in colonial India. The Birlas too were handicapped by colonial restrictions. I examined this in my biography of Aditya Birla: 'By 1918, Ghanshyamdas had established a company called Birla Brothers & Co. in which he, Jugalkishore, Rameshwardas and Brijmohan held an equal number of shares. Trading in jute brought profits and enhanced the status of the four young Birlas among Calcutta's entrenched Marwari community. Ghanshyamdas, however, was deeply ambitious and trading left him dissatisfied. He knew that the real profits lay in manufacturing over which British companies held a vice-like grip.

'When Ghanshyamdas attempted to buy land for his proposed jute factory, a British company, Andrew Yule, then the largest managing agency in Calcutta, promptly bought all the surrounding land, making it impossible for Birla to set up the necessary additional infrastructure. Ghanshyamdas was forced to buy land further south, towards Budge-Budge on the idyllic curve of the Hooghly river. It was there that the first Birla jute mill was eventually constructed. Against tremendous odds, the mill began operations in August 1919, marking the entry of the Birla family, hitherto traders, into industrial manufacturing.

'Apart from buying up all the land near his factory, the British harassed Ghanshyamdas in several other ways. The Imperial Bank initially refused to give him capital. When it finally did, it was at a provocatively high rate of interest compared to that charged to British firms, wrote Alan Ross in his biography of G.D. Birla, *The Emissary: G.D. Birla, Gandhi and Independence.* But not only did Birla Jute get off to a good start, it gradually began to do better than all the other jute mills in Calcutta where virtually every jute mill was British-owned as recently as twenty-five years before independence.'[7]

Revolution was rife in Europe in the 1920s. The most popular type of government to gain influence after the First World War was the republic. Europe in 1914 had 19 monarchies and 3 republics. In 1918, it had 13 monarchies, 14 republics and 2 regencies. In 1920, the Government of Ireland Act partitioned Ireland into northern and southern Ireland with Britain intending to offer both states home rule.

[7]*Aditya Vikram Birla: A Biography*, Viking-Penguin.

Economically, the war resulted in the devastation of several European economies and paved the way for the United States to become the world's creditor and leading industrial power. Much of Europe had suffered devastating losses of physical and financial property. At the start of the war, Europe was the world's most reliable money-lender. By its end, she owed her allies $10 billion. To pay back the debt, some governments resorted to printing vast sums of money leading to hyperinflation.

Though, France and Britain also suffered heavy war losses, they were eventually able to claw their way back to economic health. Expectedly, it was the German economy that was annihilated. Under the humiliating terms of the Treaty of Versailles, Germany was forced to accept complete responsibility for the war and make financial reparations to the allies.

Devastated infrastructure throughout Germany, political tension under the Weimar Republic and the reduced size of the German state led to unprecedented economic depression. The Reichsmark, the German currency, was steeply devalued. In 1923, it plunged in just three months from 4.6 million marks to the dollar to 4.2 trillion marks to the dollar.

In hindsight, the First World War marked the beginning of the end of the British Empire. Though, Britain emerged from the war with even more colonial possessions than it had before including Germany's former colonies like Tanganyika and Namibia as well as former Ottoman possessions in the Middle-East, it began to find it increasingly difficult to control the numerous strands of Empire. Rising nationalist demands from non-European countries became more strident. The arrival of Mahatma Gandhi in India from South Africa in 1915 would ignite the freedom movement in Britain's largest colony.

The massacre of civilians by members of the British Indian Army in Jallianwallah Bagh, Amritsar, in 1919, a year after the end of the First World War, prompted large-scale protests against British rule in India. They would morph through the 1920s and 1930s into a non-cooperation movement – a political strategy associated with Gandhi's philosophy of non-violent direct action. It was obvious that Indian nationalism was becoming an unstoppable movement – a template for anti-colonial nationalist movements globally. Disparate social issues were subsumed into the dominant motif of the day: national independence across Asia and Africa from European colonial rule.

Seksaria's business and trading activities meanwhile grew steadily. The Cotton Contracts Board, of which Seksaria was a member, established the East India Cotton Association in 1922 in which Seksaria would have automatically received membership. The Bombay Bullion Exchange was formed a year later. Still only 34, Seksaria was inducted as a member. Govindram's star was now rising rapidly.

Britain had always enjoyed the role it played on the global stage, providing shipping and insurance services worldwide. During the war years, however, England consumed all of its credits and became heavily indebted to the United States. The world's financial centre began to shift from London to New York. Though, Britain was determined to restore London's role as the leading international financial centre, this ambition was stymied by deflationary policies that attempted to maintain an overvalued pound sterling at its pre-war parity.

Following its timely military intervention in the First World War and President Woodrow Wilson's astute diplomatic leadership, the United States was hailed as the saviour of Europe. Having joined the war as late as 1917, it did not suffer from Europe's catastrophic losses in men and material. Though nearly 1,00,000 Americans lost their lives, this toll was relatively low compared to the numbers who died in Europe. Its geographical location, insulated by an ocean, kept American factories and land safe from destruction. Mass production of military hardware, the use of machinery to perform human labour tasks and the new eight-hour workday stimulated the US economy. Productivity rose sharply.

Even before the Great War broke out, the US had institutionalised innovation moving from individual inventors to government sponsored scientific research. In 1913, the US had 370 research institutes manned by 3,500 people. These figures increased steadily and by the 1940s the country had 2,300 institutes that employed 1,18,000 people. Technology too received a great boost after the war. The production of automobiles, airplanes, radios and chemicals skyrocketed. The first US coast-to-coast long-distance telephone call had been inaugurated in 1915 by A.G. Bell in New York speaking across the wires with his former assistant Thomas Augustus Watson in San Francisco. The invention would help integrate financial markets in the 1920s. Access to information was now instantaneous. It provided Govindram the means to trade across the world with real-time knowledge of market trends.

The First World War proved to be a defining moment in the complex imperial relationship between Britain and India. When the war erupted, political unrest across India was simmering. The Indian National Congress, in its thirtieth year since inception in 1885, had been demanding more self-government. It was believed that as soon as Britain got involved in the war, Indian nationalists would press their cause strongly. Author William Archer wrote: 'The moment Britain gets into trouble elsewhere, India, in her present temper, would burst into a blaze of rebellion.'[8]

India was to prove the Cassandras wrong. When war was declared on 4th August, 1914, India unexpectedly rallied behind Britain. Offers of financial and military help poured in from all over the country. The railway network in India, built assiduously by the British with Indian labour and Indian taxpayers' money, was used to transport troops, grains and raw materials to the ports of Bombay and Karachi en route to Britain, Mesopotamia and East Africa. These large shipments were often made at the

[8]William Archer was an author, playwright, essayist and critic. He was a friend and contemporary of George Bernard Shaw in the early-twentieth century.

expense of local people. India contributed 146 million pounds sterling to the war effort. Thousands enlisted both from within and outside India. Nepal sent 1,00,000 gurkhas and the Dalai Lama in Tibet offered 1,000 of his own troops.

By the winter of 1914, Indian troops were on the Western front. A large number of them were ill-equipped. Indian soldiers fought at Ypres, Neuve Chapelle, the Somme and Passchendaele. They suffered alarming casualties. Of the 1.5 million Indians deployed in all theatres of the war, over 50 per cent were either killed or went missing.

Right up to the very end, Indians were encouraged to join the war effort. Mahatma Gandhi said: 'Seek ye first the recruiting office and everything will be added unto you.' The fact that Indian soldiers fought in the war beside British, Canadian and Australian troops was commended all over the world. It led to India being invited to be a founder member of the League of Nations in 1920 under the name Les Indes Anglaises or The British Indies.

Govindram lived modestly in Bombay through the war years. Chaotic markets gave operators with gumption many profit-making opportunities. The experience would stand Govindram in good stead for sterner tests and greater opportunities in the unfolding century.

The reasons for Indians' robust response to the call for arms in aid of its colonial master were less heroic than it seemed: poverty and unemployment. The British army paid its Indian recruits well. The wounded were well looked after in hospitals in France and England. Many married local girls had settled down in Europe after the war.

The Indian corps was awarded 13,000 medals for gallantry, including 12 Victoria Crosses. Khudadad Khan won the corps' first Victoria Cross. But other than these superficial tokens of appreciation, Britain showed no signs of giving India what it wanted – self-government. Despite India having proved its loyalty to the King and the Empire when it was most needed, Britain was increasingly insecure about its vulnerability as the conflict in Europe and the Middle East ebbed and flowed.

As more British troops were withdrawn from India to fight in Europe and Mesopotamia, the Defence of India Act was passed in 1915. This allowed the government to intern 'politically dangerous' dissidents without due process. Under the Press Act, journalists could be imprisoned without trial. The press was closely censored. In 1917, a sedition committee chaired by S.A.T. Rowlatt was tasked with investigating war-time revolutionary conspiracies and German and Bolshevik links to violence in India. His report became the basis of the Rowlatt Act which created widespread indignation amongst Indians.

British promises of greater self-government embodied in the Montagu-Chelmsford reforms that were the basis of the Government of India Act of 1919, were contradicted by the fact that ultimate power still lay in the hands of the viceroy and the India office in London. Though it created national legislatures for India and gave five per cent of India's wealthiest the right to vote, providing berths in provincial governments to Indians, a veto vested with the British. They controlled the central government and within the provincial governments kept control of the key posts of taxation and law and order.

India's political infirmities were exacerbated by economic difficulties. An increase in taxes coupled with disruptions in both domestic and international trade doubled the index of overall prices between 1914 and 1920. Returning war veterans, especially in Punjab, contributed to growing unemployment. Post-war inflation led to food riots in Bombay, Madras and Bengal. The failure of the 1918-19 monsoon and profiteering and speculation added to the problem. The influenza pandemic of 1918 took an estimated 10-20 million Indian lives, leading to a depletion of meagre resources. Anti-British sentiment hardened. The public mood had turned. Britain's hold over India began to weaken. Within a generation, India would be free.

Govindram, now in his early 30s, would over the next 27

eventful years, emerge along with the Birlas, Tatas and Bajajs as one of India's most successful industrialists. Jawaharlal Nehru, 30 years old and on the cusp of his own glittering political career, was officially inducted into the Indian National Congress in 1919. The trajectories of the two men would ascend rapidly.

The shortage of British goods during the First World War strengthened domestic textiles and steel. Indian firms in industry, insurance and banking had been given a boost by the *Swadeshi* movement. In Bengal, coal mining output in 1914 reached 15.7 million tonnes, comfortably meeting the demands of the railways. For Govindram, the First World War had opened up avenues in speculative trading. He entered cotton speculation under the mentorship of Juharmal Roongta of Swaroopchand Prithviraj. An established figure in the cotton market, Roongta was impressed with young Govindram's work ethic and vision. The Roongtas and Seksarias also had a family connection so important to Marwari business families: Govindram's nephew, Baijnath had married Roongta's daughter.

Roongtas were also purchase agents for the Currimbhoy group from whom, two decades later, Govindram would acquire Indore Malwa Mills (initially in partnership with the Roongtas, Brijmohan Podar and Sitaram Parasrampuria)—the jewel in Govindram's industrial crown. Juharmal's solid financial base as well as his established firm gave Govindram the financial muscle to speculate with aplomb.

Recounting those early days, Govindram's nephew, Mangtulal Seksaria, says: 'My father Kanhaiyalalji worked with the Roongtas for a short period. He introduced Govindramji to the family. The Roongtas were established speculators in cotton. They were brokers for the Currimbhoy group which was one of the largest at the time. The Roongtas were members of the cotton exchange and they facilitated Govindramji's entry into cotton trading. Govindramji started trading under the guidance of

Juharmalji and enjoyed immense support from him. Juharmalji recognised the mettle and tenacity in Govindramji.'

Mangtulal further describes the affection between the cousin brothers Govindram and Kanhaiyalal: 'Thakurao was the family driver. Govindramji had a white convertible open-hood Chrysler car. He used to tell Kanhaiyalalji, "*Bhaiji* you take the motor car." Kanhaiyalalji would say, "No, you take the car." *Unke beech me jo pyar tha,* I have not seen anywhere else in the world. Govindramji used to say: "*Mere to yeh hi bhai hain.*"'

Mangtulal recalls: 'While speculating, Govindramji would lose money. In the early days, when he suffered losses he would avoid going to the market and remain in his room at home. Juharmal Roongta would come home and encourage him to continue speculating and not get disheartened. At times he could not make a payment, he would come to Kanhaiyalalji and just sit. He never said a word, kept completely silent. Then Kanhaiyalalji would say: "Why do you worry? I am there for you. I will ensure that the payment is done." And Kanhaiyalalji would arrange the payment for Govindramji.'

In a rare interview, Kanhaiyalal Seksaria's widow reminisces about her brother-in-law: 'When Govindramji used to come to talk to my husband, I would sit in the corner and just listen to them. Goma (as he was affectionately called) would tell me, "Despite being my *bhabhi,* you don't talk to me at all!" I went to meet Basantibai when I came to Bombay after Govindramji's death. Bai started crying. She told me that even before he went, Govindramji spoke about his elder cousin Kanhaiyalalji who had stood by him through thick and thin.'

Ironically, despite making his fortune in speculation, Govindram was known to say: 'If you want to make anyone your enemy, put him into speculation. If you want to destroy someone put him into speculation.' When people asked him why despite his dismal opinion of speculation he had immersed himself in it, he would touch his forehead and reply with a smile: 'It is my luck, my destiny, that is earning for me.'

Prafulbhai Hirji, a veteran cotton merchant, recalls Govindram visiting his uncles occasionally. He also remembers hearing that Govindram never did *satta* against a person whom he considered to be lucky. And there was one person in the market by the name of Chunilal Manekchand, popularly known as Chuni Manka, against whom he would never do *satta*.

But it was more than just destiny or luck that brought Govindram success. It was a result of intuition, a delight in risk-taking, a lifelong passion for speculation and a sharp, analytical mind that helped him reap rich rewards. In those early days, no one who saw the tall, thin man dressed in a dhoti, long cotton coat and black shoes could have imagined that in less than two decades he would be an influential member of the New York Cotton Exchange (NYCE) and that *The New York Times* would write copiously of his growing clout to set prices in global markets.

Though, the United States stumbled through a brief economic recession at the start of the 1920s, as the decade unfolded the American economy boomed, fuelled partly by the war economy and manufacturing innovation. The Great Depression of 1929 lay ahead but, for the moment, America was resurgent. The age of consumerism had arrived. Americans bought cars, radios, refrigerators—the bigger the better.

In India, Govindram, now a respected commodity trader well into his thirties, tracked developments in the US and Europe with interest. Major cities like New York and Chicago saw a surge in new construction through the 1920s. A slew of sky-scrapers spiralled upwards. So buoyant was the economy that the decade came to be known as the 'Roaring Twenties'. Ripples of excitement spread from America all over the world. Speakeasies, short skirts, the Charleston and jazz music dominated the cultural landscape. Charlie Chaplin and Babe Ruth were the icons of the day. The discovery of King Tut's Tomb, insulin, the lie detector and penicillin; the inventions of bubble gum, sliced bread and the car radio; the screening of the first talking film *The Jazz Singer* and the first Mickey Mouse cartoon; the launch of *Reader's Digest, Time* magazine and the Oxford English dictionary as well as the founding of the BBC stimulated the world. All of these lent energy and vigour to a world scarred by years of war.

Yet it would be the Great Depression of 1929 that would eventually define the decade. It would also be the decade when Govindram would come into his own as a businessman and in short order, as an industrialist, educationist and philanthropist.

The Great Depression began in America in the summer of 1929, deepening as the decade drew to a close. It would continue relentlessly for another decade. Between the peak and the trough of the downturn, industrial production in America plunged 47 per cent. The unemployment rate ballooned to over 20 per cent. In 1928 and 1929, the Federal Reserve had raised interest rates to slow the unnatural rise in stock prices. In October 1929, the New York Stock Exchange (NYSE) plummeted by 33 per cent from its peak in September 1929. 24th October was mourned as Black Tuesday.

Within two months of the crash, stockholders had lost more than $40 billion. Yet there were other factors that contributed to the Depression spreading across the country. The United States experienced widespread banking panic in 1930, 1931 and 1932 that took a severe toll of its financial system. The worst depredations of the crisis would end only with the national 'bank holiday' declared by President Franklin D. Roosevelt in March 1933 when all banks closed and reopened only after being deemed solvent.

Over 9,000 banks failed. As bank deposits were uninsured, people lost their life savings. For the first time the American economy was seen as being vulnerable. Americans from different strata of society began to cut back on spending. This inevitably led to a slowdown in production and consumption of durable goods which in turn caused a spike in unemployment. As businesses began failing, the government created the Smoot-Hawley Tariff that imposed a high tax on imports. Trade between America and other countries fell sharply. It was in this chaotic economic environment that Govindram would make his mark as a trader on the New York Cotton Exchange.

America's economic decline was transmitted to the rest of the world largely through the gold standard. The gold standard forced countries to deflate along with the United States. Britain had adopted the gold standard as far back as the 1790s. It abolished it during the First World War but returned to it after the war ended. The value of the pound sterling, however, was only a fraction of what it was at the start of the war. It remained low until 1925 when Winston Churchill, then chancellor of the Exchequer, restored it to pre-war levels. As the price of gold fell rapidly, the rest of Europe purchased large quantities of gold from Britain. To stem the outflow, the Bank of England raised interest rates substantially. High interest rates depressed British spending and led to severe unemployment.

During the Great Depression, investors in Paris and New York lost confidence in the pound. With sterling being pegged to bullion, the pound sterling was worth a fixed amount compared to other currencies and gold itself. In order to ensure that sterling retained its value, the Bank of England was obligated to exchange gold for pounds at the specified rate. However, as political turmoil engulfed Britain, the country's first national government (a coalition between the Labour and Conservative parties) presided over a budget crisis that triggered a run on the pound.

Up until 1931, the gold standard had been preserved by loans from the US Federal Reserve and the French central bank, with the Bank of England's bullion reserves used as collateral. In May 1931, payment difficulties at the Creditanstalt, Austria's largest bank, played a key role in forcing Britain to finally abandon the gold standard. The British economy stabilised only after the country went off the gold standard in September 1931.

Amidst the global economic turbulence, Seksaria's only son, Kudilal, was born on 17th April, 1930. Mangtulal's mother recalls: 'There was no big celebration at Kudilal's birth so as to ward off the evil eye. This was because he was the first male child born to Govindramji after several years as well as the fact that there had been still-born births who were males before Kudilal.'

The return of Gandhi to India from South Africa dramatically altered the trajectory of the freedom movement. According to author A.D. Gordon, the participation of businessmen in the freedom struggle depended on the economic privileges they received from the British government. He broadly divides these businessmen into two groups: big industrialists and smaller 'marketeers' who supplied to big industries. Their response to the political priorities differed. Gordon observed that 'marketeers' with their traditional business practices had received little from the British government in terms of privileges, commercial benefits or an English education. They were, thus, unable to exert the same kind of influence on the government as the big industrialists, many of whom worked closely with the British colonial authorities and received special attention from them. This led small marketeers and brokers to support the freedom movement. In Gordon's view, therefore, when it was reported that businessmen backed the movement, it necessarily referred to this group of smaller businessmen.

Writing in a similar vein, Markovits observed that the rising sentiment in favour of the national freedom movement called for new measures. British political, strategic and fiscal thinking continued to shift in favour of large Indian entrepreneurs and businessmen. They received fiscal concessions and 'discriminating protection' to help nascent industries.

Markovits goes on to write that colonial imperatives encouraged bourgeois elements but never to the extent that they could form any kind of class consciousness. 'In India, capitalists remained for a long time largely cut off from the intelligentsia and generally from the more advanced sections of Indian society which played a crucial role in the elaboration of a nationalistic ideology. Internally they were also split in many ways.'[9]

Caste, religious and kinship ties further weakened any prospect of a united business class. According to Markovits, Marwaris among Indian communities, however, remained the most particular about community and kinship ties.

---

[9]Claude Markovits, *Indian Business and Nationalist Politics*, p. 12.

In April 1923, when Govindram was making a mark as a commodities trader, leaders of India's deepening freedom movement began collecting donations for the struggle for independence. *The Times of India* published a report on 9th April, 1923 on the initiative of the Tilak Swaraj Fund: 'On their return from Mandalay, Maymyo, and Prome,[10] Messrs. Jamnalal Bajaj, Vallabhbhai Patel and Manilal Kothari started collections for the Tilak Swaraj fund here. During the last three days nearly one lakh rupees was collected, most of the contributions being from the Gujarati merchants, both Hindus and Mussalmans. Last night the Burma Provincial Congress Committee sanctioned a grant of Rs. 50,000 to the All-India Congress Committee. This amount was earmarked for the support of the families of political prisoners.'

The Tilak Swaraj Fund, initiated by Gandhi, had been launched following the Congress resolution at its 30th December, 1920 session to help finance the Non-Cooperation movement. At the time, Gandhi made an assurance to all Indians that if the fund reached one crore within six months, he would be able to attain *Swaraj* for India. In an article titled *How to Finance the Movement*[11] about the importance of mass participation in the Non-Cooperation movement, Gandhi wrote: 'The All-India Tilak Memorial Swaraj Fund should be large enough to meet every requirement, not excluding that of national institutions. Welcome as the thousands of monied men must be to us, we must rely upon the pice[12] of the masses. Every pice knowingly given will be a token of the determination of the giver to establish *Swaraj.*

'The movement can be financed by the nation by abandoning its superfluities, its questionable habits and its vices. We are poor people, getting poorer daily; and if we are to make collections from the masses we shall do so only by acts of self-denial. There is certainly always something which we can deny ourselves for the sake of the country.'

---

[10]Cities and regions in erstwhile Burma.

[11]*Young India,* 12th January, 1921.

[12]Pice – a former Indian monetary unit, equal to one quarter of an anna.

In another article titled *All-India Tilak Swaraj Fund,*[13] Gandhi again wrote: 'One crore rupees for the whole of India is a most modest tribute to the memory of a patriot so great as the Lokamanya. It is a trifle when we think of the object with which the memory of the deceased is to be associated. To contribute one crore rupees towards the attainment of *Swaraj* is not much. And it may be noted here that the money is not to be spent in foreign or other propaganda, but largely in spinning, weaving and other educational activity. It is to be spent in educating our children. The collection has to be distributed among the twenty-one provinces and should be finished before the 30th June next. Each province will on an average be expected to collect about five lakhs of rupees. But Bombay, Gujarat, Bengal, Punjab and such other provinces, may be expected to collect much more than Orissa or Andhra for instance.'

Over a decade later, *The Times of India* testily reported on 20th May, 1936, that the fund, having reached and surpassed its target of one crore rupees, 'was ostensibly collected to further the cause of *Swaraj*, was actually used for any object under the sun which the Congress authorities chose to call "constructive". The auditor intimates that "substantial sums have been expended on famine and flood relief and work among the depressed classes."'

The *Times* report though, not opposed to the relief work, cautioned against the fund being utilised for something other than what it had been collected for, namely *Swaraj.* The fund had in fact attracted criticism much earlier. There were allegations of misuse of money and opaque accounting, drawing Jawaharlal Nehru in 1924 to defend the fund thus: 'We may mention that out of rupees fifty-four lakhs which have been given for specific earmarked objects, rupees twenty-two lakhs are invested in immovable properties, trusts, valuable securities, etc., and the income accruing from them is spent on the objects named.'

---

[13]*Young India,* 16th March, 1921

While the causes of the Great Depression, as successive recessions have proved, were largely economic, they were also demographic (migration and mobility), social (growing localism, income inequality and distrust of the elite), and geopolitical (rising isolationism, nationalism and authoritarianism). The unemployment and poverty that swept the world had far-reaching consequences. Authoritarian regimes were established in several countries in Europe and South America. Hitler was appointed chancellor of Germany in 1933. The first Nazi concentration camp was set up in the same year. Ethiopia, China and Poland were invaded by expansionist world powers.

Most of the world, however, still grappling with the seismic tremors of the Depression, failed to see or accept these changing global contours until it was too late. The Second World War would unleash within years as a reign of destruction the world had never seen. It would also mark a new era in business and trading worldwide as global stock and commodities markets fluctuated widely, throwing up new opportunities and challenges.

The Great Depression affected the US economy more than it did any major European or Asian country. America's GDP dropped by 26 per cent from 1929 to 1933. This compared to a six per cent decline in Britain's GDP and an 11 per cent fall in GDP across continental Europe during the same period. Though, the effects of the Depression were felt till the late-1930s, economic recovery in affected countries was relatively quick. From 1933 onwards US GDP grew at over 8 per cent per year. By 1941, it was 41 per cent higher than in 1933. British GDP too had, by 1934, risen above its 1929 level.

At the start of the 1930s, with more than 15 million Americans, a quarter of the country's workforce unemployed, not many could foresee that there would soon be a change for the better. Though, President Herbert Hoover was unable to alleviate the crisis, his successor in 1932, President Roosevelt, pledged to use the power of the federal government to improve the lives of Americans. His new deal created an enlarged role for government in American life and provided an unprecedented safety net to millions. As the US struggled to get back on its feet, Seksaria had his eyes fixed firmly on New York.

Chapter Three

THE FIRST CALL OF FREEDOM

The seminal events of the period between 1905 and 1940 shaped Govindram's worldview, life and work. This was the most decisive era in modern history. The empires of Britain, France, Portugal and Spain teetered on the edge. Where others saw apocalypse, Govindram and other rising Indian business leaders saw opportunity. A challenging but rewarding future beckoned.

In 1930, a formal declaration of national independence (unrecognised by the British) was made by the Indian National Congress under Gandhi's leadership. To an informed Indian or even within the insulated confines of the British establishment, it was becoming impossible to feign ignorance of swelling popular sentiment for Independence. Indians increasingly saw the British Raj as morally, economically and politically bankrupt. No matter how humble, simply spoken and non-violent the leaders of the *Swaraj* movement sought to be, by the 1930s they represented more than just an existential threat to colonial rule. Mahatma Gandhi, Jawaharlal Nehru, Sardar Vallabhbhai Patel and Subash Chandra Bose made an uncompromising statement: colonial rule was over. The British Raj, as historical fact and as a system of government, had effectively ended by the late-1930s.

The Congress leaders declared: 'We hold it to be a crime against man and God to submit any longer to a rule that has caused [...] disaster to our country. We recognise, however, that the most effective way of gaining our freedom is through non-violence. We will, therefore, prepare ourselves by withdrawing, so far as we can, all voluntary association from the British government and will prepare for civil disobedience, including non-payment of taxes. We are convinced that if we can but withdraw our voluntary help and stop payment of taxes without doing violence, even under provocation, the end of this inhuman rule is assured. We, hereby, solemnly resolve to carry out the instructions issued by the Congress from time to time for the purpose of establishing *Purna Swaraj*'[14].

Cotton was destined to lie at the heart of Govindram's success. It is important, therefore, to examine its provenance. According to the Tata Institute of Fundamental Research (TIFR): 'In the mid-19th century, India would export cotton to Britain. Then textiles made from the same cotton were re-imported into India. Between 1820 and 1860, the total cost of textile imports rose from Rs 3.50 lakh to Rs 1.93 crore.'

Indian entrepreneurs, however, felt the need to set up a domestic cotton industry. India's first cotton mill was opened in 1854 by Cowasji Nanabhai Davar. It was called The Bombay Spinning Mill. Though, initial opposition came from the mill owners in Lancashire, this was offset by British manufacturers of textile machinery.

'The American Civil War (1861-1865) interrupted Britain's cotton supply. This led to the growth of cotton exports from

[14]Indian National Congress Declaration, 26th January, 1930, in Nehru, Jawaharlal. *Toward Freedom: The Autobiography of Jawaharlal Nehru*. New York: John Day, 1942.

India. Before the Civil War, English mills imported only 20 per cent of their cotton from India. By 1865, when General Lee's army surrendered, Bombay had earned 70 million pounds sterling. This money spurred a financial bubble, with land reclamation schemes and the dockyards attracting huge investments. By January 1865, Bombay had 31 banks, eight reclamation companies, 16 cotton pressing companies, 10 shipping companies, 20 insurance companies and 62 joint stock companies. Within two months of the American Civil War ending, most of these companies went into liquidation. Large numbers of speculators became bankrupt. However, wealth had been created and this immediately led to industrial growth.'

TIFR elaborates on how cotton gained prominence over the years: 'By 1870, there were 13 cotton mills in Bombay and at the end of 1895, there were 70 mills. This number grew to 83 in 1915. There was a period of stagnation during the recession in the 1920s. In 1925, there were 81 mills in the city. After World War II, due to strong competition from Japan, the mills declined. By 1953 only 53 mills remained in the city. The cotton mills of Bombay, and the rest of India, were owned and managed mainly by Indians. The initial investments came from families of the mill owners, mainly obtained from trading. Later, when shares became available to the public, much of the ownership still remained Indian. The management and directorships of these mills were also mainly Indian.'

Both World Wars and the *Swadeshi* movement gave a strong boost to the Indian cotton textile industry. Despite this, during a slump between 1922 and 1937, a number of Bombay mills changed hands. However, with the onset of the Second World War and imports from Japan ceasing, the industry experienced an unprecedented period of growth. The 1930s and 1940s were the Golden Age of King Cotton.[15] The East India Cotton Exchange reached the pinnacle of its success during the war years, humming with activity day and night.

---

[15]A.D. Gordon p. 87.

In 1918, there had been a deeply felt need for reforms in the raw cotton market. Mill owners required the free flow of cotton to feed their industries and were growing impatient with the cornering of cotton by speculators. Thus, by 1920 Sir Ibrahim Rahimtoolah and other members of the Bombay Millowners' Association (BMA) began to strongly express the need for regulation to check the *kutcha khandi* and *teji-mandi* market.[16]

Efforts were made to implement practical suggestions from the Indian Cotton Committee. After several meetings and proposals on 19th June, 1922 the East India Cotton Association approached the Government of Bombay to recognise it as a statutory body, enabling it to regulate the trade effectively.[17] Sir Purshottamdas Thakurdas, a close friend of Govindram, was one of the chief propagators of such uniform control.

This was not the only frustration felt by industrialists. By 1922, when Govindram was rising rapidly through the traders' hierarchy, Japanese competition had affected the Bombay cotton industry to such an extent that it practically ceased to exist. It would take years of concerted effort by Indian traders to revive the industry.

Gordon divides the politics of India into two stages. According to him the period between 1918 and 1922 (Non-Cooperation movement) was one of 'agitational' politics while the period between 1922 and 1930 was one of 'constitutional' politics. In the 'agitational' period, most big industrialists and mill owners had steered away from Gandhi's passive resistance. In 1920-21, when the Tilak Swaraj Fund was initiated, Gandhi remarked on the lack of contributions by big industrialists.

A chief propagator of the fund was Jamnalal Bajaj and Seksaria reportedly contributed monthly to it. Gordon also notes that contributions by many Indian businessmen might

---

[16]*Saga of the Cotton Exchange,* Madhoo Pavaskar, p. 54.

[17]http://theory.tifr.res.in/bombay/history/cotton.html

have taken place confidentially to avoid the wrath of the British colonial government. In this period, Marwaris and Gujaratis were consistently pro-nationalist.[18] This was because they believed that the fiscal and currency exchange policies of the British government targeted them instead of industrialists and British companies operating in India. Markovits voices a similar opinion. In the 1920s, wealthy industrialists were supportive of the British government to such an extent that, between 1920 and 1922, Sir Purshottamdas Thakurdas spearheaded the short-lived anti-non-cooperation movement.

Factionalism among Indian businessmen was based on common interests rather than community or kin relationships. Indian businessmen's relations with the British colonial state also depended on their personal rapport with officials. G.D. Birla, for instance, was close to Sir George Schuster, finance member of the Government of India between 1929 and 1934, but had no relationship with his successor.[19]

However, the post-War period created severe economic difficulties. Industries experienced a slump. The Great Depression rippled around the world. This affected the big industrialists, leading to an increase in their support to nationalists within the 'constitutional' political framework. It was a critical time for Indian businessmen, caught as they were between the need to maintain cordial ties with British colonial authorities and the rising tide of nationalist fervour for Independence.

Meanwhile, far from being unnerved by the economic crisis in America and the charged political atmosphere in India, 40 year old Seksaria prepared for his great leap forward. Within a short period, as the global economy slumped in the early-1930s, he would morph into an international commodities trader and homespun industrialist.

---

[18]A.D. Gordon, pp 155-161.

[19]*Indian Business and Nationalist Politics,* Claude Markovits, pp 37-39.

As a colonial power, Britain differed vastly from its nautical rivals Portugal and Spain, even indeed from France. While Portugal and Spain's conquests were imbued with clinical proselytising, France was committed to cultural diffusion. To the British though, all that mattered was commerce. In 1858, thirty years before Govindram Seksaria was born, India had come under the control of the British Crown. The first war of Independence, often wrongly called the Mutiny of 1857, had proved to be the trigger. Direct colonial rule, coupled with the technological advances of the Industrial Revolution, ensured that the economies of Britain and India would be inextricably linked over the next century.

Britain was the first country in the world to industrialise. It was technologically ahead of other European countries through most of the nineteenth century. Britain's economy was the world's largest—ahead of the United States and Germany, its closest rivals. As a result, Britain was insulated from the effects of the first long Depression that stretched from 1873 to 1896. The worldwide price recession crippled several economies. It was only at the end of the nineteenth century that Germany, Italy, Russia and the United States challenged Britain's technological and economic dominance.

Though, the world's per capita income between 1870 and 1913 increased nearly three times faster than it had in the past, India's economy grew at less than one per cent per year. With its population rising rapidly, per capita income stagnated. Poverty remained endemic. The world's average per capita income had risen at an annual rate of 1.3 per cent in 1870-1913 compared to 0.5 per cent a year in 1820-1870. This relatively buoyant global economy was a result of technological advances made in the aftermath of the Industrial Revolution as well as a growing educated and skilled labour force and the absence of global military conflicts. In contrast, between 1688 and 1815, six major wars had erupted.

Britain's colonial rule in India led to several social and economic depredations. However, as Professor Dwijendra Tripathi, one of India's leading business historians says, by virtue of being part of the British Empire India's economy absorbed the benefit of technology, the rule of law and global business practices. This would play an important role in Seksaria's business career as the new century wore on.

India was a strategic possession, both geographically and economically. Queen Victoria was proclaimed Empress of India in 1876. She replaced East India Company officials with a cadre of trained bureaucrats who increased the monopolies held by the company. This club of all-white men had nothing in common with those it ruled. Fortunately though, corruption in civil administration was relatively low. Individual British buccaneers made personal fortunes (as Robert Clive had done over a century ago) but institutionalised graft was rare. Law and order was efficient and the judicial process swift, if occasionally biased against Indians.

The new business and social elite enjoyed a western lifestyle in an Eastern milieu. Having no interest in proselytising Indians, the British established themselves as a separate ruling class. Like regimented Indian castes, they lived insular lives. They did not socialise with Indians except with those in the highest echelons: Maharajas and Nawabs. Their children, when old enough were packed off to Britain to experience the rigours of the public school system. And at the end of their professional careers nearly all of them returned home to what they believed was well-earned retirement. Their lifestyle would soon be adopted by a new class of professional Indians—businessmen, lawyers, doctors, teachers and traders—who would over the next few decades play a crucial role in India's freedom movement.

In rural India the impact of the British was minimal. It did not create a significant change in their traditional way of life or in the production techniques employed in agriculture. For Govindram, living as he did in Nawalgarh as a young boy in the 1890s, the British would have had little impact on his life. There was no need to learn English as those in urban India often did. In fact, so insulated was his early life from the mainstream that besides his mother tongue Marwari, he was not exposed to even Hindi which would become the official national language in 1949. It is a measure of his acuity that, despite this linguistic disadvantage, he became a remarkably successful businessman with a global trading footprint and a vast industrial empire.

In the economic history of India, therefore, lie clues to the key factors that would, a century later, enable a generation of businessmen like Govindram Seksaria to build a fortune in cotton trading and manufacturing industry and, through philanthropy, especially in education, contribute to the nation's development.

By the turn of the eighteenth century and the early nineteenth century, the political and economic environment in India had changed dramatically. Centuries-old Mughal power had declined, reorienting power centres from Mughal fiefs to new regional capitals. This change led to a series of events. Merchants and business groups were becoming not just economically important but politically influential. These trading and banking communities provided credit to the new regional rulers. In turn they gained important political positions.

The Industrial Revolution in England had spawned rapid growth in manufacturing, especially, in the textiles sector. Modern industries soon spread to other parts of Europe. In need of markets and raw materials, these countries shifted their focus to Asia and Africa, leading to a scramble for colonies. By the end of the eighteenth century, the British had effectively defeated other European powers in India. By the nineteenth century, it had taken political control over most of the Indian dominion. This led to a change in trading patterns. The produce of British colonies was used to finance Britain's imperial ambitions as well as keep its factories at home busy. In this kind of trade, cotton especially, from the slave plantations of America became an important commodity.

Britain needed raw materials to feed its industries as well as discover markets for its finished products. This greatly affected the Indian economy, leading Indian nationalists like Dadabhai

Naoroji to propose the 'drain theory', criticising the British government for rampant exploitation. Despite the increasing discontent, the Bombay Presidency stayed for the most part aloof. The primary reason was the growing commercial relationships between indigenous business communities and the British. However, a need for peaceful protests was soon felt, leading to the formation of the Indian National Congress in 1885. Born three years later, Govindram would play an important role as a donor to the Congress as the freedom movement entered its decisive phase 50 years later.

The British transformed the financial and industrial infrastructure of India. Indian textiles and spices had once been bought in exchange for bullion. Now farmers were forced to grow cash crops like cotton and tea for export instead of food crops. Huge revenues from land rent and taxes on commodities like salt were inflicted on the country. The policy of fair trade that the British adopted in India to create a market for British products was inherently flawed. British capitalists who invested in India or provided services like banking, insurance and shipping enjoyed monopolies. India was also the ideal arena for Britain's middle classes to find employment. They went on to remit their generous salaries home.

With his family engaged in cloth trading, Govindram had spent hours in the family's small shop playing with cloth as a young child. Cotton would play a pivotal role in Govindram's life though, he was obviously unaware then of the major role cotton had always enjoyed in world economies. In the United States, for instance, the term King Cotton was coined by over-zealous Southern politicians who believed, erroneously as it turned out, that Britain's reliance on cotton would ensure its intervention in America's Civil War and that an independent confederacy would be economically successful. Senator James Henry Hammond famously said in 1858: 'What would happen if no cotton was furnished for three years? England would topple headlong and carry the whole civilised world with her. No, you dare not make war on cotton! No power on earth dares make war upon it. Cotton is King.'

Cotton diplomacy, unfortunately for the South, proved unsuccessful. Some historians believe that America's Civil War, which led to an interruption in the supply of baled cotton exports, triggered the Lancashire Cotton Famine of 1861-1865. Others, however, argue that the 'famine' was primarily due to over-production and price inflation caused by an expectation of future shortages. The American Civil War nonetheless catalysed the cultivation of cotton in more land acreage across India. It would have a significant impact on Govindram Seksaria's career more than half a century later.

Henry Louis Gates, Jr., the Harvard University scholar, describes vividly in *The African Americans* the seminal role cotton played in shaping America's economy, politics and society: 'The most commonly used phrase describing the growth of the American economy in the 1830s and 1840s was "Cotton Is King". We think of this slogan today as describing the plantation economy of the slavery states in the Deep South, which led to the creation of "the second Middle Passage". But it is important to understand that this was not simply a Southern phenomenon. Cotton was one of the world's first luxury commodities, after sugar and tobacco, and was also the commodity whose production most dramatically turned millions of black human beings in the United States themselves into commodities. Cotton became the first mass consumer commodity.

'Understanding both how extraordinarily profitable cotton was and how interconnected and overlapping were the economies of the cotton plantation, the Northern banking industry, New England textile factories and a huge proportion of the economy of Great Britain helps us to understand why it was something of a miracle that slavery was finally abolished in this country at all. Let me try to break this down quickly, since it is so fascinating.

'Let's start with the value of the slave population. Steven Deyle shows that in 1860, the value of the slaves was roughly three times greater than the total amount invested in banks, and it was equal to about seven times the total value of all currency in circulation in the country, three times the value of the entire livestock population, twelve times the value of the entire US cotton crop and forty-eight times the total expenditure of the federal government that year.' The invention of cotton greatly increased the productivity of cotton harvesting by slaves. This resulted in dramatically higher profits for planters, which in turn led to a seemingly insatiable increase in the demand for more slaves, in a savage, brutal and vicious cycle.

'Now, the value of cotton: slave-produced cotton 'brought commercial ascendancy to New York City, and was the driving force for territorial expansion in the Old Southwest and fostered trade between Europe and the United States,' according to Gene Dattel. 'In fact, cotton productivity, no doubt due to the sharecropping system that replaced slavery, remained central to the American economy for a very long time: cotton was the leading American export from 1803 to 1937.'

What did cotton production and slavery have to do with Great Britain? The figures are astonishing. As Dattel explains: 'Britain, the most powerful nation in the world, relied on slave-produced American cotton for over 80 per cent of its essential industrial raw material. English textile mills accounted for 40 percent of Britain's exports. One-fifth of Britain's twenty-two million people were directly or indirectly involved with cotton textiles.'

And, finally, New England. As Ronald Bailey shows, cotton fed the textile revolution in the United States. 'In 1860, for example, New England had 52 per cent of the manufacturing establishments and 75 per cent of the 5.14 million spindles in operation,' he explains. The same goes for looms. In fact, 'Massachusetts alone had 30 per cent of all spindles and Rhode Island another 18 per cent.' Most impressive of all, 'New England mills consumed 283.7 million pounds of cotton, or 67 per cent of the 422.6 million pounds of cotton used by US mills in 1860.' In other words, on the eve of the Civil War, New England's economy so fundamentally dependent upon the textile industry, was inextricably intertwined, as Bailey puts it, 'to the labor of black people working as slaves in the US South.'

'If there was one ultimate cause of the Civil War, it was King Cotton—black slave-grown cotton—"the most important determinant of American history in the nineteenth century," Dattel concludes. 'Cotton prolonged America's most serious social tragedy, slavery, and slave-produced cotton caused the American Civil War.' And that is why it was something of a miracle that even the New England states joined the war to end slavery.

'Once we understand the paramount economic importance of cotton to the economies of the United States and Great Britain, we can begin to appreciate the enormity of the achievements of the black and white abolitionists who managed to marshal moral support for the abolition of slavery, as well as those half-a-million slaves who "marched with their feet" and fled to Union lines as soon as they could following the signing of the Emancipation Proclamation.'

Cotton has historically been an important commodity for the Indian economy. It was known from as far back as the Indus Valley Civilisation. Trading in the commodity has its roots in 60 AD[20]. Almost every household wove cotton textiles, making it a widespread industry. It is no surprise then that cotton was to a large extent the mainstay of the Indian economy. As author and historian Madan Gaur writes, 'King Cotton, though a fibre, cannot be defined merely as a commodity. It is a culture which wields royal spectre, which symbolises both authority and power, but which has also been a blend of service and sacrifice.'[21]

---

[20]M.P. Gandhi, p 3.

[21]*Saga of the Cotton Exchange*, by Madan Gaur pp 3-4.

By 1800, cotton exports from India had risen to 150,000 bales. Recognising the importance of Indian cotton, the British Governor-General India, Lord Ellenborough, stated in 1842 that the objective of the East India Company was not only to improve the quality but also the quantity of cotton grown in India and thereby, to gradually substitute it for the cotton imported from the United States.

According to author Amalendu Guha, the geographical specialisation of cotton began even before the development of the railways. However, with the growth of railway networks this specialisation became more prominent.[22] Around 1825, exports from Bombay became significant. From 1832, a rise in the price of American cotton resulted in increased imports of Indian cotton. These imports touched a new high of almost a million bales a year.

Though the first cotton mill was set up in Calcutta in 1818, major developments took place only after 1851 with the establishment of Bombay Spinning and Weaving Mill. For the export and import of cotton, port cities became points of embarkation and disembarkation. Their importance also depended on their proximity to production centres. Surat was the most important port in the time of the Mughals. However, by the end of the seventeenth century and the beginning of the eighteenth, Surat lost its importance to Bombay which was being developed specifically for this purpose by the British. The period between 1885 and 1895 represented the third phase in the expansion of the cotton textile industry in India. An additional 21 mills were set up, taking the total to 70 mills. These new mills included those established by Currimbhoy and Sons, Sassoon J. David and Co. and E.D. Sassoon and Co.[23]

A newspaper article observed astutely: 'As the Civil War ravaged America and its cotton economy collapsed, Bombay stepped in to plug that void with its own cotton industry.

---

[22]*Growth of Acreage Under Raw Cotton in India 1851-1901*, Amalendu Guha, p 1.
[23]*Cotton Production in India*, Henry W Spielman, p 3.

Picking up from the mercantile decline of Calcutta, Bombay really became the urbs prima.'[24]

During the American Civil War Britain and France turned to Egyptian cotton, tempting the Egyptian government of Viceroy Isma'il to accept substantial loans from European bankers and stock exchanges. When the war ended, British and French traders unceremoniously abandoned Egyptian cotton for its cheaper American version. This sent Egypt into a deficit spiral that led to the country declaring bankruptcy in 1876. It gave the British Empire the leverage it had been seeking to occupy Egypt in 1882.

Following its victory in the Franco-Prussian War in 1870, Germany had extracted a huge indemnity from France of £200 million. It then joined Britain on a gold standard for its currency. France, the United States and other industrialising countries followed suit. India, subject to imperial policies, remained on a silver standard. With discovery of more silver reserves, currencies based on gold rose in value and those based on silver declined due to the demonetisation of silver. As the price of silver continued to fall, there was massive depreciation of the rupee against the pound sterling. British imports became prohibitively expensive.

British colonialism did, however, as business historian Professor Dwijendra Tripathi and others have said, imbue India with key advantages. Britain introduced a modified version of the English education system in 1835. It established three universities in Calcutta, Madras and Bombay. Though they were initially merely examining bodies, they gave India's elite access to modern education.

Britain also modernised India's legal, justice and civil service systems. It built roads, railways, canals and bridges across India. In the mid-1850s, two new railway companies, the Great Indian Peninsular Railway and the East Indian Railway began to construct and operate lines near Bombay and Calcutta. By

---

[24]*Mumbai Mirror,* 10th January, 2016

1909, the railway network was the fourth largest in the world. By 1913, India had a bigger railway network than Britain. This helped relocate business and economic activities, opened new lands for development, enhanced markets and increased the scope for urban migration.

The objective, though superficially altruistic, was to enable the smooth passage of raw materials, especially cotton, from India's hinterland to ports like Bombay and from there to Liverpool in England. Unfortunately, while in Britain private investors voluntarily funded its infrastructural development, in India it was local taxpayers who were compelled to do so.

The growth of Bombay as a commercial port city encouraged several business communities to migrate to the island. These communities entered into partnerships with private British agents and began trading with other Asian countries, especially China. Several Parsi and Gujarati business communities prospered in such trade. Principal among these were Jamshetjee Jeejeebhoy, the Sassoons, the Wadias (who were also shipbuilders), the Mafatlals and the Petits.

The author and economist Dr. Madhoo Pavaskar explains how the increase in trading and production of commodities also carried increasing risks in the form of natural or man-made disasters, leading to the development of insurance mechanisms. One such mechanism was the growth of commodity speculation markets. It follows that speculation in cotton existed in rudimentary form during this period. In the aftermath of the American Civil War, speculation became so profitable that several merchants made small fortunes. Premchand Roychand, who became known as the 'Cotton King', stood out.

It is a title Govindram Seksaria would inherit.

New technology meanwhile transformed India's agricultural economy. Though agriculture still dominated the economy and extensive irrigation systems were built, providing a boost for raw materials like cotton and jute, most farmers lived in relative poverty. Shipping too received an impetus from the technological boom. While the first steamship appeared in Britain in 1812, by the 1880s iron and steel ships were primarily used in India. Being bigger, quicker and more reliable, they helped boost commodity exports.

The opening of the Suez Canal in 1869 cut the distance between London and Bombay by 41 per cent. By the late-1890s, a large fraction of cotton was being exported to distant overseas markets. Small farmers, dependent on the caprice of foreign markets, lost their land to moneylenders. All these apparently unconnected developments would lay the foundation for Indian business to flourish in the 1900s, allowing pioneers like Govindram Seksaria to prosper through, first, trading and then industry.

Under British rule, India became increasingly vulnerable to recurrent famines and epidemic diseases. In 1876-78 and 1899-1900, famine killed millions. Official figures place the number of Indians who died of starvation between 1854 and 1901 at 28 million. In the 1890s, there was also a widespread outbreak of bubonic plague. And in 1919, India reeled under the great influenza epidemic. The monolithic colonial administration was inept or unwilling to truly help. However, the overall death rate in India gradually reduced during British rule. Internal warfare and local banditry were controlled and the British contributed to overall public health by introducing Western medicine.

The economic fallout of continual degradations of India's agrarian economy led to the migration of Indians to countries in southeast Asia such as Burma, Malaya, Ceylon, Thailand and Vietnam. This raised the incomes of migrants whose remittances to families back home helped invigorate the Indian economy. The migration was facilitated by cheap passenger services that transcontinental liners offered. It also led to over 4,50,000 indentured workers being forcibly shipped to the British Caribbean to compensate for the loss of slaves and bonded labour from Africa.

The British government, with its constitutional monarchy,

was ironically considered a model of liberal democracy. Its strength lay in its ability to stifle revolution through calibrated reform. European Imperialism was widespread and Britain zealously set out to add to its possessions. By 1870, the United Kingdom possessed the world's largest Empire that covered one-sixth of the earth's land surface. The crown jewel of the Empire was of course India. It accounted for three-fourths of the Empire's population. Indian taxes financed British military presence and conquests around the world.

From the 1860s to the 1940s, the drain of resources from India to Britain fluctuated between 0.9 and 1.3 per cent of national income. Additionally, over a fifth of net savings were transferred to Britain—funds that could have been used to import capital goods and finance Indian infrastructure. Britain also sent half its Indian savings abroad, a massive outflow of capital that was used by the British government for overseas investment.

Fortunately, the impact on India of this outflow was cushioned since most of it was in the form of bonds or in the construction of the railways. The telegraph was invented in 1850. By 1870, having laid cables on the floor of the sea, Britain was in direct contact with India. The telegraph helped immeasurably in integrating global financial markets. It would serve as a crucial tool in Seksaria's future business, especially in the 1930s when he needed to be in constant touch with traders in the New York Cotton Exchange.

The engine that powered Britain's industrialisation was its textiles sector. The mills of Lancashire were well-lubricated cogs in that engine. In the efflorescent years of the Industrial Revolution, British inventors furnished the textile industry with a number of implements that propelled its growth. John Kay's flying shuttle, James Hargreaves' spinning jenny, Crompton's mule and Boulton and Watt's steam engine were some of the inventions that helped place the English Midlands at the vanguard of the global textile industry. The creation of chemical bleaches and dyes ensured that bleaching, dyeing and printing could all be done in the same factory. Robert's power loom enabled every stage in the making of cotton textiles to be conducted under one roof.

With Britain having conquered Bengal in 1757, less than two decades before the Industrial Revolution began, it was determined to scuttle India's textile industry in order to lay the ground for British textile imports. Apocryphal stories swirl about the ways in which this was initially done. In one version, the East India Company is said to have ordered the hands of hundreds of Bengali weavers to be cut off. In another, the thumbs of weavers were slashed. Yet another account alleges that many weavers cut off their own hands to protest their deplorable working conditions. Wherever the truth lies, the fact is that Britain was successful in seriously damaging India's textile industry.

Britain looked at India as a cradle for capital, raw materials, labour and a readymade market for its finished goods. Tax revenue and raw cotton were appropriated and sent to Britain. Manufactured textiles that had the advantage of zero duties and tariffs were sold back to colonial India. The Indian textile market reeled under the combined onslaught of Britain's lower production costs, greater supplies and manipulated tariffs.

As the British cotton industry underwent a technological revolution in the late-eighteenth century, India's cotton industry stagnated. India would have to wait till the early-twentieth century for industrialisation to take firm root. If Britain had been willing to extend tariff protection, India could have imbibed the technological advancements of the Lancashire mills and enjoyed a level playing field to compete as the United States and France successfully did. British imports, however, entered India duty-free.

When a small tariff was required for revenue purposes, pressure from the Lancashire mills led to the imposition of a corresponding excise duty on Indian products in order to prevent them gaining a competitive advantage. This handicapped India's industrial development. In the 1880s, Indian customs revenues were only 2.2 per cent of trade turnover, the lowest ratio of any country. In Brazil, by contrast, import duties during that period were 21 per cent of trade turnover. If India had enjoyed duty protection, there is little doubt its textile industry would have prospered far earlier than it eventually did.

Indian industrial efficiency was also hampered by the British administration's neglect of technical education and the reluctance of British firms and managing agencies to provide training and managerial experience to Indians. Though most of the capital in the textile mills was Indian in the late-1800s, 42 per cent of management and supervisory staff was British. This contributed to spiralling overhead costs. As a consequence, Indian mills supplied only 8 per cent of Indian cloth consumption, a figure that gradually rose to 20 per cent in 1913 and as Indian industry evolved, to 76 per cent in 1945 on the eve of Independence.

Despite handicaps, the establishment of textile mills in India preceded those in Japan by 20 years and in China by 40 years, making India the first Asian country to harbour a modern textile industry. In 1861, Seth Ranchhodmal Chotalal set up a cotton spinning wheel with machines brought from England. Production in cotton mills was concentrated on coarse yarn sold to China and Japan. Exports were half of total output. In 1874, The Central India Spinning, Weaving and Manufacturing Company was established by Jamsetji Tata, marking the Tata group's entry into textiles—and its first large-scale industrial venture. It also signalled the beginning of Jamsetji's stellar industrial career.

As with all Tata ventures, Jamsetji sought to create quality products. He spurned the cheap coarse yarn and cloth that was produced in other mills using indigenous short-staple cotton and cheap British machines in favour of more expensive longer-stapled cotton from Egypt and more sophisticated ring-spindle American machines. The result was finer yarn that could compete with the best in the world.

Exports to Britain had been on the decline from the second half of the nineteenth century as the British textile industry began to favour long-staple American cotton over medium and short-staple Indian cotton. The loss in exports to Britain was, however, compensated by exports to China and, more particularly, Japan. As the dependence on Japan grew, the Japanese began to dump cheap manufactured textiles into India. This succeeded in depressing the prices of Indian cotton. After the First World War in 1918, the price of Indian cotton slumped. Now an avid trader, Govindram cut his teeth on such cotton price swings. It would sharpen his instincts as a speculator, trader and in years to come, manufacturer.

Yarn exports to Japan had meanwhile dropped precipitously from 8,400 tonnes in 1890 to practically nothing in 1898. India also suffered from Japanese competition in its trade with China. The Japanese had set up factories in China after the Sino-Japanese War of 1894-95. Before this, India had supplied 96 per cent of Chinese yarn imports. Within three years the Japanese, with exemplary commercial acumen, were supplying a quarter of Chinese imports. By 1914, India was exporting less yarn to China than Japan was doing. During the First World War, Japan made further progress in the Chinese market. By 1924, it accounted for three-quarters of Chinese imports. By 1928, India was exporting only three per cent of its yarn output. And by the end of the 1930s, Indian exports of yarn to China and Japan had all but stopped. Soon after, India was forced to import both yarn and finished goods from China and Japan. It was a period in which Seksaria would have to strain every nerve and sinew to prosper in a difficult and rapidly changing environment.

The explosive growth in the number of mills and the temptation to make fortunes in cotton speculation gave rise to a new wave of migrations, especially from Gujarat and Rajasthan. Marwari traders initially came mostly from the Shekhawati region of Rajasthan. These merchants had become so economically prominent in their own region that they acted as advisers to royalty.

As they were mostly known for long-distance trade, the

major towns of the Shekhawati region such as Nawalgarh, Dundlod, Ramgarh, Sikar, Mandawa, Fatehpur, Lachhmangarh, Jhunjhunu, Bissau, Khetri and Bagar were linked to important trade routes.[25] Of all the villages in this region, Nawalgarh produced the greatest number of billionaires—23 in total.[26] Govindram Seksaria was among the most prominent but also among the most low profile.

To keep a semblance of control over the rapid rise in speculative activities after the American Civil War, the Bombay Cotton Trade Association had been formed in 1875. However, the association did not involve Indians in important positions. This led to the rise of the Bombay Native Cotton Merchants Association as a reaction. The cotton industry soon expanded to the extent that leaders in cotton such as Jamsetji Tata, Dinshaw Petit, Cursandas Vallabhdas and Narayandas Purshottamdas came together to establish the Bombay Cotton Exchange Limited which was registered in 1893.

Throughout Seksaria's life, and well into the 1950s, Indian cotton cultivation remained non-mechanical. Cotton farms were small. Farmers preferred to use traditional, oxen-pulled ploughs and planters, and short-handled hoes or more commonly, a *kharpa,* which has a flat blade and short handle. Cotton picking was traditionally the role of women and was usually taken care of by the farmer's wife and children. For slightly bigger farms, neighbours or other villagers were hired to help with the picking. Instead of using sacks, pickers in India would traditionally use a part of their sari to place the gathered cotton.

The planting season for cotton was from April to November. Harvesting was from September to July. However, in the Oomra tract and northern Bombay Province, planting was done from June to July and harvesting from October to March. In 1950, the average yield for cotton in India was 39 kg per acre, though it was considerably higher than the average in the Broach region.

---

[25]*Cotton Production in India,* Harry Spielman, 1950.

[26]*Nawalgarh* in History.

Once plucked, the cotton was passed through a cleaner before being pressed.

The cleaning process allowed the dealer to mix various qualities of cotton to form uniform bales. According to Spielman, each bale was secured using a wrapping of burlap and three metal straps, each wound two or three times around the bale. Bales were then marked with relevant information including the number of the gin, the number of the press, and the quality of the cotton. A pressed bale wasn't sampled until it was ready for sale either to a mill or an exporter. Samples were taken from random bales out of each sales lot. By the time cotton reached the mill owner or exporter it changed hands on average three to four times.

Depending on local customs, how a farmer sells his cotton varied from place to place. According to Spielman, around 70 per cent of the crop was sold in village markets, which was later resold in town markets. In village markets, it was usually the local buyer or a small local merchant who bought from farmers. Travelling buyers usually purchased cotton from local merchants: they could buy for themselves or be commissioned by a larger merchant, a ginner, a mill owner or an exporter.

Once a sale was conducted, it was usually the farmer's duty to transport the seed cotton. Sales were made through brokers who tried to get the highest price possible for the farmer, especially in organised town markets. It was the broker's job to weigh the cotton, both for the farmer and the buyers. These brokers took buyers through the market to examine the cotton and took down their bids.

Spielman writes: 'The broker covers his hands with a piece of cloth and each buyer in turn conveys his price by means of a code using finger signs. After the price is conveyed, there may be a long discussion of the price without mentioning a specific figure. If a buyer desires to revise his bid, he again covers his hands and passes the new price under cover. If the cultivator thinks the price is too low, he may ask the broker to store the cotton and sell it later.'

Apart from brokers, Spielman describes cooperative selling societies that help in the sale of cotton: 'Their goal is to reduce the cost of marketing cotton and to benefit the cultivators. The Indian Central Cotton Committee, with the help of government bodies, organised 104 such societies. These societies started coming up in the 1920s. At the Gadag Cooperative Cotton Sales Society Limited, Gadag, Bombay Province, cotton is collected at these societies, where each farmer's contribution is recorded. When a large amount of cotton is collected, an auction is held. Buyers from the region come to this auction, where samples of different grades of the cotton on sale are passed around. The chairman holds the auction and has the right to refuse to sell a batch of cotton if the bidding is too low.

'In the Surat district, there is a different form of sales, also organised by the Indian Central Cotton Committee. Five cooperative cotton gins, owned by cultivators, are set up within 35 miles of Surat. At these gins the farmers' cotton is processed and the bales are pooled together for a joint auction sale. Again, bales are organised by grade of cotton. These auctions are a rare example of farmers selling their cotton after it is ginned. In both auction markets, farmers receive the average price for the grade of the cotton they supplied. Once the cotton has passed from farmer to ginner, it passes hands once again. Cotton ginners usually sell their cotton to mills or to cotton merchants in Bombay. Cotton can also be shipped to Bombay for sale on the spot market (sellers would carry their samples from office to office, and interested buyers would place their bids).'

In the late 1940s, shortly after Seksaria's death it became common for merchants and exporters in Bombay to send a number of buyers to all the major cotton producing areas. These buyers would be instructed to either buy directly from farmers or village merchants. Mill buyers also adopted this practice with great success, at times making it difficult for the Bombay merchants to buy enough cotton to operate their cotton gins. Prior to the

1948-49 season, 45 per cent of the cotton in the Oomra tract was purchased by foreign cotton merchants, 30 per cent by other Bombay merchants and textile mills, and only 25 per cent by local merchants.

The East India Cotton Association maintained a futures market in Bombay where trading was run along the same lines as futures around the world. There were four delivery months in a year – February, May, July and September. It was up to the seller to deliver his cotton between the 7th and 25th of the delivery month. If the seller failed to do so, he was subject to a penalty. (At the time of publication of Spielman's book in 1950, four years after Seksaria's death, the penalty was fixed at $1.57 per khandi over the spot price fixed by the association on the last delivery date.) Deliveries were to be made in Bombay warehouses.

Writing in *The Saga of the Cotton Exchange,* Dr. Madhoo Pavaskar observes: 'Futures (hedge) trading in cotton took place in two sessions in Bombay. The midday session took place at Marwari Bazaar, Kalbadevi in a small, dingy room under the control of the Bombay Cotton Brokers' Association. The second session, called the afternoon session, took place at the cotton market in Colaba (before it moved to Sewri in 1923), between 4:30 and 6:30 pm, at the Bombay Cotton Trade Association. Marwari Bazaar was the heart of the cotton trade, though the commute to Sewri was inconvenient for futures trading. Hindu-Muslim riots in 1929 disrupted the afternoon sessions at Sewri, and though an attempt was made to revive this practice after the situation settled down, the afternoon session was soon abandoned altogether. After February 1929, only ready business in cotton was carried out at Sewri between 11 am and 2 pm, and futures remained restricted to Marwari Bazaar.

'Finally, after the Bombay Cotton Contract Act of 1932 was passed, the EICA acquired property in Marwari Bazaar, where construction of a new Cotton Exchange Building began. The foundation stone was laid on 12th February, 1936, in the presence of eminent cotton traders, notably Anandilal Podar and Sir Purshottamdas Thakurdas. The building was opened on August

1938. While the top floor was reserved for administration offices, the 113 rooms in the remaining floors were occupied by various members of the exchange. The trading hall of the building was filled with activity day and night till its decline in 1966.'

The importance of cotton to the Indian economy was reflected in the fact that, as early as 1917, there were eight associations in the cotton trade: Bombay Cotton Trade Association, Bombay Cotton Exchange, Bombay Cotton Brokers' Association, Cotton Merchants and Muccaddums' Association, Marwadi Chamber of Commerce, Japanese Cotton Shippers' Association, Gujarati Shroff Mahajan and Bombay Millowners' Association.[27]

With several associations competing with one another and fluctuations in prices due to the First World War, panic set in among speculators. According to A.D. Gordon, 'Within the raw cotton market the most infamous speculation was that which took place in the fine-staple Broach contract towards the end of 1917. When Broach cotton, in short supply for some years before, was driven to a high point of Rs. 800-850 per khandi or 188 per cent above par, Bombay was in a 'state of upheaval in which were all the signs of dissolution'.

To maintain control, the government appointed the Indian Cotton (Mackenna) Committee headed by Sir Gilbert Wiles. It suggested the establishment of one central association to control the cotton trade. Gordon observed that the press reported speculation during the war years by largely blaming smaller merchants, particularly Marwaris, rather than large operators even though they were heavy speculators as well.

Speculation also provided capital for cotton mills. Gordon wrote that most speculators entered the market as brokers and were drawn to speculation due to the availability of small contracts as well as a flourishing trade in 'options' (*teji mandi*) and forward/futures trading (*satta*). Brokers became enormously prosperous and linked their speculation profits to their 'legitimate trade'. Many invested in setting up cotton mills.

---

[27]*A Time of Transformation for the Global Cotton Market,* Madhoo Pavaskar.

The forward contracts also increased the opportunities for cornering markets, which became a common feature by 1919. It was this buoyant but wildly oscillating market that Govindram Seksaria plunged headlong into.

Chapter Four

Cotton is King

Govindram Seksaria began his career as an ambitious young businessman at a fortuitous time for Indian entrepreneurs. In 1888, when he was born, a year before Jawaharlal Nehru and five years before G.D. Birla, cotton industrialists around the world were engaged in a concerted attempt to develop new sources of raw cotton after the cotton famine of the 1860s.

This period of growth in the first two decades of the twentieth century corresponded with Seksaria's own entrance into the cotton trade, later leading to cotton ginning factories, cotton seed oil extraction plants and textile mills. Seksaria, like numerous others in his generation, recognised the significant opportunity for Indian business that this historical moment held and worked to make the most of it.

In her book *Three Merchants of Bombay,* Subramanian Lakshmi notes that much of Bombay's prosperity, starting early in the nineteenth century, was generated out of credit and bills supplied by local merchants. While Seksaria was born after the cotton industry had already begun to develop in Bombay, he soon became part of a larger Marwari network in the city which was known for providing credit and which later founded some of the most important banks in India.

Between 1932 and 1934, Seksaria bought a plot of land at Juhu beach in Bombay. The plot was large, around 9,000 sq yards. He acquired it for Rs. 1.32 lakh and also purchased a bungalow in Koregaon Park, Poona. Shrinarayan Seksaria, Govindram's nephew and brother Makhanlal's son, says: 'My mother says that *jethji* (elder brother-in-law) bought the Poona bungalow as he used to regularly visit Poona for the horse races.' These two purchases, collectively for around Rs. 2 lakh, show how well Seksaria's business was doing. He had earned enough money to afford two holiday homes in the 1930s when entire buildings in upscale areas of cities like Bombay were available for less than Rs. 1 lakh.

By the early 1930s, Seksaria's status as a key figure in cotton and as a creditor was so well established that even members of royal families turned to him in times of urgent need for funds. Diwan Jarmani Dass notes Seksaria's influence when he narrates the political fall of Jai Singh Prabhakar, Maharaja of Alwar, in the 1930s. Writing of the Maharaja's exile to Paris in 1933 by the governor-general of India for corruption and for his anti-British orientation, Diwan Jarmani Dass inadvertently also describes Seksaria's financial clout in India in the 1930s:

> 'The Government took this step on the pretext of bad finances and administration for which the Maharaja was charged. The State's finances were so depleted that it called for the disposition of the Maharaja. Shortly afterwards, he went to Europe with a staff of about 40 men and women after getting a loan from Seth Govind Ram Seksaria of Bombay, known as the Cotton King, after mortgaging part of his best jewellery.'[28]

In the first half of the twentieth century, when industry and

[28]*Diwan Jarmani Dass, Maharaja,* Hind Pocket Books, India 2007: 270.

politics were undergoing a significant transformation, Seksaria was at their financial centre of gravity. It was during this period that British and American businessmen found themselves competing with their counterparts in countries such as Brazil, China, Korea, Egypt and India. They had never had to do so in the past. England was compelled to compete with Japan and India in the production of finished goods for markets in India and China.

And although, Britain had a measure of advantage in India and Egypt due to its imperial presence in both countries, strong nationalist movements throughout the colonised world worked to transfer power into the hands of a new generation of political and business leaders. Additionally, in Britain and the United States wages for industrial workers were rising as a result of strong labour movements. Higher wages meant American and British industrialists had to work harder for their goods to be competitive in global markets.

As Sven Beckert explains in *The Empire of Cotton:*[29]

> 'Two groups played a decisive role in northeastern United States, and aspiring cotton capitalists in the global South (Asia). They contributed independently to a pair of mutually reinforcing processes: nationalising social conflicts and strengthening states. At the same time, capitalists in the global South (Asia) supported state policies conducive to their own project of domestic industrialisation . . . rising labor costs opened up new possibilities for manufacturing in those parts of the world in which labor was cheaper and less constrained by state regulations.'

The United States continued to expand its cotton agricultural industry since the cheap labour wages of former slaves allowed it to better compete in agricultural output. However in the 1920s,

[29]Beckert 2014, pp 383 and 391.

US growers also struggled against the devastating Boll Weevil which decimated its cotton crops in 1921, lowering the value of its cotton and forfeiting its market share of cotton supplies. As a result, the price of cotton registered on the Liverpool Cotton Futures Market fell significantly throughout the 1920s:

- February 1920: 29.19 pence per pound.
- March 1921: 6.68 pence per pound.
- March 1931: 3.38 pence per pound.

Speaking of the mid-1930s, Beckert observed '. . . the North Atlantic moment in cotton was over, its vaulted productivity and state sponsors no match for the precipitous wage differentials and the burgeoning nation-states of the global South (Asia).'

In such an environment, Seksaria, now a seasoned businessman in his forties, showed financial foresight. He invested his energies and capital into industries which were beginning to form the backbone of India's increased global financial competitiveness. India's manufacturing industries in cotton and other commodities did, of course, suffer from the worldwide recession of the 1930s. And indeed, in 1933, after witnessing riots in 1932 and an alarming drop in the price of cotton, Bombay's cotton industrialists broke with their usual stance of solidarity with the Indian National Congress.

In 1933, they withdrew their support of the Civil Disobedience campaign in which they had been asked to refuse to trade with European cotton merchants.[30] Nonetheless, although weakened by the recession, India's cotton industry prior to the Second World War was poised to grow. This was because the low cost of labour in India would soon allow Indian industries to undercut British, American and European products in international markets.

Seksaria's success cannot be attributed solely to his role as an Indian businessman during a period when the market for

---

[30]Madan Gaur, 1994, p 155.

Indian cotton production was expanding rapidly. Nor was it merely a consequence of diversifying his investments into other commodity markets poised to grow in India. Clearly, Seksaria's success was also a byproduct of his risk-taking ability and calm judgement. As an entrepreneur who had used trading profits to invest heavily in industry, it was natural that he extended this chain of 'continuum' to trading in commodities futures.

As a Marwari, Seksaria was not alone in speculation activity. Thomas Timberg observed:

> 'A considerable number of the larger Marwari business groups made their money in the speculative markets of the nineteenth century and especially, in the early-twentieth century during the First and Second World Wars. These funds they then sometimes invested in new industrial ventures.
>
> 'Though records of the great speculators are under-documented, there exists a body of anecdotes and stories which emphasizes how much they operated on intuition, perhaps based on superior commercial intelligence, and maybe even inside information before tapping into such information became illegal.'

This describes Seksaria well. He used profits made through speculation to launch and support industrial ventures. He maintained an impressive commercial network across India. And the daily phone call he received from market advisors in New York showed he had ready sources of information on the Bombay, New York and Liverpool cotton exchanges.

But what sets Seksaria apart from other Indian businessmen of the era is that he established his reputation in the 1930s far beyond India. He was unusually adept at international trading compared not only to other Indians but also to American and British traders. Most traders based in Liverpool and New York did not command the knowledge of trading on global markets necessary to undertake the scale of speculative trading that Seksaria managed across three continents.

The antecedents of trading in futures predates the development of cotton exchanges. The origins of contemporary stock trading are commonly attributed to the moneylenders of the Venetian Empire who traded securities from various governments in the fourteenth century.

These traders listed relevant sale information on slates for use in consultation with clients, not unlike contemporary brokers. In the seventeenth century, as the number of imperial trading ships expanded, the British, French and Dutch governments all extended charters to companies with 'East India' in their title. The practice allowed these companies to raise funds for what were essentially expensive and risky business ventures.

Debt and sales notifications were posted on shop doors or distributed through newsletters for the benefit of people who had invested in these voyages. This process of garnering investments for single commercial voyages gave way to a more effective system developed by the British East India Company which had the benefit of a government-backed monopoly. The East India Company created a system of dividends for investments (stocks) that were not paid in relation to a single voyage but paid in relation to the proceeds from all of the commercial voyages the company undertook during a specified period of time.

The London Stock Exchange was established in 1773, followed shortly by stock exchanges in Philadelphia and New York (1792). The global cotton market expanded so rapidly over the course of the nineteenth century that the industry developed its own exchanges. The New York Cotton Exchange was established in 1870 and the Liverpool Cotton Exchange in 1906.

During the heady days of cotton speculation, the price for a seat on the New York Cotton Exchange rose steeply. Between 1878 and 1880, an NYCE seat was sold for up to $45,000 (equivalent to several million dollars in today's money). In 1965, a seat on the exchange was listed for a mere $770.[31] These figures suggest

[31]*The Story of Indian Business*, Thomas A Timberg, pp 60-61.

that large profits were made by cotton traders and speculators during the nineteenth century and the first half of the twentieth century when Seksaria was a member of the NYCE and an avid trader.

The evolution of technology that enabled swift, accurate trading was pivotal to the extraordinary financial boom witnessed by the cotton industry. In the eighteenth and early-nineteenth century, cotton prices and sales were circulated through newsletters and posted in public venues. Liverpool was the hub of cotton trading in the first half of the nineteenth century. It relied first on the 'General Circular' for listing details of sales, import prices and other important information. This circular helped manage negotiations between cotton growers in the American South and merchants in Liverpool who wished to purchase cotton at the best prices when it was unloaded in the Liverpool docks a month after ships began their journey across the Atlantic Ocean.

As the cotton industry expanded in the nineteenth century, Liverpool developed a number of institutions and systems for managing the large amounts of money being exchanged during every trading day at the 'New Exchange'. One such development was the Bank of Liverpool, founded to enable a system of credit that would facilitate the transactions of cotton brokers. Just as advances in industry were fuelled by developments in new technologies, cotton trading was bolstered by the development of the transatlantic telegraph cable. It spawned a degree of speculation not possible with earlier market mechanisms. The telegraph meant that messages which took weeks to cross the Atlantic Ocean aboard ships became available in minutes.

According to the International Cotton Association, John Rew, a former employee of the Liverpool Bank and later a broker in his own right, invented the hedge fund in 1866. Able to receive quotations from US cotton sellers in the American South instantaneously through cable instead of through the slow circulation of letters, Rew's original hedge fund is described thus:

> 'The cotton would be scheduled to arrive in Liverpool in two or three months' time. But as soon as he had bought his actual cotton, Rew could go to the arrivals market in Liverpool where he sold the exact quantity of cotton he had bought speculatively, selling it for delivery far enough ahead to cover the time it took for the cotton to arrive. So Rew had two cotton contracts, one actual and the other speculative, which had been bought and sold simultaneously. When the cotton arrived in Liverpool, Rew sold it to his spinner and bought back his speculative contract in the arrivals market. If the price of cotton had dropped, say, four pence since his purchase, Rew lost that amount on his cotton; but he would also have made a profit of four pence on his speculative contract in the arrivals market. This is the first example of a hedge fund.'[32]

The futures market doubled the level of cotton trade in the Liverpool cotton market. It came to be the principal manner in which cotton was bought and sold. Futures markets allowed both buyers and sellers more leeway to choose when they would engage in trading. As the ICA describes it, 'Cotton growers could take advantage of high prices when they came rather than be forced to sell at harvest time every year; spinners could book yarn orders for delivery much further than previously and could avoid loss through falling prices while carrying unsold yarn stocks by selling futures as a hedge against loss.'[33]

Sven Beckert's history of the global cotton industry deals very little with the role of trading despite the fact that the global cotton market's development was closely intertwined with the development of futures markets. However, he does suggest that, in the years between 1898 and 1913, traders had already developed methods for manipulating prices through trading futures on the new cotton exchanges. Beckert explains that,

---

[32]cf. Foreword in Dickson G. Watts' *Speculation as a Fine Art and Thoughts on Life*, reprinted in 1965 by Fraser Publishing Company Editions.

[33]www.ica-ltd.org/about-ica/our-history/1830-1913.

'concerns were further amplified by the temporarily successful efforts of some speculators to corner the market and force higher prices by manipulating future and spot transactions on the newly established cotton exchanges.'

What Beckert's historical work suggests is that not only did trading develop alongside the modern cotton market, but that market manipulation has also been part of the warp and woof of the cotton market for a very long time.

One of India's most astute financial minds, Suresh Kotak, who is the chairman of Kotak & Co. says: 'Indian cotton, and its initial roots in India, were as a fibre product. We used to grow cotton and spin it as well, but that cotton was of a different variety from what they grew in America. The British influx brought a kind of reactive growth. They wanted an alternate source of supply of cotton. So they introduced a competing type of American cotton, hirsutum [*Gossypium hirsutum*], to India, whereas, we were originally growing arboreum [*Gossypium arboreum*].'

Kotak continues: 'Before the Second World War, Japan dominated the cotton trade. In fact, Japan's industrialisation started with the textile industry. It was the biggest importer. But two countries were competing with each other industrially - Britain in the West and Japan in the East. China developed a little later. In Japan they're very meticulous. They used to do such a methodical study even in those days which helped them develop a very fine industry. Their way of training is also remarkable. It is a very, very great work culture. But they don't have resources. It's an industrial country with no resources. It's the same in the UK—no resources, which is how they're both similar. They may have different cultures, but both competed in the same industry. So, here was Lancashire and Manchester and there was Japan.'

'The cotton market is based on the resource. Two countries had the resource, India and America. China, Japan and Britain were all importers and in the commodity markets, basically, the supplier determines the price. This is a truth that Govindramji understood. His mind was never inert, it was dynamic. That is where his greatness came from!'

Pausing to reflect, Kotak adds: 'Let me give you the example of my father. He was also very calculating. He used to write down the Kotak company's profit and loss in his small diary every day. Then he would say, "We're running with this profit" or "We're running with this loss." My father was a contemporary of Govindramji, and he's told me so much about him. My father was a great learner himself. To be frank, what my son (Uday Kotak) has learned, he has learned more from my father, who was a great visionary too. He would say that people like Govindramji are very rare. So the point is, we must remove from people's minds that Govindramji was just a speculator. He was not only a speculator—that was just one of his qualities. He was a man of multiple personalities. He was a man of vision, he was a man of commitment. He had certain targets, certain understandings; he could interpret information to the advantage of a situation and that is what is contextual. He understood the environment he was in.'

Despite being experienced traders on the Bombay cotton exchange, the sellers in cotton contracts with whom Govindram Seksaria entered into in 1938 were disappointed by the price for which they sold Seksaria 200,000 bales of cotton that summer. They would have consoled themselves with the thought that the anticipated drop in the price of cotton would have at least yielded some profit in the time they had until settlement. They would have expected and wanted to arrange to buy the cotton bales at a price that suited them prior to settling with Seksaria.

What they certainly would not have expected is that Seksaria would request delivery. Their calculations went haywire when Seksaria demanded deliveries at the time of settlement of the contracts. They would thus have to buy the amount of cotton they owed Seksaria at a higher price and doing so would result in a substantial loss at the time of the settlement with Seksaria.

As analyst L.C. Gupta suggests, 'Such a mechanism for securities sales, while not unheard of in the US, was uncommon in Britain. But it was typical of the Indian cotton exchange.'

It was in this fast-changing world of the 1930s that Seksaria made his leap into the big league. Seksaria's trading profits catapulted him into the NYCE. *The New York Times* on 29th August, 1934 announced his membership of the world's premier cotton exchange with a terse but laudatory notice. So did *The Wall Street Journal* which reported on 30th August, 1934: 'Edward Valentine Jaeger, of this city and Govindram Seksaria of Bombay, India, have been elected to membership in the New York Cotton Exchange. Mr. Jaeger is a partner of Redmond & Co., commission brokers. Mr. Seksaria is a member of various associations in India and is engaged in the spot cotton business, wheat and jute merchandising.'

After he became a member of the NYCE, Seksaria garnered even more interest among Americans. *The New Orleans Cotton Journal* reported on 7th May, 1938, 'Govindram Seksaria, one of the biggest of the Bombay operators, is coming about as close to cornering the Indian cotton market as is possible under changed world conditions.'

However, Seksaria was not a typical trader. The wealth he had amassed by 1938 attested to his uncanny ability to identify good market strategies for himself. Having acquired membership of the New York Cotton Exchange in 1934, Seksaria was clearly not content to maintain a peripheral position confined to the Bombay Cotton Exchange. He had set his sights on the most powerful cotton exchanges in the world in New York and Liverpool. His trading volumes had outgrown Indian markets. He needed a larger canvas.

In May 1938, six other Indian businessmen were elected as members of the NYCE: Hemraj Anandilal, Piramal Chaturbhuj, Ramanlal Dahyabhai, Chimanlal B. Parikh, Jamnadas B. Thakkar and Vadilal Chunilal. All were either directors of the Indian Stock Exchange (ISE) along with Seksaria, bankers or cotton traders of repute. Along with Seksaria, they traded on the

NYCE with gusto. Interestingly in May 1938, the *Oakland Tribune* wrote about six applications for membership received by the NYCE from Bombay. It said that Seksaria had sponsored the six applicants to facilitate his operations in the United States.

An experienced derivatives specialist at Kotak Securities, Vikram Gupta, outlines Seksaria's trading strategy. 'Seksaria took a call on New York prices and kept buying Bombay cotton futures (trading cheaper to their replica contracts in New York) till there was no spread left (after which buying in New York would start becoming more viable). Seeing this gap reduce, other arbitragers kept selling their positions to Seksaria in the hope of covering them back when the spread improved back again. The amount of cornering also highlights a unique ability of Seksaria to gauge how much capital would be needed to complete his objective. Had he bought more than he could finance, the trade could have gone against him.'

Seated in a compact room in South Mumbai's business hub, Suresh Kotak, widely regarded as one of India's leading experts on commodities, leans forward to make a point: 'Govindramji understood the economics of commodities. You can't do speculation without understanding economics. What did Govindramji do? In a transaction there is a buyer and a seller. So a transaction is made up of what? *Make* the transaction and *take* the transaction. What is a taker? Takers, though they are speculators, are also risk providers. Don't call them just speculators. They are risk providers. They are in the business of providing a risk. You may call it speculation, but no, they actually provide a risk. And that provides the greatest liquidity to the hedgers.

'The point is how can I sell if I don't have a counter-party transaction in the trade? Govindramji, without any education, was calculating this like an actuarial science! He had a scientific bent of mind. Even insurance is based on actuarial science and this kind of calculation is what made Govindramji so great.

'Now consider "straddles"—*badla* in our language is also

known as straddles. Straddles are a simultaneous purchase of options to buy and sell a security or commodity at a fixed price, allowing the purchaser to make a profit whether the price of the security or commodity goes up or down. There are many types of straddles. Straddle is not speculation. It's the kind of business where two are symmetrical—two different kinds or strata of prices are traded. Either it's a straddle of the month where the carrying charges are involved or straddle of quality. What hedge funds are thinking today, Govindramji thought in those days. That is why he was so great. His success was based on a study of straddles of commodities.'

In his book *All About Futures,* Russel Wasendorf[34] explains how the options and futures market works: 'An option is the right, but not the obligation, to buy or sell an underlying futures contract at a specified price (called the strike price) during a specified period of time. Just like futures contracts, all options on futures are bought and sold at competitive auctions in the options pits on the floors and the futures exchanges. Also, just like the futures contracts, at the end of each trading day all options transactions are accepted and cleared by the clearing association, assuring performance on all contract obligations. This frees buyers and sellers of any direct obligation to each other.

'A call option conveys the right, but not the obligation, to buy a futures contract at a specific price during a specified time period. You would buy a call option if you expected prices of an underlying futures contract to rise. A put option conveys the right, but not the obligation, to sell a futures contract at a specific price during a specified time period. You would buy a put option if you expected prices of an underlying contract to decline.'

'The strike price of an option is the price at which you may buy (in the case of a call option) or sell (in the case of a put option) the underlying futures contract. The various exchanges

[34]McGraw Hill, USA

that offer options determine the strike prices for put and call options. Additional strike prices are added by the exchanges in accordance with futures price movements by applying a formula.'

'Volatility is probably the most obvious and least understood influence on options prices. While there may be mathematical explanations for volatility, common sense is the best rule. If soybean futures are at $5.60 per bushel and will remain at that price for a year, there is little risk in selling a $6.00 call option. However, if soybean futures trade between $5.25 per bushel and $5.95 per bushel in the same week, there is significantly greater risk associated with the $6.00 call option.'

'Once again, the writer of the option must be paid for assuming the risk. The greater the likelihood that the option will trade through the strike price, thus increasing the chance of the buyer exercising the option, the higher the premium must be to accommodate the risk taken by the writer. The common thread running through each of these components of time value is risk. Anything that increases the writer's risk will increase option premiums, regardless of the source of risk. Any time the amount of risk decreases, option premiums fall.'

Suresh Kotak adds that, 'Govindramji understood the value of cotton, not just the price of cotton. That's what led to his strategy of forward integration. That's how he could develop an idea further. He was a visionary. Today industry is run with the concept of supply chain management. He understood value additions. Not only did he have a deep understanding of the economics and context of the times, Govindramji understood what was happening around him. He could interpret every point. He was a great visionary. The important point is he understood and utilised information to his benefit.'

Seksaria's membership of the New York Cotton Exchange raised his profile internationally. The exchange had been established in 1870 by a group of 100 cotton brokers and merchants at

1 Hanover Square. The historic commodities exchange traded futures and options on cotton and cotton derivatives. The NYCE was an important exchange in the late nineteenth and twentieth centuries because of the centrality of cotton in the American economy. It marked the end of the factorage system for marketing America's most important domestic crop and the beginning of today's futures trading system for buying and selling commodities. Brokers and investors in the NYCE traded on the Bombay Cotton Exchange and vice versa. Seksaria controlled the New York cotton market, especially during the war years. Most textile industrialists too were hedging in cotton.

Seksaria's entry into the New York Cotton Exchange continued to raise both eyebrows and hackles in the US four years after he acquired membership. The *Oakland Tribune* in a piece by Louis M. Schneider wrote on 8th May, 1938: 'Not long ago the New York Cotton Exchange posted a new list of applications for membership. Of the seven names published six were from Bombay. It started a lot of talk but few had inside knowledge. Here's the story: the Bombay Cotton Exchange doesn't turn over in volume the amount done in New York. But it is a colorful market. It is loaded with speculators. We call them plungers in this country. The most popular of the lot is Govindram Seksaria. He's a member of the New York Cotton Exchange, too.'

'Right now Seksaria has the Bombay cotton market in the palm of his hand. He is said to have cornered the April-May contracts. To offset the position he is short of the July-August delivery. He aims to accept May deliveries and dump on the July-August buyers. It's a cold manipulative deal. There aren't any trading restrictions on the Bombay Cotton Exchange. He does as he pleases. He is currently hedging part of his operations on the New York cotton Exchange. To help his work in the United States, he is the sponsor of the six who have made applications for memberships on the New York cotton mart.'

The fact that Seksaria preceded his colleagues from the Bombay Cotton Exchange to membership of the NYCE underlines his leadership within an ambitious community of Bombay traders. Some of them had also partnered with him in founding the Indian Stock Exchange at the end of 1937. This was an inflection point in Seksaria's career: the historical moment when he went from being a successful and wealthy Indian businessman to the man whose bold trading created ripples in all of the 'cotton markets of the world,' as *The New York Times* wrote on 24th April, 1938.

Seksaria could afford, literally, to innovate within the system of short-selling on the Bombay Cotton Exchange. He had attempted to 'squeeze the shorts' by actually taking delivery of the 200,000 bales of cotton purchased as part of the April-May 1938 contracts. He could take delivery because he was financially capable of paying for his enormous purchase of Indian cotton. This strategy meant that he was squeezing the sellers out of their short position, forcing them to secure enough bales of cotton to deliver them in accordance to their contract with Seksaria rather than wait and purchase the cotton when prices dropped.

Requiring delivery of the stock that was purchased in a short sale was within a buyer's right. But it was a deviation from the expectations many sellers would have had operating on the Bombay Cotton Exchange where most sales were short sales (80-90 per cent of all sales). These never required delivery. Indeed many buyers on the Bombay Cotton Exchange were not interested in taking delivery since it was not the material goods they profited from but the trading.

Thus, squeezing the shorts was a competitive position reserved for only those who could accept the risk that the price of goods might keep falling. It also required enough capital to pay for stock purchased when it arrived in material form upon delivery two weeks after the trade deal was agreed. Seksaria could undertake a short squeeze as the price of cotton held and because there was now increased demand for Indian cotton thanks to his huge purchase.

Squeezing the shorts in this instance meant that Seksaria

forced his sellers to quickly purchase enough cotton to cover their commitment to him at whatever price they could, probably at a higher price than they would have liked to pay. With this enormous purchase, Seksaria had cornered the Indian cotton market, the second largest after New York.

But Seksaria was not finished. With 200,000 bales of cotton to his name to be delivered in May 1938, he did a short sale of his own for Indian cotton for the July-August contracts. However, it was not a typical short sale because Seksaria had the 200,000 bales of cotton as back-up for his July-August contracts should he not find cotton at a cheaper price on the market before he needed to make good on these new contracts. In doing so he could buy more cotton for these sales if the price of cotton dropped enough to ensure a profit on his July-August short sale contracts or, if the market went against his hedge, he could use the large amount of cotton he had purchased several months earlier. Seksaria had holding power to deliver on his 'sell' contracts because he owned textile mills which possessed ready stocks of cotton. Forward integration was the key to his trading success.

In the middle of this two-stage creative operation in which Seksaria first figured as buyer and then as seller, *The New York Times* highlighted the significance of his actions and predicted: 'If all goes well, he stands to profit on both positions.' Seksaria did in fact profit from both positions. He nudged the market in a direction that suited him—first in his position as buyer and then as seller.

Doing so involved gaining enough control of cotton securities to be able to successfully manipulate the pricing, resulting in large profits for him. Seksaria's success resonated through the Bombay Cotton Exchange. Its relatively light regulations over short-selling enabled Seksaria to simultaneously 'game' the market to his benefit and produce a significant effect on cotton markets across the world. It made him even more of a figure to watch in both New York and Bombay.

Placing bets on the opening and closing prices of futures in the NYCE had become very popular in Bombay. Traders were getting hooked onto it and the bets continued until late night because of the time difference between the US and India. Seksaria too was very active in this. Prafulbhai Hirji narrates an incident: 'Once an astrologer advised a member of the royalty to play the open and close prices of the New York Cotton futures. Govindramji got a whiff of it and said let's see whether the astrologer goes right or I do. He is supposed to have instructed his brokers to ensure that those expected figures don't come and that's what happened. The royalty lost a big amount. Such was his *naseeb* (luck).'

Kishorilal Jhunjhunwala of Fatehchand Paliram and Sons, an old established cotton firm, elaborates: 'As far as cotton *vaida* (forward trading) was concerned, the US was the largest market and Mumbai was number two. Probably because of the time difference, this was the position, otherwise as far as *vaida* is concerned, Mumbai could have been the largest. India was not the largest or number two in production, it was lower, but in *vaida* trading volume it was number two. I reckon that during the lifetime of Govindramji, in actual cotton production, India would have been number 4 or 5. There were times, not always, when the *vaida* trading volumes in Bombay, on EICA, were even higher than NYCE. Although, predominantly the turnover of NYCE was higher.'

'Normally the trend that followed in the local market was of NYCE. Therefore, in India the *vaida* trading would take place in the day up to about 4 pm, while NYCE opened in the night our time and the effect of NYCE would come onto the Indian/Bombay market the next day. The NYCE opened at around 9 pm IST and closed at around 3 am IST. The trend in the Bombay market would be based on the New York market, but not necessarily always. And at one juncture the time came when people were looking to see what Govindramji's views were rather than New York market trends. We know that everybody looks up to a person who is successful, and Govindramji was invariably successful in his trades. Even Govindramji when asked by people for advice would always say 'follow those who are successful—those whose luck is favouring them, follow them.'

When the New York Cotton Exchange posted a list for applications for membership, the fact that six of the seven aspirants were Indians from the Bombay Cotton Exchange had caused some 'comment', as the *Oakland Tribune* had then put it, but not much sustained attention. However, when Govindram Seksaria made huge profits and roiled global cotton markets in the summer of 1938, stronger opinions crystallised around Seksaria, among the first Indians to be admitted into the NYCE. An element of prejudice infused the discourse.

Seksaria's success on both the Bombay Cotton Exchange in British India and the New York Cotton Exchange took place within a larger context of the Indian anti-colonial movement. Seksaria was compared with Mahatma Gandhi by New York financiers. They had limited knowledge of other Indian public figures. Few were written about in the international press. Besides, many of Seksaria's views were in fact congruent with the Indian National Congress' agenda of self-sufficiency for India and the promotion of key Indian industries such as cotton.

However, Seksaria's market leadership in 1938 resonated with Americans in particular because it illustrated the potential of resourceful international traders outside hegemonic financial centres like New York and Liverpool to profit from diverse markets. US newspapers worked to reinforce an imperial hierarchy. Indians, this theory held, had much to learn from Western powers like the United States and Britain. US media poured scorn on Seksaria and members of the Bombay Cotton Exchange for being plungers. They labelled practices such as night trading and short-selling as behaviour that western traders had given up years ago.

Such characterisations of Seksaria's market success attempted to show him as not being 'fully modern'. Ironically, American traders in future decades would be jailed for illegal insider trading and other crimes which Seksaria, despite his predilection for speculation, was never guilty of. American media cynically ignored the fact that Seksaria's trading success showed how from a position outside the centre of western financial and political power he had anticipated and adapted to contemporary global markets.

Seksaria monitored several international markets at the same time. A daily call from New York would give him an instant analysis of Wall Street's trading without waiting for information from local media sources. He also benefitted, along with his Bombay trading allies, from reports and analysis provided by the East India Cotton Association. This enabled him to make decisions based on data circulating among his New York associates who could gather and analyse information relating to Wall Street traders.

Today, brokers access several markets online throughout the day. They evaluate when night trading might suit their aims. In the 1930s, Seksaria was already navigating several major global markets without the aid of instant internet updates. There is little evidence that New York traders were active in Indian markets or were able to leverage the difference in pricing between two different global markets. In contrast, global arbitrage was a potent tool in Seksaria's trading armoury.

Puranmal Jiwarajka, one of Govindram's munims, tells the story of Seksaria's purchase of India government bonds which proved extremely profitable: 'Govindramji had an eye for arbitrage so he spotted arbitrage opportunities between bonds, whether it was India government bonds or Royal bonds between London and Bombay, I don't know—but he seized that opportunity. One of his leading business contemporaries got a whiff that Govindramji is buying the bonds. He came to Govindramji and asked him, "Govindramji, what are you doing, I am told you are buying?" Govindramji said innocently, "What are you saying? I don't understand all these things." He made a cool packet out of that transaction. Later, the business community was surprised that Govindramji, sitting in Bombay, was able to spot and seize opportunities such as these that arose in global markets while his more savvy and widely travelled peers were unable to do so.'

Computerised systems of recording and trading now mean that people have real-time information about other markets. It is extraordinary that 80 years ago Seksaria had created his own system of informants in New York and had a Bombay telephone operator on his payroll. Live streaming information today ensures there is rarely a price gap in different markets of the same commodity or stock. Seksaria's organised system of information gathering and analysis, aimed at detecting price gaps between unconnected markets across the world trading the same security, made him a more cosmopolitan international trader than most traders on the New York and Liverpool exchanges at the time.

Western observers of Seksaria's deft navigation of global markets could not bring themselves to acknowledge it as being tactically astute. Like Europeans criticising Marwari speculation at the turn of the century, American commentators chose their words and imagery to recast as 'backward' what were actually sophisticated and advanced trading practices ahead of their time, as today's hedge fund managers would attest. In the 1930s however, Seksaria's triumph across continents grated on his global peers.

Volatility in the cotton market in 1938 had been exacerbated by the continuing impact of the US stock market crash in 1929. This reverberated across a recession-hit American and world economy. Almost all industries and securities languished at profit levels far below those prior to 1929. But by 1938, as war clouds gathered over Europe, an end to the long recession ironically seemed in sight. War spurred the armaments industry. The knock-on effect would spark an industrial revival.

In England, Liverpool's pre-war cotton imports were at

their lowest for 62 years, indicating how the cotton economy had changed significantly in only a couple of decades since the boom period at the turn of the nineteenth century. Following the 1929 market crash, the US government pursued an agenda of reforming stock market trading. Extensive investigations were carried out into the speculation and market manipulation that many believed was responsible for destabilising the financial system.

As a result of this process, President Franklin Roosevelt established the Securities Exchange Commission (SEC) in 1937, a regulatory body which introduced measures to regulate trading practices in the United States. It is telling that during this period traders were represented in the popular imagination as figures of suspicion and a threat to the well-being of society. Speaking out against the excesses and instability caused by rogue trading practices, the first Chairman of the SEC described predatory traders as 'termites who feed and thrive on other people's money.'

The US government had additionally begun to insert itself more actively in financial markets by adopting policies designed to buttress US financial interests. Given the economic importance of cotton, a market that the US had dominated for many years (with India advancing its claim as the world's second largest supplier), Washington in 1938 formulated a twin strategy to maintain the domestic competitiveness of US cotton: first, through a new agricultural policy and second, through the tactical use of tariffs to decrease the competitiveness of imported cotton.

Protectionism was a hallmark of state involvement in cotton markets. Beckert notes that the United States had strengthened its 'protectionist regime' in the second half of the nineteenth century, a move that helped establish its dominance of the cotton market. In the first decades of the twentieth century, the US government's interventions were aimed at leveraging the cotton market to its advantage in the face of serious challenges of war, crop blight and increased competition from emerging independent, post-colonial nations.

To Seksaria, war unlike to his Western peers in Washington, New York, London and Liverpool meant a suspension of the traditional rules of empire: rules guaranteeing control of trade routes, access to supplies of cheap labour and raw materials like cotton, and market monopolies on essential goods such as copper, sugar and wheat as well as bullion.

For India 1937-1938 was a period of significant developments and transformation in futures trading. A group of business leaders in Bombay in 1937 registered their trading forum as the newly established Indian Stock Exchange Ltd. (ISE) and occupied its new office in Laxmi building at Fort in August 1938. This arrangement reflected the strength of the financial syndicate in Bombay. Govindram Seksaria was a key player and one of the founding members of the exchange. The ISE commenced business in February 1938.

The establishment of the exchange gave this pivotal generation of Indian stock traders a more secure platform for their market activities. The Indian cotton market was also more volatile during this period because of the fluctuations in the market for US cotton. Nonetheless, the value and strength of Indian cotton was being transformed for other reasons as well. Three factors predominated.

First, the symbolic significance of cotton and khadi to Gandhi's nationalist *Swadeshi* campaign which directed Indians to wear khadi produced in India (rather than textiles imported from England). Second, workers' strikes in cotton mills and other industries happened across India in 1938 in support of the nationalist movement. And third, the increase in ownership of production, cotton and otherwise happened, by Indian capitalists after many decades of being dominated by the British.

Towards the end of 1937, many analysts were trying to anticipate what would happen to the price and supply of cotton in the coming months. *The Times of India* reported on 15th November, 1937 that a large cotton yield by American farmers meant that the price of American cotton was in decline. This news would have interested Indian speculators as much as Americans because a drop in the price of US cotton would inevitably affect the price of Indian cotton. This prediction proved accurate several months later, prompting *The New York Times* to report the following April: 'Normally the spread between New York and Bombay prices is about 2 cents a pound. In January, it narrowed to about one-fifth of 1 cent.'[35]

Other factors were also threatening to destabilise the price of Indian cotton at the end of 1937. European countries were importing US cotton on easy credit terms. *The Times of India* in November 1937 observed: 'The spot demand in the local market has completely dried up. With the parity becoming still narrower, the outlook is well-nigh hopeless.'

Although, the Roosevelt administration pledged to boost the value of US cotton through the Agricultural Bill it would release in January 1938, Indian newspapers rightly predicted that this would have little impact on the narrowing price differential between US cotton and Indian cotton. Additionally, those watching the market in Bombay and elsewhere in India were aware that although the demand for Indian cotton in Indian mills was robust there were increasing signs of labour strikes in 1938, including in the Seksaria Mills.

This was a mixed blessing: plenty of Indian cotton would be available for trading on the cotton exchange in 1938 since India had enjoyed a bumper cotton crop in the final months of 1937.

When the price of Indian cotton continued to fall in January 1938, many traders made a calculated choice to sell their Indian cotton contracts for a lower price. They were apprehensive that the market would keep falling for all of the reasons the Indian press had forecast several months ago. Seksaria immediately saw the opportunity. His acumen in trading and the financial

---

[35]*The New York Times,* 24th April, 1938.

capital he had assiduously built emboldened him to take risks. The speculative set of transactions Seksaria undertook in the first quarter of 1938 was mitigated by his holding power: he held physical commodity stocks for delivery from his mills to fulfil sell orders. And he had liquid funds to fulfil buy orders. Almost no one else in the market could match these strengths.

Kishorilal Jhunjhunwala adds a caveat: 'Although, Govindramji was a member of EICA, he never did trading through his own card but always did it through other brokers who were members of the exchange. I have heard of big *khelas* (corners) in Bombay. They were done by large groups and prominent personalities of that time, contemporaries of Govindramji. However, three of them failed and they lost big money, but being large groups they were able to bear the loss. Then two big transactions were done by Govindramji, and he was successful in both of them. He had also acquired textile mills by then. Look, you can buy even one lakh bales of cotton in forward trade but you also need to have the capacity to take delivery otherwise the *khela* can fail. So what I'm trying to say is that rarely do people make money in speculation. Govindramji was successful on his own *balbutha* (on his own conviction and luck), but otherwise it was not a wise thing to do.'

On the Bombay Cotton Exchange, like other Indian markets, the badla system was part of a general widespread practice of short-selling. In markets where delivery is required within a fortnight, as on the Liverpool Cotton Exchange, short-selling is greatly reduced. Moreover, short-selling was much curtailed in the United States after 1937 by the Securities Exchange Commission which passed regulations limiting opportunities for short-selling on Wall Street.

The badla system, a form of securities lending at rates that averaged between 8 and 18 per cent, fuelled short-selling in India. It had long been a key feature of the Bombay Cotton Exchange. Short-selling was a prominent feature of Indian Stock Exchanges throughout the twentieth century. Its critics charged that this practice made Indian Stock Exchanges more vulnerable to fluctuations, manipulation and frequent market crises and should be strictly regulated as in the US.

L.C. Gupta, one of the critics of short-selling, argues that it functioned in India throughout the 1900s and for a while beyond. This was because, compared with Britain and the US, the agrarian character of India's economy meant that crises in the stock market would not destabilise the entire economic structure of the country the way it did in the US during the stock market crash of October 1929.

Urging greater trading governance by Indian regulators in 2002, Gupta describes the system in India thus:

> 'Because of the badla system, India's stock market environment till recently had been conducive to excessive speculation and all kinds of speculative abuses. The badla system promoted a wildly spurious kind of share trading in which neither buyer had the money to pay for the shares at the time of settlement nor the seller had the shares to deliver but settlement took place by payment of differences along with carry forward of outstanding positions. Only about 10 per cent of the trading volume was settled by delivery.'

Following the meltdown in the New York Stock Exchange in October 1929, short-selling was identified as one of the reckless market practices that had destabilised the economic system and created a debilitating recession. Gupta explains some of the illegitimate market manipulation with which short-selling came to be associated: 'It was often found to take an organised and malicious form of bear raiding to drive down prices artificially. Even (many) Wall Street firms had perfected the art of forming pools or syndicates for rigging stock prices upwards or downwards.'[36]

In the face of economic crisis in the 1930s, manipulative practices came in for harsh criticism. This statement, issued by

---

[36]2002, NSE Research Initiative paper no. 12, p 18.

William O. Douglas, chairman of the SEC in 1938, captured the general mood of disquiet in the American financial community:

> 'The financial and industrial world has been afflicted with termites as insidious and destructive as the insect termites. Instead of feeding on wood they feed and thrive on other people's money . . . these financial termites are those who practice the art of predatory high finance. They destroy the legitimate function of finance and become a common enemy of investors and business . . . one of the chief characteristics of such finance has been its inhumanity, its disregard of social and human values.'[37]

The SEC chairman's speech underscored the mood that prevailed. Traders were seen as 'predators', inhumane and a danger to social values. As an antidote, the SEC imposed 'plus-tick' and 'zero-plus tick' tests to ensure that short-selling was possible only above the last reported market price to limit the ways it can be used to manipulate prices. Ironically, Seksaria and other Indian traders struck US traders just one year later as 'colourful' and 'lively' because their Bombay trading communities, operating under the Bombay Cotton Exchange, continued to be free to make short sales throughout the twentieth century.

In the US and elsewhere, less cynical traders noted the fact that Seksaria undertook a risky but highly successful set of purchases and sales that left him with a profit on cotton trades. He did this at a time when many other Indian cotton traders had been forced to accept losses. In contrast, Seksaria ended up with control of a large stock of Indian cotton. He could trade when the market suited him. His peers in the US were mere traders. Seksaria was trader and industrialist rolled into one. That gave him an edge others were beginning to notice with more than a tinge of envy.

---

[37]2002 NSE Research Initiative; paper no. 12.

Seventy years after Seksaria's death, cotton remains an important commodity for the Indian economy. *Business Standard* noted[38]: 'The government estimates output in India to decline this year to 36.5 million bales, as compared to 38 million bales last year. This is due to a fall in sowing area to 11.76 million hectares, from 13.08 million hectares last year. The yield is actually estimated to rise significantly this year to 527.49 kg a hectare from 493.77 kg last year, on sowing of higher yielding seed. Bangladesh was India's largest importer of cotton in 2014-15, for the first time, due to a sharp slump in Chinese offtake. Bangladesh imported 2.29 million bales from India in 2014-15, up from 2.16 million bales a year before. China's imports were 1.68 million bales, down from 6.48 million bales in 2013-14.'

In Maharashtra, where Seksaria ran most of his industrial enterprises, cotton has today acquired, with government blessing, the sobriquet 'white gold'. According to an *Indian Express* report, 'The Maharashtra government is working on a comprehensive policy to integrate six distressed districts of Vidarbha through 80 per cent cotton industry to restore its tag of white gold. The policy intends to address problems of farmers in the country's largest cotton growing belt across Nagpur, Amravati, Akola, Buldhana, Yavatmal, Washim and Wardha. In the 2016-17 budget, it plans to earmark a special allocation to promote cotton-based industries in Vidarbha to address its socio-economic problems. Chief Minister Devendra Fadnavis directed officials to expedite work to transform Amravati district as the international textiles hub of country. The detailed plan includes integrating three nodal departments of textile, finance and agriculture to work towards attaining the target of the ambitious project. The state government intends to promote the textile sector through public-private-partnership. Vidarbha is amongst the maximum cotton growing region of India. It contributes 30 per cent of the crop. Next is Marathwada.'[39]

---

[38] 5th December, 2015.

[39] *The Indian Express*, 2015.

The International Cotton Association (ICA), based in England, once described accurately the characteristics of the market in cotton futures in the twentieth century: 'Subsidies, duties and currency imbalances became increasingly common and meant that, effectively, there was no longer a price for cotton, as cotton of equal value in quality could command widely differing prices according to their country of origin and destination.'[40]

If a stable and standard value does not determine the price of cotton on the cotton exchange, then the strategic calculations of the trader would clearly be increasingly important when it comes to making a profit on either buying or selling. This would mean that traders must make assessments in relation to numerous variables. The pattern of trading in international markets highlighted how Seksaria was actually ahead of New York trading practices in 1938 when he navigated a complicated set of variables to move the market in a direction that served his financial interests. Seksaria's remarkable success in 1938, when most others were struggling to make any profits at all and when India had yet to become a dominant presence in the international cotton market, suggests that he was anticipating the internationalisation of trading which would characterise the modern futures market fifty years later.

Grandson Nandkumar recalls: 'We have heard old-timers say that Govindramji used to speculate big on the NYCE. One interesting anecdote is that Govindramji's bull operation in cotton was leading to cotton prices spiralling out of control in the US which was in turn leading to cotton mills facing hardships due to high prices of cotton. His agent in America informed him that the way cotton prices are rising the authorities in the US are threatening to take all necessary and corrective action to bring down cotton prices, including release of buffer stock. Govindramji replied that in such a situation he would consider asking for physical delivery of cotton! That would entail a huge amount of cotton leaving American shores! However,

---

[40]2002 NSE Research Initiative; paper no. 12.

Govindramji slowly started to unwind his trades and he made a huge profit in the process.'

Nandkumar adds: 'We have also heard old-timers say that after Govindramji's death his portrait was shipped to the NYCE which was put in the NYCE hall. Efforts to confirm this have not yielded any results as yet. Minute books are not traceable and the records had not been digitized. The NYCE building no longer exists.'

Seksaria's success flew in the face of US interests in another respect as well. America had dominated the cotton market for raw material for many years. Throughout the 1920s and 1930s, however, the balance of power in cotton was shifting away from the United States as a dominant cotton producer and Britain as a dominant cotton manufacturer. Additionally, the United States battled against the deterioration of the quality of its crops after the infestation of the resilient boll weevil. It struggled to maintain the price of its cotton against less expensively marketed cotton from markets such as India.

In the face of these threats, the US government tried to influence the value and price of US cotton with the 1938 Agricultural Adjustment Act. Despite the government's attempts to protect the national market, the price of US cotton dropped sharply at the beginning of 1938, creating a cascade of effects the US could not control and which Seksaria's adventurous trading would take full advantage of.

Chapter Five

America Wakes Up To Seksaria

What did Govindram Seksaria, the 'cotton king of the world', as he was popularly known, have in common with Mahatma Gandhi? The answer of course is cotton and khadi. Cotton is what both men embraced: cotton spelt prosperity, monopolies and markets that would someday belong to, and be regulated by, sovereign India.

This is where Gandhi's and Seksaria's worldviews converged. Seksaria was the quiet nationalist businessman, Gandhi the political messiah. In their own distinct ways they sought the same ideal for India: a free country, a liberalised economy and the sovereign rule of law. Both men unnerved the West, though in very different ways. It is necessary to rewind to the American media's obsession with Seksaria to discern the latent cause.

Seksaria's trading in cotton bales had first intrigued *The New York Times* on 22nd May, 1937: 'Owing to a holiday in Liverpool, foreign business was turned to the local market and Bombay interests bought actively early. For a time, holders were able to liquidate at a slight advance in quotations, but steady pressure on the near month and less disposition by domestic consumers to follow the advance caused an easier market.'

The buying helped raise the price of cotton. Six months later, on 13th November, 1937, *The New York Times* again reported on the strength of Liverpool cotton and the narrowing of the Bombay-New York spread: 'Further improvement marked the course of prices on the Cotton Exchange here yesterday, the upward movement carrying December to 8 cents and all later months above the even figure. Closing quotations were at gains of 9 to 13 points. Hedging operations continued on an extremely light scale, despite the rise of about a half cent from Monday's low levels. Merchants reported that few growers were offering cotton on a basis that would warrant sales of contracts at current prices.'

Shortly after its article on Seksaria's growing influence on global commodity markets, and how he was 'cornering' the cotton market, *The New York Times* on 12th June, 1938, wrote: 'According to Liverpool advices, buying power there was augmented by a firmer tone in Bombay and absence of offerings from any quarter. Bombay interests bought distant positions here while aggressive covering of July obligations, anticipating notices a week from today, helped to strengthen the whole market.'

Days later, on 14th July, 1938 the newspaper reported: 'Because of the sharp advance here since June 1, straddle accounts between New York and Bombay showed profits and a reversal of operations supplied contracts. From less than 10 points last winter, differences have widened to around 165 points. With the marketing movement in India diminishing and that in the South just beginning, Bombay traders showed more disposition to take profits.'

The condescending undertone in several *The New York Times* articles suggested that, 'as an Indian subject of the British crown, Seksaria should not try to emulate his civilised betters and should, like Gandhi, adopt humbler, simpler, cotton attire.' This was ironic at best, ignorant at worst. For whether he was meeting with the president of the New York Stock Exchange in

Bombay or confabulating with bullion traders in India, Seksaria was invariably seen wearing his trademark *dhoti* and long coat. Seksaria's high-volume speculative trades in cotton seemed to the international press to pose as much a threat to British and American cotton empires as Gandhi's political nationalism did to Britain's Indian empire.

So intrigued were Americans by Seksaria that the president of the New York Stock Exchange (NYSE) and member of the NYCE travelled to India to see for himself how the Indians operated. On his arrival at Seksaria's modest office, the NYSE president was astonished to see Govindram sitting cross-legged on a white *gaddi* dressed in a simple *kurta* and *dhoti*. The president returned to New York to tell his disbelieving American colleagues how this seemingly humble Indian trader was running rings around them, comparing him to Gandhi.

The Free Press Journal reported on the visit with understated delight: 'The story goes that the president of the New York Stock Exchange and head of New York's leading cotton firm, in Bombay on a globe-trotting tour, paid a visit to the office of this Indian member of his exchange and met with an experience he is never likely to forget. He found Seth Govindramji squatting on a *"gaddi"*, a group of people about him, each discussing a different matter but contriving to get the Seth's ear. No one demanded the American visitor's card, there was no need for a secretary to conduct the visitor around. The whole atmosphere was so simple, so informal, that the visitor took some time to reassure himself that he was really at the headquarters of Bombay's leading cotton magnate and an important member of the New York Cotton Exchange.'[41]

Kishorilal recounts an unrelated incident of Americans being intrigued by Seksaria's operations: 'Another thing I've heard is one about an American coming to India to meet him. After all, even in America he had become a known figure and it was accepted that he was a market mover. The American gentleman

[41]*The Free Press Journal*, June 1946.

came to meet Govindramji and was shocked to see this person squatting on the *gadda* in his *dhoti,* coat and *pagdi.* Through translators they started conversing.

The American said: "I want to do a trade with you."
Seksaria agreed and asked: "What do you want to do?"
American: "I want to sell."
Seksaria: "Okay, I'll buy."
The American then said, "No I've changed my mind, I want to buy."
Seksaria: "Okay, I'll sell!"
The American asked, "What is your desire? Are you willing to do both?"
Seksaria: "I want to do the opposite of what you want to do."
American: "What quantity?"
Seksaria: "Whatever you want."
American: "One hundred thousand bales."
Seksaria: "Done, you fix the price today and at four annas difference, I'm willing to do any quantity that you name."
'Such was the confidence and financial power Govindramji had over the outcome of the trades he entered into,' says Kishorilal.

The heavy-handed tactics of US market authorities towards Indian cotton exports meanwhile drew the ire of G.D. Birla. According to one published report[42], the doyen of Indian industry responded sharply with regard to the reported threat that in case India did not regulate her cotton exports, the United States of America would dump cotton in the world market, and thus reduce the price of cotton to the disadvantage of all exporting countries. Mr. G.D. Birla remarked that he did not understand what advantage there would be for India to regulate her exports, except that it would cheapen cotton within the country to the

[42]*The Times of India.*

benefit of Indian cotton mills. However, this would not help the agriculturists.

'India enjoyed a unique position in respect of her cotton exports. Firstly, most of the Indian cotton that was exported was of the short staple variety, and the world wanted this type of cotton. Indian cotton generally did not come into competition with the long-stapled American, African or Egyptian cotton. Secondly, India had definitely earmarked markets. Out of the balance a small part is taken by Lancashire which would continue to take in the future, because she is eager to sell her cloth in the Indian market. The rest is taken by the continent and China because they want it for special purposes. They cannot do without it.'

'It is thus, clear that it is not to our advantage to restrict our exports, and neither will it be necessary for us to do so. It was the United States of America that produced a few years back more cotton that the world market would absorb and it is she who had to and must restrict her production and also exports if necessary. India has neither extended her production nor exports. It does not therefore, lie in the mouth of America to come to India and say, "Well, we are restricting our production because we can't sell. You also should restrict your sales, although you have a ready market for your products."'

It was a spirited intervention by G.D. Birla whose elder brother R.D. Birla was a friend and contemporary of Seksaria. The two men enjoyed a cordial relationship. In the future they would collaborate on a major philanthropic medical institution: Bombay Hospital.

Western paranoia of Seksaria explains some of the seemingly patronising depictions of him in the American press. Hardened New York speculators saw Seksaria's successful financial strategies undercutting their traditional trade and market monopolies. Like Gandhi's nationalist movement, this was regarded in some circles as evidence of the increased bargaining power of countries like India. As Seksaria's financial acumen began to pay off in the wake of the new monetary order that followed America's break with the gold standard in 1933, there was a palpable sense that a united, independent populous India could one day rise to be one of the world's most powerful global economies.

What Goldman Sachs would predict 70 years later in 2013 about the stellar future of the Indian economy was already an uneasy seedling germinating in perceptive Western minds—independent India would be a force to reckon with. The lesson of India's cotton nationalism, moreover, conveyed a powerful message to other colonised regions of the world: the key to development and freedom lay in their own hands.

The Indian cotton market meanwhile continued to burgeon. It clearly aspired to global dominance. This led US commentators to make even more disparaging remarks. One commented acerbically that while the Bombay Cotton Exchange was 'well behind' that of New York when it came to 'trading volume', it nevertheless eclipsed New York 'in the matter of *colourful operations*.'

But 'colourful' was also code for speculation conducted by colonial subjects. Not just Seksaria, but the whole of Bombay was, according to *The New York Times'* Louis M. Schneider, 'a colourful market loaded with speculators.' Men like Seksaria were not men to be admired, this reportage implied, but rather to be resented for any tactical (and subversive) maneuvering on their part. They were compared negatively to the supposedly extinct gamblers or 'plungers' of America's hoary past (before President Roosevelt's New Deal). The Indians were inveterate risk-takers prepared to break rules and destroy the world for material gain. To jaundiced Western eyes, their behaviour was not acceptable.

Had Govindram Seksaria been a speculator of Western extraction in New York, his trading success would have been shrugged off, even quietly admired for its audacity. It certainly wouldn't have been described as 'colourful'. In the febrile political climate of the 1930s, when racial segregation was lawful in several parts of America, speculators and traders in New York looked upon Seksaria with a mixture of awe and apprehension, laced with disbelief. How could an unlettered Indian with no working knowledge of English, or even his native Hindi, outwit some of the cleverest, most well-informed traders in the NYCE?

Reportedly, Mr. Albrecht, the biggest cotton speculator in New York, upon learning that even a bigger speculator operated in Bombay wanted to meet Govindram Seksaria. He came to Bombay and after learning about Seksaria's trading operations, said to him, 'In my entire career, it is my good fortune to meet such a unique large chested speculator and I can reiterate that you are one of a kind in the entire world.' He then doffed his hat at Govindram and after exchanging pleasantries, he left.[43]

Though not overtly political, Seksaria meanwhile kept himself fully informed of global developments. He knew freedom was but years away. His business was flourishing. As he turned to philanthropy and building educational institutions, Seksaria continued to donate generously to the Congress. And even as *The New York Times* was playfully comparing Seksaria with Gandhi in 1938, the Indian movement for political and intellectual independence from Britain was well underway.

The call for *Swadeshi* and *Swaraj* resonated across the country. Self-rule lay tantalisingly within reach. Anxious rumours circulated in London and New York's financial communities, where Seksaria had made for himself a larger-than-life reputation, over the imminent dissolution of the British Raj. Fervid commentators debated the consequences of this for British, European and North American hegemony. Another world war was brewing in 1939 and for many it seemed that the world, once again, was about to change dramatically.

The national independence movement was a vehicle for powerful lobbies within India: urban-based Indian business elites who sought indigenous control of domestic industrial production and foreign imports. Cotton in particular was seen

---

[43]Source: Bharat Bubna, as told to him by his grandfather, the Late Puranmal Bubna

by capital-rich merchants and bankers in Bombay and Gujarat as an obvious avenue for investment. Cotton industrialisation in India was heralded as the most effective way to challenge cotton monopolies held by the British since the early-nineteenth century. It would pave the way for a modernised Indian economy that could thrive on the growth of unfettered domestic industries and free trade in independent India. That was the promise of national independence for India's cotton merchants. It led to the birth of what Sven Beckert has named 'cotton nationalism'.[44]

'More so than perhaps anywhere else in the world,' writes Beckert, 'cotton and nationalism became intertwined in India.' Cotton was absolutely central to India's anti-colonial policy. For example, protectionism and a celebration of domestically manufactured cotton were key economic and ideological strategies advocated from the 1890s onwards in order to counter excise taxes and cotton duties imposed on Indian textile manufacturers by the British colonial government. The dream of cotton entrepreneurs and nationalist politicians alike was to build a global industrial powerhouse based on Indian cotton which would leverage lucrative East African markets against British competition.

As Beckert has pointed out in his masterly historical survey of cotton and modern capitalism, cotton merchants were the most significant, if historically overlooked, agents of change within the Indian independence movement. They worked indirectly through economic investments in industry rather than through explicit political agitation. But these two areas were not separate: both cotton entrepreneurs and nationalists in India shared a common goal: an independent nation state. It was a goal Seksaria too espoused throughout his career.

The cotton merchants needed a government that would facilitate the development of import-substitution industrialisation and help them gain access to foreign markets. Nationalist politicians needed a state that would not prioritise British

---

[44]Beckert, pp 421-422.

over indigenous interests. These unlikely bedfellows were prepared to work together to achieve their goals. Their cause was strengthened by other disenfranchised groups, including mill workers and peasants who formed the backbone of non-cooperation and the independence movement.

Gandhi, as the physical and poetic embodiment of the nationalist cause, dedicated a great deal of his political career to cotton. Aware of his increasing international celebrity, he used everything he could—diet, fasting, lifestyle and dress to promote the independence movement through khadi. For Gandhi, cotton was a symbol of *Swadeshi,* of Indian self-sufficiency. It was essential to Gandhi's nationalist politics.

Beckert writes:

> 'Symbolizing the great significance of cotton to nationalism and anticolonialism [. . .], Gandhi not only wrote a history of cotton in India, but also publicly spun cotton on a spinning wheel, the same mechanism that the Indian National Congress chose in 1930 as the centerpiece for its flag.'

While cotton occupied a central role in the Independence movement, its economic viability faced diverse challenges. Why did Japan pose a threat to India's cotton and textile industry? The *quality* of cloth from Japan was superior to most others. Canny investments and cost-effective methods of production added to Japan's success in the textile industry.

M.P. Gandhi in his book *The Indian Cotton Textile Industry: Its Past, Present And Future,* written in 1930, when Seksaria was on the path to acquire the sobriquet 'king of cotton', analyses Japan's role in riveting detail: 'Mixing of cotton is an art of which the Japanese mills are justly proud. Each mill has its own mixings which differ according to the price at which the yarn is to be sold or the purpose for which it is wanted. Frequently, two kinds of Indian cotton are mixed such as 60 per cent Oomrahs and 50 per cent Bengal. It is also interesting to note that the Japanese mills do no hedging in regard to their purchases of raw cotton. Large quantities of cotton are purchased and, if prices drop after purchasing, another lot of cotton is purchased and the price is averaged. This speculation in the purchase of cotton is one cause responsible for Japan's rapid industrial advance.

'At the commencement of the First World War, several mills purchased their cotton requirements for a year at ¥.30 per picul[45] for fear that the development of hostilities might prevent them from obtaining their regular supply of cotton. In course of time the price of cotton advanced to ¥100 and over, followed by a still greater advance in prices of yarn. None of this was hedged and this lucky gamble in cotton was responsible for huge profits which enabled the Japanese mills to build up very high reserves, amounting to nearly 60 per cent of their paid-up capital to pay higher dividends and to extend the mills. Not only did the Japanese manufacturers find themselves freed from competition in their chief market in China, due to the incapacity of England and other regular suppliers to meet the demand, but they were enabled to build up a great trade to substitute goods in other markets such as India, South America, Africa, the Netherlands, East Indies and other countries.

'Another cause for the rapid development of the mill industry in Japan is their organisation and management. Four mill-combines control 60 per cent of the industry. There are three large cotton purchasing firms who also undertake selling of manufactured goods, and who have therefore, cut out the intermediaries between themselves and the wholesale dealers in China, India, etc. There is also another factor, viz. cheaper cost of spinning and weaving. With this super-abundance of their money, the Japanese also built a large number of mills in China which represent more than one-third of the total spindles of China. China has now a tariff autonomy and is very likely to enhance the protective duties on cotton goods like what Japan

[45]A picul or tam is a traditional Asian unit of weight, defined as 'a shoulder-load, as much as a man can carry on a shoulder-pole'.

did and whose example is serving the Chinese Government as an excellent model. Having realised the danger to their export trade in good time and having acquired large sums of money due to the lucky speculation in cotton during the war, Japan staged her own cotton industry in China to take advantage of the cheaper labour conditions and to escape any taxation on her goods exported from Japan to China.

'The Chinese mills work almost exclusively for the home market, while the Japanese mills both in China and Japan are anxious to develop their export business. The Chinese mills have not yet reached the high standard achieved during the last few years by the best Japanese mills. Chinese labour is the crudest material in China. China has labour unions of a political nature while Japan can boast of an absence of unions amongst the cotton mill operatives. Living conditions in China are much lower than in Japan, the general lack of school education is prominent and only about 10 per cent of the labour force is able to read and write while in Japan almost all the cotton operatives are literate.'

Aspirations in India were now set in stone: improvement of infrastructure; economic growth; job creation; new wealth reinvested in public works nationwide on a major scale; schools, hospitals, new industries; urban sanitation and most importantly opportunities for the poor who had suffered the most during colonial rule. The corollary of Seksaria's and Gandhi's message to Western nations was two-fold: first that the West's days of exploiting Indian taxes and labour were numbered and second, that a new global order was in the making. It would transform the world.

By now Seksaria had diversified from trading into industry in a classical move: forward integration. It would pay rich dividends.

Chapter Six

The Making of An Industrialist

Seksaria's first industrial venture was the Shree Krishna Rice and Oil Mills Ltd. established at Masaurhi around today's Bihar in 1924. He was 36. Labour problems though were endemic in British India. Seksaria's rapidly-growing group of industries in the years ahead would not be immune. As one report stated: 'The conciliation proceedings in the dispute between the India United Mills Limited, No. 4, Bombay, and their employees in the weaving departments ended in failure,' stated Mr. E.J.S. Ram, conciliator, in a report to the Government. The report was published in the Government Gazette on Thursday. The dispute related to the proposed retrenchment of 62 weavers working in the mill.

Seksaria set up a few greenfield manufacturing units and also made strategic acquisitions. He invested across sectors: sugar, oil, textiles, minerals, banking, printing presses, motion pictures and real estate. Industry and trading were now ticking along in synchrony—one complementing the other. Indore Malwa Mills, founded in 1909 by Seth Hukumchand and others and inaugurated by Maharaja Holkar of Indore, was managed by the Currimbhoys. It ran into trouble in the late-1920s. By 1933 shareholders had filed cases of criminal breach of trust and cheating against the Currimbhoys. Following their exit, Seksaria took charge of the company.

Nandkumar explains the background to the acquisition: 'Govindramji bought Indore Malwa Mill in 1934. Malwa Mill was acquired along with the Roongtas and two other families. The mill was originally set up by Sir Hukumchand along with others. He gave it to the Currimbhoys to run. The Currimbhoys took over. Then it developed problems and was closed. There were a lot of bidders. It was, however, awarded to a consortium formed by Govindramji along with Roongtas of Swaroopchand Prithviraj, Brijmohan Podar and Sitaram Parasrampuria. Govindramji acquired 5½ annas (around 34 per cent) partnership, along with Roongta (5½ annas) and others. Soon, however, there were more problems. Differences started between Govindramji and the Roongtas.'

Seksaria had been awarded the agency of Indore Malwa Mills in August 1934 following an arbitration by Rai Bahadur S.M. Bapna, prime minister of Indore. The plea of the other contender Kanhaiyalal Bhandari was rejected. The prime minister concluded: 'The important feature in the offer of Seth Govindram Seksaria that appeals to me most is the provision regarding cash payment to the depositors against possession of the mills and, considered along with some of its other provisions, I consider that the extra burden that it imposes on the company is nothing in comparison to the advantages the company is likely to get by accepting it.'

It was an important victory for Seksaria and marked a milestone in his ascent as an industrialist. In 1941, a dispute over the management of Indore Malwa Mills was again referred to the then prime minister of Indore in Princely India. One report, published in *The Times of India* on 10th February, 1941, elaborated on the arbitration: 'Rai Bahadur Col. Dinanath, prime minister of Indore, gave his award on Saturday in the cases which had been referred to him for arbitration by several partners of Seth

Govindram Seksaria and Sons, managing agent of the Indore Malwa United Mills, deciding that Seth Govindram Seksaria shall have the right to take over the actual management of the mills. Seth Govindram Seksaria and Sons have many partners. Seth Govindram Seksaria and some of his relatives hold eleven annas in the rupee shares in the managing agency concern and Seths Brijlal Ramjidas and Bilasrai Juharmal have five annas. Sometime ago differences arose between the parties as to who should manage the concern. The question was referred to the prime minister of Indore for arbitration.'

With the verdict once again going in favour of Seksaria, his reputation as an industrialist was further cemented. According to *The New York Times* (5th January, 1945), 'American manufacturers are being contacted by H. Chaudhary representing Govindram Brothers, Bombay, India, to enter the production of goods in India on a capital-sharing basis with the Indian company, it was announced yesterday. The interests of Govindram Brothers, it was explained, include the management of textile, sugar and vegetable oil mills. Mr. Chaudhary is making his headquarters with Orvis Brothers & Co., 14 Wall Street.'

Nandkumar Seksaria traces his grandfather's industrial lineage: 'Interestingly from old records we find that Govindramji had business establishments in Madhya Pradesh prior to the takeover of Indore Malwa Mills. Archival papers mention that he had a shop in Ujjain in the early 1930s. Indore was a very big centre for speculation. "Speculation *ka gadh tha*" and it was not covered by British tax laws in pre-Independence India. So, this probably could have been an important link to his interest in Indore. The documents further say that he had shops all over the country. In Masaurhi there used to be a shop dealing in commodities like oil seeds. So Govindramji set up a crushing plant in Masaurhi. Even in Karachi, there was a shop. For his cotton purchases and trading, he had a network of *gaddis* in several parts of the country.'

An associate recalls the sequence of events that led to the expansion of Seksaria's industrial empire: 'In 1934, Seksaria, in partnership with the Roongtas, Brijmohan Podar and Sitaram Parasrampuria, purchased the Indore Malwa Mills. Indore Malwa was one of the largest textile mills of the central provinces region (as it was then known). It was also the first acquisition for Seksaria in the textiles space and would play a pivotal role in bolstering his trading activities. The mill had 52,000 spindles and 1,400 looms. It employed around 3,400 people. This constituted 10-12 per cent of the total capacity of the region. Indore Malwa Mills also owned two ginning and pressing factories. One was in Indore and the other in Kannauj. The mill also had a resplendent *kothi* spread over 10 acres which served as a residence for the owners.'

There is an interesting anecdote about Seksaria and H.H. Yeshwantrao Holkar II related to Indore Malwa Mills. Apparently when Seksaria was bidding for the venture, some local businessmen petitioned the Maharaj against giving the management to Seksaria, saying how will this speculator, sitting in Bombay, run the mill. Seksaria was summoned and when this question was put to him he replied, 'Maharaj, like your PM/ Diwan runs your state in your absence, my managers will run the mill.'

Ultimately Seksaria's proposal, being the best, management was awarded to him. Interestingly, archival records reveal that Seth Hukumchand, though he said that at the beginning he was not attracted by taking a share in the managing agency firm as the condition of the mill was not good, within two months became so anxious to have a share that he pressed Seksaria several times to give him a stake and take him as a partner if, 'no writing had been executed and completed' between Govindramji and anybody else.

Nandkumar says: 'We have heard Govindramji used to visit Indore every year for the AGM of Indore Malwa United Mills. For him it was a not-to-be-missed calendar event. During the visit he used to call upon H.H. Holkar Maharaj and it is said that H.H. Holkar, Sir Saab (as Sir Hukumchand was fondly known), and Govindramji would get together. Another aspect is that due to Govindramji's industrial and business interests in Madhya Pradesh, Indore became an important centre for his philanthropic and charitable activities. In 1945, he set up the Shree Govindram Seksaria Charity Trust in Indore with corpus of Rs. 50 lakh which was later increased to Rs. 1 crore.'

H.H. Maharaja Indore Yashwant Rao Holkar II was felicitated in the mill campus in the late 1940s. Grandson Harigopal Podar, son of Seksaria's elder daughter Anaribai and grandson of Brijmohan Podar, recalls 'seeing photographs and leaflets which were distributed at a grand function to felicitate Holkar Maharaj at Indore Malwa Mills.'

Kishorilal Jhunjhunwala relates an interesting incident: 'At that time there was a restriction on holding of stocks of cotton in mills. I've also heard that during that period there were huge stocks in Indore Malwa Mills. Govindramji came to know that the next day there was going to be an inspection at Indore Malwa Mills, so he ordered that, overnight, whatever extra bales they had were to be thrown in the boiler. Although, he incurred losses, which he was able to bear, he did not want to come under the clutches of the law for holding extra stocks.'

Messrs Govindram Seksaria had been formed in December 1935 along with Seksaria's two brothers, Bholaram and Makhanlal, and cousin Nagarmal Dharnidharka. In September 1937, Seksaria acquired the well-known Currimbhoy Mills at Bombay by purchasing debentures issued by the company to the state of Gondal for Rs. 12.5 lakh, in accordance with a scheme of arrangement sanctioned by the High Court of Bombay. The Maharaja of Gondal held the first mortgage debentures of land, building and machinery. The mill was lying closed.

Soon after the purchase of the mill Seksaria introduced further working capital to start the defunct mill. He modernised it by bringing in equipment for fine counts spinning (from Platt Bros) and humidification with a modern dye and bleach house

(Mather & Platt), which was said to be the best in the country at the time, according to the *Indian Textile Journal* (June 1946).

Seksaria's total investment in Currimbhoy Mills would have been approximately Rs. 40-50 lakh, including working capital. The mill was subsequently renamed Seksaria Cotton Mills Pvt. Ltd. It was one of the largest mills in Bombay at the time with a total capacity of about 75,000 spindles and 1,000 looms while employing around 3,400 people. It also stood on one of the largest plots of land.

Puranmal Jiwarajka recalls: 'I went for the *muhurat puja* of Seksaria Cotton Mills with Seth Govindramji. Govindramji *badi puja karayi. Lugayian sab wahan gaye.* (Govindramji got a big *muhurat puja* done, the ladies of the house also attended the *puja*.)'

Around 1941 Seksaria made a 'crore-plus' bid for Apollo textile mill, Bombay. The mill was part of the Victor Sassoon group. The bid, however though being the highest, did not materialise. The mill was eventually purchased by Puranmal Bubna, a wealthy cloth merchant from Bombay and a good friend of Seksaria.

Bharat Bubna, Puranmal's grandson narrates an interesting account of the incident as told to him by Puranmal: 'Sir Victor Sassoon had invited Puranmalji to buy Apollo Textile Mill in Bombay and had indicated to his chief executive, one Mr. Smith, a price of Rs. 1 crore for the transaction. Puranmalji requested for a time of one week to decide and revert. He came back to Mr. Smith and said that he was interested in purchasing the mill. Mr. Smith asked him at what price would he like to finalise the deal.' Puranmalji replied, 'Sir Victor Sassoon has always said that Apollo is your son and so I have sentiments attached to it. I, thus, cannot mandate any price for my son.' Mr. Smith became emotional and on a piece of paper wrote the figure of '90 notwithstanding the indicative price of Rs. 1 crore fixed by Victor Sassoon. Interestingly, Govindramji had made a bid of Rs. 1.10 crore for Apollo Mill. Nevertheless, Apollo Mill was sold to Puranmalji.' Upon learning this, Govindramji called Puranmalji and said, 'I appreciate the commitment of the English business magnates, but I fail to understand that since the mandated price was Rs. 1 crore and my standing offer was of Rs. 1.10 crore how did Sir Sassoon close the deal with you for only Rs. 90 lakh? This magnanimity is beyond my imagination.' Puranmalji explained, 'Sethji, Victor Sassoon had nicknamed the mill as son of Puranmal and I have been instrumental in increasing the profits of the mill by introducing textiles with better margins.' 'Seth Puranmalji told me that upon hearing this, the expression on Govindramji's face was that of disbelief. He gave a pat on Puranmalji's back and said that his goodwill is unmatched.'

Bharat Bubna narrates another interesting conversation between the two business magnates. Japan had just entered the Second World War Around this time, Govindramji invited Puranmalji for a business discussion. He asked Puranmalji his opinion on the market trends. Puranmalji responded with humility saying, 'You are the unchallenged king of the market, so I seek your opinion.' Govindramji replied, 'Puranmalji you are the uncrowned king of the textile market, so you cast your opinion first.' Puranmalji said, 'Sethji, cotton prices will come down since cotton will not be exported to Japan and the textile market would become bullish since textiles imported from England would come to a halt.' Govindramji, with a smile on his face, concurred with him and stated, 'You have snatched my views, so why lose time now. Let us corner the textile market.'

Puranmalji requested that he would like to discuss this proposal with his sons and that he would get back to him shortly. Subsequently, he expressed his inability to participate in the operations as his sons would like to play safe but nevertheless, he offered to buy any quantity on Govindramji's behalf and market at the appropriate time. The operations were done and whatever profits accrued, Puranmalji sent a cheque to Govindramji. In his unparalleled way of appreciation, Govindramji sent a cheque of 50% of the amount he had received from Puranmalji back to him. Puranmalji, being a man of unstinted integrity, returned the same and said, 'I was not a partner in the business, I have just acted on your behalf.'

In the first week of December 1943, *The Indian Textile Journal* reported the news in large type: 'BIGGEST DEAL IN INDIAN MILL HISTORY: E.D. Sassoon's interests taken over by Indian Businessmen.'

> Mr. Seksaria was a partner in the syndicate which was constituted to take over the managing agency of E.D. Sassoon Mills for a consideration of approximately Rs. 4 crore on the understanding that the designation of the company would be altered to the India United Mills Ltd. The sanction of the government was subsequently obtained for the alteration and the agency was transferred on 1st December, 1943. The new agency firm was called Agarwal & Co.

The mills that formed part of 'the India United Mills' group under Agarwal & Co. were:

1. The Jacob mill
2. The Alex and E.D. mills
3. The Manchester mill
4. The Rachel mill
5. Turkey Red Dye works

These mills together had approximately 2,50,000 spindles and 6,000 looms, a large and well-equipped dyeing, bleaching and printing works at Mahim, Bombay, and a woollen mill at Thana. The total workforce employed in 1943 in all these undertakings was approximately 10,000. The monthly bill for wages and salaries amounted to around Rs. 12 lakh. Monthly consumption of raw cotton averaged 12,000 bales and the monthly output of cloth and yarn was 10,000 bales.

Agarwal and Co. controlled the management of what comprised roughly 8-10 per cent of the working looms and spindles installed in the island city of Bombay. The formal taking-over ceremony of the India United Mills was performed at Sassoon's office at Ballard Estate, Bombay, on 3rd December, 1943. The partners of Agarwal & Co. officiated at the religious function. Sir Victor Sassoon, speaking on the occasion wished the new managing agents good luck.

The change in the agency of the principal mills in the E.D. Sassoon group marked an important landmark in the history of cotton mills in India. The establishment and expansion of the textile industry in Bombay had been due in no small measure to the enterprise of the firm of E.D. Sassoon & Co. During the two decades between the end of the First World War and the outbreak of the Second World War, 30 mill undertakings either changed hands or were liquidated or scrapped.

Grandson Nandkumar says: 'Agarwal & Co. comprised wealthy individuals such as the Khaitans of Ganeshnarayan Onkarmal, Ramkumarji Morarka, Rai Bahadur R.P. Bagla, Shivchandraiji Podar, Kantilal Nihalchand and Govindramji. I have heard from veterans close to my grandfather that Govindramji was initially reluctant to become part of this consortium but was persuaded by others to become a partner. (Seksaria's nephew Radheshyam was married to Khetan's daughter by then). Ramkumarji Morarka was like a family member. The group could hardly afford to have the "cotton king" sitting out! Having him as a partner was therefore strategic and necessary. A win-win situation for all.'

In 1941, Seksaria, now 53, commissioned the Bharat Vanaspati factory at Pachora in Khandesh which was an important groundnut centre for making hydrogenated ghee. It was one of the most modern vegetable oil factories of the time. In 1938, Seksaria had entered into a contract with Francke Werke A.Q. of Bremen, Germany, and Hansa (India) Trading Company Limited of Bombay for the supply of machinery and accessories for a complete oil refining and hydrogenated plant to produce 25 tonnes of faultless hydrogenated ghee. The total price for the plant was 1,77,500 Reichmarks (approximately Rs. 2 lakh at the then exchange rate).

Continuing to expand his industrial holdings rapidly, Seksaria acquired Premier Cotton Mills, later renamed Prakash Cotton Mills. Gauri Shankar Modi, Seksaria's grandnephew (Bholaram's daughter's son) recalls, 'I went to work at Prakash Cotton Mills which was acquired after Indore Malwa and Seksaria Cotton

Mill. The mill would also recycle waste cotton.' Seksaria was also associated with Shree Mahadeo Cotton Mills and Shri Bijay Cotton Mills, Bhilwara. The mills had a combined capacity of around 16,000 spindles and 330 looms and employed about 1,100 people. The Mansinghka's were managing agents. The firm Govindram Ramnath, comprising the two brothers, was also the managing agents for the three Johns mills in Agra for a year.

Seksaria was the prime mover and guiding force of the New Jack Printing Works Ltd., Bombay; The Seksaria Trading Company Ltd., Bombay and The Estate Investment Company Pvt. Ltd., Bombay, which acquired the khoti rights to what was known as the Bhayender Estate, comprising lands at Bhayender, Mire and Ghodbunder, as well as, about 500 acres in Chincholi and Dindoshi near Malad.

Seksaria held several important directorships. In November 1940, he was re-elected director of Powells. Other directors included R.D. Birla, Haridas Madhavdas, D.M. Khatau and Vithaldas Kanji. In February 1943, *The Times of India* named Seksaria as one of the directors of Bank of Jaipur. He was also a director of Hindustan Commercial Bank where Mangtu Ram Jaipuria, his close friend, was the chairman. Seksaria was also a partner in Anand Sugar Mills in Khalilabad along with Mangtu Ram who was the owner of the Swadeshi Mills, Kanpur.

As his career blossomed in the early 1930s Seksaria had set up a greenfield sugar factory called Seksaria Sugar Mills in Bhabhnan in present day Uttar Pradesh. Messrs Govindram Ramnath (Seksaria's partnership firm with his brother Ramnath) were managing agents of the mill. In 1938, Biswan Sugar Mills was the first cooperative unit of present day Uttar Pradesh which went into liquidation. It was bought by Seksaria in an auction in 1939 for approximately Rs. 11.25 lakh.

Prakash Seksaria, grandson of Bholaram, narrates an intriguing incident related to the purchase of Biswan Sugar: 'An ordinary man turned up at the auction, and when he gave his bid everyone was surprised to see such an ordinary looking

Seth Govindram Seksaria (1888-1946)

Smt. Basantibai Govindram Seksaria (1890-1959)

Young Kudilal Seksaria (1930-1996),
Govindram's only son, born 13th April, 1930

Basantibai Seksaria with eldest daughter Anaribai (standing),
second daughter Bhagwatibai (seated), and son Kudilal on the lap

Govindram Gordhandas Seksaria (1888-1946)

Bholaram Gordhandas Seksaria (1890–1946)

Ramnath Gordhandas Seksaria (1902–1944)

Makhanlal Gordhandas Seksaria (1904–1951)

Govindram Seksaria (seated first from left) with relatives

Kudilal Seksaria with wife Pushpabai

Standing left to right: Harsh Nandkumar Seksaria (Great-Grandson), Arnav Sharanya Harsh Seksaria (Great-Great-Grandson), Tarun Nandkumar Seksaria (Great-Grandson)
Seated left to right: Nandkumar Kudilal Seksaria (Grandson), Rajkumar Kudilal Seksaria (Grandson)

The main entrance of the haveli in Nawalgarh, where Govindram was born

The entrance to the haveli in Nawalgarh that was later home to the Seksaria family

A pillar adorned with the paintings of Lord Vishnu and Goddess Laxmi in the old Seksaria haveli

Paintings that depict Govindram and his three younger brothers on the wall of the old Seksaria haveli in Nawalgarh

Govindram would go for his daily morning walk on Marine Drive, where he lived, followed by a coterie of businessmen and traders all hoping for a tip or intel from one of Bombay's most prominent speculators

The former East India Cotton Exchange building at Kalbadevi, Mumbai

The road leading from the cotton exchange in Kalbadevi to Mumbadevi Mandir. Govindram's pedi was in the next building in this lane

As a horse racing enthusiast, Govindram would visit Poona often during the race season, where he would stay at his Koregaon Park bungalow

While Govindram rarely stepped into the public sphere, he was a true patriot and was keenly interested in national politics. One of the rare occasions he allowed himself to be photographed was when he played host to the members of the Congress Working Committee (pictured here), at his Koregaon Park bungalow, during the July, 1940 All India Congress Committee (AICC) session in Poona.

Among the seated dignitaries are (from left to right): Shri Bhulabhai Desai, Shri Prafulla Chandra Ghosh, Seth Govindram Seksaria, Sardar Vallabhbhai Patel, Maulana Abdul Kalam Azad, Pandit Jawaharlal Nehru, Shri C. Rajagopalachari, Shri Jamnalal Bajaj, and Shri Shankar Rao Deo

Govindram was a quiet but firm supporter of the Freedom struggle led by Mahatma Gandhi and donated large sums to the cause

Govindram (seated on the left) was present at the presentation of an address to Netaji Subhas Chandra Bose (seated Centre) at Madhav Baug, Bombay in 1938. Bose was the President of the Indian National Congress at the time

Maharana Bhupal Singh of Udaipur (r. 1930-1955)
(Courtesy: Museum Archives of the Maharanas of Mewar, © MMFC, Udaipur)
Maharana Bhupal Singh granted Govindram the right of wearing gold while attending the Durbar of Udaipur. In those days, it was deemed a big honour to Govindram for his services for Mewar

Maharaja Yeshwant Rao Holkar II of Indore (r. 1926–1948)
Maharaja Yeshwant Rao Holkar II was the ruler of Indore when Management of Indore Malwa Mills was awarded to Govindram. Govindram would meet the Maharaja whenever he visited Indore

Govindram with Sir Hukumchand of Indore at Kudilal's wedding at Nawalgarh

Govindram with Seth Mangtu Ram Jaipuria. Mangtu Ram was a close friend of Govindram and was the owner of The Swadeshi Mills, Kanpur

The New York Cotton Exchange building (in the early 1900s), where Govindram was a member

ALONG WALL STREET

By EDWARD J. CONDLON

There were several interesting features in the markets last week. Spurred by the injection of the erstwhile desterilized gold into the credit stream and the change in bank reserve requirements, trading in United States Government bonds was the heaviest in nearly a year and all issues touched new highs for 1938 or longer. Corporate bonds moved higher, so that the gains thus far in April are the best of any month since December, 1933. THE NEW YORK TIMES index of fifty stocks declined 2.20 points on the week. On the month, thus far, the index is up 11.77 points. Unless prices move down sharply this week, the April gain will be the best of any month in nearly five years. On the year, thus far, the loss shown by the index is only 3.43 points.

The Compromise on Taxes

It is fair to state that Wall Street was a little disappointed over the compromise worked out on the Tax Revision Bill. It had hoped to see the undistributed profits tax eliminated entirely and the capital gains tax drastically modified. At the same time, there is general recognition that the compromise as now outlined will lift some of the tax burden at present borne by business and will aid the investment situation. There is no question but what the tax on undistributed profits has curbed business expansion, and that the "heads-I-win,-tails-you-lose" feature of the capital gains tax has greatly hampered the investing public. The principal of the undistributed profits tax is retained, but it is not of paramount importance at a time when corporate earnings are low anyway; relaxation of the capital gains tax will, of course, constitute the main source of gratification in the markets.

East Texas Field

The battle over the Mexican oil properties goes on, but it is well to remember that the most important oil-producing area in the world is the East Texas field. Discovered less than a decade ago, nearly thirty years after the renowned Texas Gulf Coast district, the field has yielded its 25,000th oil well. The outlay, necessarily, has been tremendous. If it be assumed that the cost of each well, including tankage, pipelines and other essentials, as well as actual drilling expenses, averages $20,000, the field itself represents an investment of about $500,000,000.

Dividend Outlook

Even if the government's spending-lending program is put into operation in the near future, it is unlikely that corporate dividends this year will match those of 1937. Corporate earnings in the first quarter bulked considerably less than in the same period last year. Indications are that earnings in the present quarter will show little or no improvement over the preceding three months. Thus far in 1938 the oil companies have made a far better showing than have many other industries. The steel and automotive groups have been hard hit, and the utilities, as a group, have felt the pinch. Even under favorable business conditions it may take some corporations a year or so to make up the ground already lost. Last year, according to THE NEW YORK TIMES compilation, dividends of corporations with stock outstanding in the hands of the public totaled $4,550,460,671, largest of any year since 1931. The extremes in recent financial history were $4,982,668,635 in 1930, and $2,910,584,076 in 1932.

Cornering Indian Cotton

The Bombay Cotton Exchange is well behind the New York Cotton Exchange from the standpoint of trading volume, but it quite eclipses the New York mart in the matter of colorful operations. Bombay abounds with big-time speculators—plungers, they used to call them here. But New York witnessed the passing of "plungers" many years ago. Occasionally the Bombay Exchange indulges in night trading. Just now, Govindram Seksaria, one of the biggest of the Bombay operators, is coming about as close to cornering the Indian cotton market as is possible under changed world conditions. And it is to be remembered that India ranks next to the United States in cotton production. Normally, the spread between New York and Bombay prices is about 2 cents a pound. In January it narrowed to about one-fifth of 1 cent. As a result, many Indian traders sold Bombay's April-May contract heavily, and Mr. Seksaria loaded up with some 200,000 bales. The story is that he will take delivery and attempt to squeeze the shorts; meanwhile, he has sold short the July-August delivery, holding his earlier cotton to make good in case the market goes against him. But if all goes well he stands to profit on both positions. At present the effect of Mr. Seksaria's operations is being felt in all of the cotton markets of the world. Mr. Seksaria also holds a membership in the New York Cotton Exchange; those who recall having seen him say that he resembles Mahatma Gandhi in modern dress.

Railroads and Aviation

From the time when Commodore Cornelius Vanderbilt forsook steamboating for railroading before the last century was far advanced, the Vanderbilt name in finance and industry has been linked closely with railroads in general and with the New York Central in particular. Last week, the news that Harold S. Vanderbilt, a director of the New York Central and of other roads, had bought out one of the nation's largest airlines contained the element of mild surprise. Mr. Vanderbilt and his associates purchased the Eastern Air Lines properties from North American Aviation, Inc., for $3,500,000, and installed Edward V. Rickenbacker, America's war-time ace, as president. The railroads, of course, have not been inhospitable to the airlines. For many months one of the huge TWA passenger planes was on exhibition in the Pennsylvania Station. It is interesting to note, however, that the airline purchased by Mr. Vanderbilt and his associates serves territory to the south and does not directly compete with the New York Central.

The New York Times article published on 24th April, 1938

"That's Mr. Seksaria?!" the surprised President of the New York Stock Exchange and head of New York's leading cotton firm exclaimed on his visit to Govindram's simple office in Bombay

Indore Malwa Mills, Indore
Now a part of National Textile Corporation –
a Government of India Undertaking
Indore Malwa Mills was the first textile mill acquired by Govindram. It was one of the largest mills in Central India

Seksaria Biswan Sugar Factory, Biswan, UP
Biswan Sugar Mills was the first cooperative unit of present day Uttar Pradesh which went into liquidation and was bought by Govindram in an auction in 1939

India United Mills in Mumbai. Now a part of National Textile Corporation - a Government of India Undertaking
Govindram was a partner in Agarwal and Co. which went on to become the managing agents of India United Mills Ltd., Bombay, in 1943. It was the biggest deal in Indian mill history at the time. The group of mills, formerly known as the E.D. Sassoon United Mills, was the largest textile company in Asia

Bank of Rajasthan
Bank of Rajasthan was established in 1943
with Govindram as its Promoter and Founder-Chairman

Set up in 1927, Seksaria Saraswati Kanya Pathshala
was the first girls' school in Nawalgarh

Established in 1942, the Govindram Seksaria Teachers' Training College is part of Udaipur's Vidya Bhawan Society

Bust of Govindram at the Govindram Seksaria Teachers' Training College, Udaipur

Established in 1945, the Govindram Seksaria College of Commerce and Economics in Nagpur was one of three colleges set up by Shiksha Mandal in Govindrams' name with generous donations made by him. The other colleges are in Wardha and Jabalpur

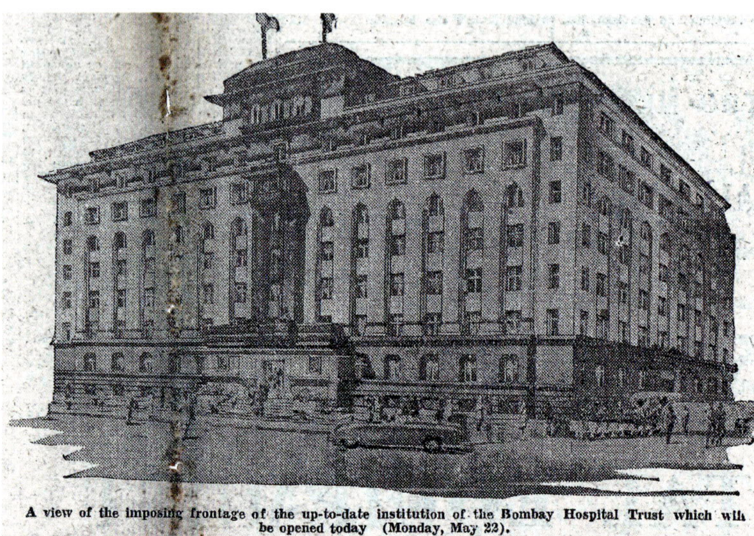

Govindram was amongst the leading donors of Bombay Hospital

The Shrimati Basantidevi Govindram Seksaria Maternity Ward at Bombay Hospital

In memory of Govindram, the Shri Govindram Seksaria Institute of Technology and Science, Indore, was established in 1952 and is one of the leading educational institutes in the state of Madhya Pradesh and Western India

In memory of Govindram and in consonance with his own policy a generous donation was made to the Hindustan Scout Association for the Govindram Seksaria Scout-Guide Pavillion at Shivaji Park

The Shri Govindram Seksaria Institute of Dacryology was inaugurated by His Excellency Shri E.S.L. Narasimhan, the Governor of Andhra Pradesh and Telengana on 7th October, 2016

Map of Shekhawati

Shekhawati is a Region in Rajasthan that falls under the modern districts of Sikar and Jhunjhunu, often dubbed the "open air art gallery of India". Nawalgarh lies close to the centre of the Shekhawati region. Govindram's ancestors used to live in a village called Seksar, hence the family name Seksaria

Govindram Seksaria Institute of Management and Research (GSIMR) is a Business School located in Indore.
It was set up by Shri Govindram Seksaria Technological Society in 1997

person making a bid. He was threatened by the district collector of the area, who told him, "See, if you give a bid and you can't pay the necessary deposit, you'll be put behind bars." So the man said, "Sir, let the bid get over. At that time, you have all the right to do as you need to." When the bidding was complete, the collector was confident that he would have to put the man behind bars, but to his shock and surprise, the man took out the money, which was rolled into his *dhoti*, because at that time high denomination notes were available! The moment he saw the bundles of notes, the collector refused to accept the money on the spot. But the man said, "Sir, before this I was unknown, now everyone knows I'm carrying so much cash, so I will not budge an inch until you accept this money and pass on a receipt to me." So the man had to be taken to Sitapur under police escort to deposit the money.'

Subsequently, it became known that the man was the representative of Govindram Seksaria and had gone for the bidding on his behalf because Seksaria was concerned that if his name was brought up, the bidding would go too high.

From available financial documents with the Seksaria group it can be assumed that, between 1944 and 1946, the India United Mills group registered profits of approximately Rs. 2.25 crore per year. It had a capacity of 2,50,000 spindles. Indore Malwa Mills recorded profits of around Rs. 40 lakh per year with a capacity of 52,000 spindles. Seksaria Cotton Mills, which was an unlisted company, had estimated annual profits of around Rs. 60 lakh and a capacity of 75,000 spindles. Seksaria Cotton Mills' spindles capacity was a little less than a one-third of India United's and 50 per cent higher than Indore Malwa's. Similarly, Premier Cotton and Bijay Cotton Mill, in which Seksaria had an interest, would have had an estimated profit of Rs. 15-20 lakh per year since the combined spindleage was about 25,000.

In the late 1930s, Seksaria's income from his trading activities was assessed at about Rs. 35 lakh a year. Keeping in view that the early 1940s were war years, profitability during that period would have been higher. A conservative estimate would place it at around Rs. 50 lakh a year. Considering his other manifold business activities, Seksaria's profits from these would have been another Rs. 50 lakh a year.

Thus, it would be fair to estimate that Seksaria's private business group was collectively recording a profit of approximately Rs. 1.75-2.00 crore per year in the 1940s. Separately, mills like Indu Group and Indore Malwa were making profits of Rs. 2.50-3.00 crore per year. This excludes income from assets which were held by people on trust. These were substantial.

Appendix 4 on page 198 of *Indian Business and Nationalist Politics,* 1931-39, by Claude Markovits, carries a table of the main business groups in the cotton textile industry from 1931 to 1939. This shows that Seksaria, who had bought two textile units by 1939, was consuming 2.9 per cent of the country's cotton consumption and was ranked No. 4 in the industry in 1939. Subsequently, with the addition of the Indu Group in 1943, Premier Textile Mills (later renamed Prakash Cotton Mills) and Bijay Cotton Mills, he would have directly and through partnerships been the largest consumer of cotton in India in the 1940s. At the time of his death in 1946, Seksaria directly and through partnerships controlled about four lakh spindles.

Even as Seksaria deepened his trading in New York, Liverpool and Bombay, he continued to expand his industrial assets. The Mahalaxmi Oil Mill was set up in Agra in 1935. In 1937, he registered Govindram Brothers Pvt. Ltd. which acted as purchase, selling and managing agents of his various companies. Rajkumar Seksaria recalls: 'My father, Kudilalji, was very young when my grandfather died. He was only 16. The empire was so big at the time and, unfortunately, as it happens in many families, the business interests were divided among the members of the family soon after. My grandmother Basantibai was magnanimous but very firm. After partition, she realised that her teenage son Kudilal wouldn't be able to handle such a large business empire himself. She saw the importance of banking on the senior associates of our group to help my father and look after the business. One of the main lieutenants was Prahladraiji Seksaria. There were others too who were in Indore—Pyarelalji Seksaria and Chandansinghji Bharkatiya, who looked after Indore Malwa Mills. They would come to Bombay often.'

'Our main interest was in textiles. We were partners in the biggest group in Bombay. India United Mills Ltd. which was the largest textile company in Asia. It had five mills in Bombay and one dye works at Bombay's Cadell Road with 2.5 lakh spindles and nearly 6,000 looms. In Bombay, in addition we had two other cotton mills - Seksaria Cotton Mills and Prakash Cotton Mills. In Indore, we had Indore Malwa United Mills. So, our main concentration in industry was textiles, sugar and oil. My father was particularly interested in India United Mills. When Govindramji died, Agarwal and Co. which was managing India United Mills, had six partners at the time. Progressively, we went on increasing our share and in the end by the late 1950s, early 1960s, we were one of the largest partners/shareholders in India United Mills.'

Seksaria did not diversify into industry only to de-risk his speculation and trading business in British India's turbulent economy. It was in order to prove that there were significant profits to be made from manufacturing that Seksaria set up industrial projects. As a report in *The Free Press Journal* noted: 'There was hardly any line of business in which Seksaria was not interested and none that he did not manage ably.'

Seksaria was also an excellent judge of men. His choice of colleagues and employees was sound. His confidence in them was based on an astute reading of their abilities and integrity. For each department of his business he picked up men of a different mould. Honesty and industry were the only common qualifications he looked for.

'Never leave until tomorrow what you can do today,' is a motto that Seksaria shared with all successful men. But he consistently differed from other successful leaders in his constant and deliberate breach of the other adage: 'Never let others do what you can do yourself.' His own version of that precept was:

'Never do yourself what you can get a right man to do.' That was how he enjoyed not only the respect and loyalty of partners and employees alike, but managed to run a large variety of activities and yet was always free to interest himself in new propositions.

'Seksaria's style of management was delegation,' says Nandkumar. There is a quote from him: 'Why should I do something myself when I have competent people to do it for me?' He had a very keen eye to spot talented people. We also heard anecdotes that when people used to come and complain to him, 'Look so-and-so is making money,' he would say, 'I am very happy with such people, if they are making money for me and on top of that making money for themselves, I would rather have such people working for me.'

There were occasions when Seksaria was let down. Often trusted colleagues would bring friendly warnings against new associates. On all such occasions, Seksaria had only one observation to make, 'I have lost or may lose a few lakhs but that man will have lost his soul. For myself, I would have earned a valuable experience of men. Surely, a little money is not too much price for that experience.'

That willingness to trust people was carried into Seksaria's daily business routine. He would not usually bother with the formalities of legal documents. His word was enough, and he was always willing to take other people at their word. Lakhs of rupees used to change hands without a word on paper. Businessmen and lawyers long remember a famous legal action he had brought against a rich businessman in which he stopped his counsel, the late Bhulabhai Desai, in the middle of his arguments and said to the court, in effect: 'I do not like this waste of time of the learned judge and learned lawyers. I myself have very little time for these things. Let my opponent solemnly declare that he does not owe me these monies and I shall gladly withdraw the suit.' The counsel's protests were to no avail. The other party did make the declaration and quite a few lakhs were written off by Seksaria without a murmur.

The strength of Seksaria's financial network and personal resources allowed him to secure capital in industry without real risk. The sheer diversity of Seksaria's industrial portfolio across sectors enabled him to reduce risk further and demonstrate that profits could be made in manufacturing industry despite the constraints of operating in a colonial economy.

Returning to Seksaria's strategy of forward integration, grandson Nandkumar says, 'Look at cotton. Govindramji was speculating in cotton, he had ginning factories, cotton seed oil extraction plants and textile mills. So what a great advantage that gave him for his speculation in cotton. If anything went wrong, he could give or take deliveries in his textile mills.'

A fourth-generation entrepreneur, Harsh Seksaria, Nandkumar's elder son, is involved in the family's various businesses. He has done a close study of his great-grandfather's business methodology. 'Another interesting point about Govindramji's forward integration with all these verticals is that it draws parallels with other industrial houses today, decades later,' observes Harsh. 'In one of the letters from our agent in the US, the Orvis Brothers, mention his move into forward integration by establishing a cotton seed extraction and crushing plant in which they played a role in supervising the purchase and shipment of the Plant and Machinery. All these were path-breaking for the era and they were carefully, strategically pre-planned.'

Tarun Seksaria, Nandkumar's younger son, adds reflectively, 'Govindramji, apart from core industries like steel, cement and coal, was present in virtually everything else. But the reason he went into certain sectors is that he was trading in them commodities like food grains, vegetable oils, cotton, sugar, etc. So core competence and domain knowledge would also have played a very important role. If you have a grip on a commodity at a certain level, it aids your trade throughout, and even going backwards in case you need to do a trade to suit you, it is helpful if you have a product which you could deploy either by giving or taking delivery.'

Mining is a good example of how this strategic thinking worked for Seksaria in the second half of his career. The discovery of mica deposits during the inter-war years in the 'Konkan stretch' located in the Sawantwadi state was no coincidence. Nor was it a coincidence that Seksaria quickly involved himself in mining operations there. The costs involved promised to be low, satisfying the first criteria of Seksaria's strategy.

As scholars of Indian entrepreneurship and industry in this period have shown, mining was a formerly European-controlled industry that Indians had studied carefully in the years leading up to the First World War. They found that there were no real technological or financial barriers to entry. 'All it needed was shovels, pails and gangs of low-paid tribal labourers,' writes Roy. 'Because the mica deposits were mainly to be found in rich supply on the land surface, extraction was a relatively simple process and mining operations could be conducted without the need for much scientific knowledge or experience, yet with a considerable amount of financial success.'

International demand was strong, the value of mica throughout the first half of the twentieth century was extremely high. This was an era of spectacular developments in electrical engineering. There was huge international interest in sheet mica which was used as a heat insulator in numerous household and electrical products. It was also a very important 'war mineral' used in the aircraft engines of allied forces during the Second World War. Deposits of the mineral were dwindling in the 1930s and 1940s across the United States, New Zealand and England (where mica had been mined traditionally), but swathes of India were found to have the mineral in abundant supply.

Seksaria was now in his element: a man able to seize the advantage in industrial diversification, such as mining. Fresh opportunities had been created in the wake of the Government of India Act (1935), which granted new forms of autonomy to the provinces of British India and made provisions for the inclusion of more elected Indian representatives in government. The Act opened up new possibilities for businessmen to buy mills, factories and manufacturing plants cheaply from the state.

All though, was not plain sailing. Seksaria's industrial career encountered troughs and crises, including slumps in the price of cotton and the general strike of Bombay cotton mill workers that swept across other industrial centres like Sholapur and Ahmedabad throughout the inter-war period. But falling prices of commodities, while putting a heavy strain on manufacturing and sales, could also be turned into a trading advantage where short-selling was commonplace—as on the Bombay Cotton Exchange.

Moreover, a nationalist appetite for domestic manufacturing enabled resourceful Indian textile industrialists to monopolise markets by presenting or branding their products as traditionally Indian or homespun. An amusing account in *The Times of India* in 1940 reported that Seksaria Cotton Mills had been taken to court by Hindustan Spinning and Weaving Co. Ltd. The latter had gained a reputation for the excellence of its homespun cotton products. This was symbolised by the special product identification number associated with the Hindustan Spinning and Weaving Company: *2588*. Such traditional homespun cotton products had long been celebrated by Gandhi and other advocates of khadi.

Seksaria Cotton Mills decided to capitalise on this national brand by stamping all their products with the special number *2588*. The case was eventually won by Hindustan Spinning and Weaving Co. Ltd. Nevertheless the example reveals Indians' penchant for branding and demonstrates Seksaria's acute awareness of how Indian industry was creating unique brands of its own that could be exploited as part of a large and rapidly expanding domestic cotton industry.

Assessing Seksaria's business assets a month after his passing in 1946, *The Free Press Journal* wrote: 'A glance at the list of the principal Seksaria concerns will indicate the sweep of Govindramji's industrial vision. Geographically, the factories are strewn over half the country. The textiles are spread over

Bombay, Indore and Rajputana; the sugar plants over UP; the oil factories and rice plants over Bihar, Sind, UP, CP, Kathiawar and Bombay; the banking interests over Bombay and Central India; the mining concession on the Western Coast; and an art woodwork factory at Mysore. Apart from these are the countless substantial shareholdings in industrial enterprises throughout the country.'

'Two of these undertakings, perhaps, are outstandingly typical of the Seksaria spirit in industry. The Seksaria Oil Mill of Hyderabad (Sind) was set up in 1938 to prevent the colossal waste of cotton seed, resulting from the fabulous increase in cotton cultivation, as a result of the Sukkur Barrage. What used to be mainly fodder for furnaces is now turned into a valuable edible product. The second instance is that of the Sawantwadi Minerals and Trading Company. A tiny Indian State, Sawantwadi has long been typical of the poverty of the Konkan. Apparently, it had underground wealth, strata of mica awaiting exploitation. But the Konkan stretch has never been in the minds of the Government or of industrial leadership, except as a comfortable recruiting ground for the army or the Bombay's textile mills. It was left to a Bombay son of Rajputana to see the opportunity to lend a hand to Sawantwadi to bring its hidden wealth to light.'

The most significant feature of Seksaria's move from trading into industry was that he did not turn away from speculation. Rather, speculation, an integral part of his cultural, familial and aesthetic identity, financed his acquisition of various industrial enterprises. Most Indian businessmen followed the same route. Resources raised from trading made industrialisation in India financially viable in the face of British and European obstacles to Indian business.

In India in 1914, for example, as the author Aditya Mukherjee points out, foreign banks held 70 per cent of all deposits.[46] For

[46]Mukherjee, *Imperialism*, p 29. On pages 27-28 he writes 'Between 1914 and 1947, the Indian capitalist class, through a process of economic and political struggle, and taking advantage of the two wars and the Great Depression

Seksaria, profits from trading and speculation were not random outcomes from gambling but strategic assets that could be used to underwrite investments in manufacturing, commerce and markets traditionally dominated by foreign capital.

Since his childhood and arrival in Bombay, Seksaria was provided with an unusual education in innovative business management and strategic thinking. This was a result of being immersed as a teenager in trade and speculation. Sensing quickly not to think of these networks as operating in separate vacuums but as mutually complementary, Seksaria learned to imagine trade and speculation as joint enterprises where information derived from speculation could provide valuable insights on where to invest in long-term trade.

This was done through meticulous analysis of the markets and powerful intuition. Seksaria used information from all manner of market trivia. He scrutinised these carefully for the slightest hint of political crises negatively impacting trade and prices. He surveyed these relentlessly in order to assess capital fluctuations and global market trends. Seksaria believed in the value of information for driving investment decisions and maintaining a highly diverse and integrated portfolio.

An example of Seksaria's pioneering approach to integrated networks and the deep analyses which formed the bedrock of his business strategy can be found in his domination of cotton market trading in the 1930s. He combined cotton speculation with the acquisition of textile manufacturing plants. An integrated strategy based on both speculation and investment

as well as the specific crisis faced by British imperialism during these years, was able to significantly increase its hold over the Indian economy vis-à-vis foreign capital' (emphasis in the original). 'The control of Indian capital on the larger industries in India extended rapidly in comparison to European control between 1915-1916 and 1937 and between 1937 and 1943-44.' In summary, the significance of the two world wars for the making of both Indian nationalism and Indian capitalism cannot be overstated.

in manufacturing meant much more to Seksaria than simply watching prices and anticipating dips and swells in one or two national markets. Seksaria developed insights beyond national boundaries, comparing trends in multiple locations across continents.

Factors impacting the Egyptian, American, English, Indian and Japanese markets were absorbed as part of an emphasis on data-mining and market research, taking into account global political and financial developments. In the 1930s, this was innovative. Strategic planning in a business context did not take hold of the public imagination until the 1960s.[47] Seksaria had developed a strong role for strategic thinking in his investment decisions decades earlier. His research strategy went well beyond mere tracking of prices of raw cotton worldwide. It also focused on marketing, handling and distribution of cotton-based commodities, including interest in spreads, straddle positions, and conversion contracts.

Specialised knowledge required a powerful network of trade contacts stationed in New York, London, Liverpool and other globally important locations. From these vantage points Seksaria's team could collate data and analyse it to establish the best investment and trading options. By taking market research seriously and exploiting well-established connections within national and transnational trading networks, Seksaria was well placed to extract large profits in raw materials and industrial commodities other than cotton (though cotton was a staple). These included profits derived from the unpredictability of cotton markets and competitive growth in key alternative cotton markets like Japan.

Seksaria, deeply engrossed in speculation throughout his career, sometimes ran into financial difficulties. The early-1920s

[47]Henry Mintzberg, *The Rise and Fall of Strategic Planning*, Pearson Education Ltd., 2000.

were a sensitive time. His daughter Anaribai's wedding was around the corner. 'Govindramji was speculating all the time,' explains grandson Nandkumar. 'In the initial years, he would make money and he would lose money. His daughter Anaribai was engaged to the son of Brijmohan Podar who was a very well-to-do businessman in Bombay. When the engagement took place, Govindramji had acquired wealth. But at the time of Anaribai's marriage around 1923 he had run into financial problems. Apparently, Brijmohan Podar told him, don't worry, you have to just send your daughter and nothing else is required. The marriage took place. And in our community there's a system that the bride went to the in-laws after six months to one year after marriage. That was known as *muklava*. So by the time that occasion arrived, Govindramji had again made money through speculation so it was done with great grace.'

Speculation in India was a serious business strategy: a mechanism for industrialisation that in turn represented the best available means of forging an alternative Indian capitalism based on domestic manufacturing. The outcome for businessmen like Seksaria was to sculpt a masterful risk-averse speculation strategy. Seksaria ingeniously deployed speculation as a novel insurance mechanism, generating capital guarantees for his industrial projects that finally paid off in the late-1930s and early-1940s. Seksaria's various, initially modest, business ventures morphed rapidly into a large industrial empire.

While Seksaria remained rooted to his origins as an intuitive trader and speculator, industry gave him added prestige and influence. And yet his identity as a man who made his mark as a speculator never diminished. Not only did speculative trading define him, it was his financial bedrock.

Dickson G. Watts, author of *Speculation As A Fine Art*, was a charter member and president of the New York Cotton Exchange between 1878 and 1880. In some ways Watts' trading philosophy mirrored Seksaria's, though they were separated by several decades and two oceans. This is how Watts described the 'fine art' of speculation in his book: 'Is there any difference between speculation and gambling? The terms are often used interchangeably, but speculation presupposes intellectual effort; gambling, blind chance. Accurately to define the two is difficult; all definitions are difficult. Wit and humor, for instance, can be defined; but notwithstanding the most subtle distinction, wit and humor blend, run into each other. This is true of speculation and gambling. The former has some of the elements of chance; the latter some of the elements of reason. We define as best we can. Speculation is a venture based upon calculation. Gambling is a venture without calculation. The law makes this distinction; it sustains speculation and condemns gambling.'

'All business is more or less speculation. The term speculation, however, is commonly restricted to business of exceptional uncertainty. The uninitiated believe that chance is so large a part of speculation that it is subject to no rules, is governed by no laws. This is a serious error. We propose to point out some of the laws in this realm. There is no royal road to success in speculation. We do not undertake, and it would be worse than folly to undertake, to show how money can be made. Those who make for themselves or others an infallible plan delude themselves and others. Our effort will be to set for the great underlying principles of the art the application of which must depend on circumstances, the time and the man.'

'Let us first consider the qualities essential to the equipment of the speculator. We name them: Self-reliance, judgment, courage, prudence and pliability.

1. Self-Reliance

   A man must think for himself, must follow his own convictions. George MacDonald says, "A man cannot have another man's ideas any more than he can another man's soul or another man's body." Self-trust is the foundation of successful effort.

2. Judgment

   That equipoise, that nice adjustment of the faculties one to the other, which is called good judgment, is an essential to the speculator.

3. Courage

   That is, confidence to act on the decisions of the mind. In speculation there is value in Mirabeau's dictum: "Be bold, still be bold; always be bold."

4. Prudence

   The power of measuring the danger, together with a certain alertness and watchfulness, is very important. There should be a balance of these two, prudence and courage; prudence in contemplation, courage in execution. Lord Bacon says, "In meditation all dangers should be seen; in execution one, unless very formidable." Connected with these qualities, properly an outgrowth of them, is a third, viz: promptness. The mind convinced, the act should follow. In the words of Macbeth; "Henceforth, the very firstlings of my heart shall be the firstlings of my hand." Think and act promptly.

5. Pliability

   The ability to change an opinion, the power of revision. "He who observes," says Emerson, "and observes again, is always formidable."

'The qualifications named are necessary to the make-up of a speculator, but they must be in well-balanced combination. A deficiency or an overplus of one quality will destroy the effectiveness of all. The possession of such faculties, in a proper adjustment is, of course, uncommon. In speculation, as in life, few succeed, many fail.'

Rajkumar Seksaria concedes that his grandfather was an

inveterate, almost compulsive, speculator. 'Govindramji would lose money and he would make money overnight,' he smiles. 'Once he lost money heavily. So he had to pay, but he was unable to. The person he had to pay filed a suit against him, and he had to go to court. In those days, they used to announce, 'Govindram Seksaria *ke vakil hazir ho*?' So the day the case came up, the judge made the announcement once, twice. Nobody came forward. But Govindram himself was in the courtroom, so he said, 'Govindram Seksaria *hazir hain*.'

Once he was in the witness box, the judge asked him where his lawyer was. Govindramji folded his hands and said, 'If I had enough money for a lawyer, I would have given it to my creditor. I don't have money.' The judge was impressed and told him to state his case. Govindramji answered, 'Sir, I've lost money, I've told my creditor I'm a *satoriya*, I'll make money and I'll give it to you.' The creditor replied, 'Sir, he's making false promises and not giving my money.' So the judge asked Govindramji how much time he wanted and Govindramji said, one month. The judge replied, 'One month? Okay, you have two!' Govindram's fortunes turned so fast that he repaid the money in one shot before the stipulated time period.

Rajkumar recalls a fascinating story that showed how luck played a part in his grandfather's life. 'Govindramji used to go to his native place quite often. He was very lucky as a speculator, you know. So in the evenings, he used to go to a small outhouse called *bageecha* in Nawalgarh. Big *seth* had come, so all the people from the village would come and sit with him. One of the people there said, "Sir, you are too lucky. Today, we want to earn money from you." So Govindramji said, "I'm happy to give it to you all but how will we do that?" So they took a *mojdi* to fling it up in the air. If it landed one way, the villagers won, but if it stood straight up, Govindramji would win. One per cent chance! So they said, *chalo*, let's do it. One fellow flung it up in the air and as luck would have it, it fell and stood straight! He was that lucky!'

While speculation is popularly characterised as risky and unpredictable, it ploughed an avenue for Seksaria into industry. Business historian, Jyoti Jumani, who has co-authored several books with one of India's pre-eminent business historians, Professor Dwijendra Tripathi, says emphatically: 'Govindramji Seksaria, I believe, was a speculation genius. He was born when the textile industry had taken root in India. Bombay and Ahmedabad were the hubs of the textile industry; textile mills in western India were promoted by Indian entrepreneurs. India at that time was still a colony and so western links and influence were a natural context. Banking, moneylending, and trading were characteristics of Indian mercantilism before industrialisation came to India.'

She elaborates on Seksaria's contribution to the evolution of Indian banking and industry: 'By the end of the nineteenth century, India with its thriving textile industry was on its way to industrialisation. The operational structure adopted by Indian textile mills was of joint stock companies. Industrialisation brought in formal, western structures in banking. A few European banks operated in India at that time. Punjab National Bank was the first bank that was set up by Indians in 1894 under Indian management with Indian capital. The *Swadeshi* movement in 1904-05 gave further impetus to the Indian textile industry. Moneylending and trade continued in western India. Trade and industry co-existed; in fact, they complemented and reinforced each other.'

'A prosperous textile industry in Indian hands, a developing banking structure, a stock exchange in Bombay in 1875 and a joint stock company business structure would naturally set the tone for a speculation-friendly culture. The First World War provided a further boost to the Indian textile industry. Speculation needs information and timely action to translate into money in the hands of the speculator. Govindram Seksaria had an appetite for information, a spirit for action, and the nerve to speculate.

'India, as we are aware, was integrated in the Western world which gave it a global feel. Seksaria, I believe, took advantage of an environment in which he successfully exhibited his speculation genius. His speculation was not limited to India. Moreover, Bombay already experienced peak speculation during the American Civil War. Setting foot into industry was the next natural step. The policy of Discriminating Protection introduced in 1921 encouraged expansion of the industrial base in India. Seksaria, with money and confidence, catapulted himself into industry. A speculation genius thus, became an Indian industrialist.'

It was impossible to separate Seksaria the speculator from Seksaria the industrialist: both were integral to his life and work. Crucially, just as speculation, which he never abandoned throughout his life, enabled him to invest in industry, industry enabled him to engage in philanthropy. The canvas was broad: charitable trusts, girls' education, institutes of learning and hospitals.

Seksaria also used his wealth unobtrusively but effectively to donate large sums to the Congress party during the freedom movement. Low-key as ever, few knew about Seksaria's meetings with Mahatma Gandhi. Nandkumar Seksaria recalls: 'They used to meet. Govindramji's daughter Bhagwatibai told us that Gandhiji visited Govindramji at Khattar Galli. One of my aunts, Savitribai Nathani and his grand-nephew Gaurishankar Modi, also recall seeing Jawaharlal Nehru and Sardar Vallabhbhai Patel coming to meet Govindramji at his Marine Drive home to which he moved from Khattar Galli in 1942. In the morning, Govindramji would partake of milk and fruit and eat lunch around 2 pm. He had simple food like curry and roti. He would sleep at 1.30 am, wake up at 5 or 6 in the morning. The drawing room would often be jam-packed with people.'

Nandkumar adds: 'He used to advance money liberally against jewellery. This is what my father Kudilalji used to say, "A person who has come to pawn his jewellery, give him more than the market would and he is not going to come back."

Through all the turmoil in India, engendered by the increasingly strident freedom movement, Seksaria maintained a low profile but continued to prosper. He had by now become something of a legend in his own lifetime. In 1942, Seksaria moved into a spacious sea-facing art deco building on 74, Marine Drive. Pushpabai Seksaria recalls, 'After my wedding, which took place in Nawalgarh, the family set up residence in the Marine Drive house. We went there straight after returning from Nawalgarh.'

Every morning at exactly 7.30 am Seksaria would walk down the Marine Drive promenade. Behind him would trail a group of brokers, traders and speculators, sometimes as many as 50, who would attempt to get trading tips from him. Well-known figures of the time, businessmen and traders would be a regular part of the coterie. Once Seksaria had given them a buy or sell tip it would become carved in stone. 'Govindramji said this, Govindramji said that,' would be a refrain carried by the breezes of Marine Drive, as one old-timer put it, to the offices and homes of investors around the city.

Chapter Seven

THE MARCH TOWARDS INDEPENDENCE

As India's economy threatened to unravel in the face of the global slowdown through the 1930s, finance member in the colonial Indian government Sir George Schuster vociferously advocated devaluation of the rupee. This step would have boosted exports. London, however, proved cold to the pragmatic suggestion. During the decade, especially when compared to previous years, the ratio of public investment to public expenditure in India fell. There was practically no new investment in the railways or in irrigation—investment that would have stimulated the economy.

In 1934, the year Seksaria acquired membership of the New York Cotton Exchange, Schuster was replaced by Sir James Griggs. He initiated further cuts in the capital budget. Griggs believed that agriculture was India's vocation. He did not support industrialisation based on customs protection or other measures. His sympathies were openly with the Lancashire mills. He was extremely hostile to emerging Indian industrialists like G.D. Birla. Despite Griggs' anathema towards Indian industry, there was a surge of industrial development in 1932-37, which had a positive impact on India's business community. Hopes for an indigenous industrial renaissance rose.

When Britain abandoned the gold standard in 1931, the colonial government had linked the rupee to sterling at the old rate. Public opinion was strongly against this policy. The minutes of an extraordinary meeting of the East India Cotton Association on 6th October, 1931 reads: 'That this extraordinary meeting of the East India Cotton Association Limited strongly condemns the decision of the secretary of state for India as well as the government of India in linking rupee with paper sterling at 18d., inasmuch as this decision works against the interests of Indian agriculturists in particular. This meeting, therefore, resolves that the rupee be left to its own value.'

London chose to ignore the opinion of Indian business chambers and industrialists. Following its departure from the gold standard, the pound sterling depreciated in terms of gold. Since the rupee-sterling ratio remained unchanged, the rupee depreciated as well against gold. Thousands of tonnes of gold began to be shipped to Britain through Bombay. Seeing the mass exodus, Lord Willingdon said: 'For the first time in history, owing to the economic situation, Indians are disgorging gold. We have sent to London in the past two or three months, £25,000,000 sterling and I hope that the process will continue.'

The resultant financial crisis was eventually stemmed by the classical route of raising taxes and reducing expenditure. This brought nationalistic sentiment to fever pitch. When the first general elections were held according to the Government of India Act, 1935 (which not only separated British Burma but increased the political autonomy of the remaining presidencies and provinces of British India), the Indian National Congress won a high percentage of vote share.

However, the 1935 Constitution had specific financial safeguards that antagonised the Indian business community. The Reserve Bank of India, set up by an Act of 1934 to replace the Imperial Bank of India, was made apolitical. Its directors could not alter the exchange rate or the currency standard of the rupee.

Although, Indians occupied half the seats on local bodies, they were powerless. It was a limited version of democracy. Though no one could have then imagined it, in just over a dozen years, India would be free.

The 1930s were a period of consolidation for big business houses in India. Though, groups like the Petits and Currimbhoys (whose mill Seksaria acquired) numbered among the casualties of the Great Depression, most existing groups survived and went on to expand their activities. Business groups such as the Dalmias, Walchands and Thapars, despite having no interest in textiles, prospered. Sugar, cement and paper as well as insurance, real estate and finance attracted new investment. In 1937, the formation of the Sugar Syndicate and the Federation of Indian Chambers of Commerce and Industry (FICCI) were early signs that Indian capitalism was maturing. The emerging Indian business families recorded significant progress, but their British counterparts still wielded real power.

During the Ottawa Conference from 21st July to 18th August, 1932 (also known as the Imperial Economic Conference or the British Empire Economic Conference), Britain's abandonment of free trade in 1931 prompted delegations from around the Empire to devise new arrangements for intra-imperial trade. Britain was keen to keep or gain privileged access to Empire markets, but it was reluctant to meet the demand of Empire countries such as New Zealand, given that it was a global trader. It did in the end exempt some countries' products from import duties. But barriers for the most part remained intact.

The Ottawa Conference accepted the failure of the gold standard and abandoned attempts to return to it. The meeting also worked to establish a zone of limited tariffs within the British Empire, but with high tariffs with the rest of the world. This was called 'Imperial preference' or 'Empire Free-Trade' on the principle of 'home producers first, empire producers second, and foreign producers last.'

The policy benefitted a few established firms in India such as the Sassoons. The Sassoons' fame had travelled widely. *The New York Times* wrote on 23rd August, 1936 about their intriguing background: 'Probably less is known or may be known, of the Sassoon family than of any other powerful banking family in the world. The family migrated from Spain to Baghdad in the sixteenth century, then to Bombay in 1832. From then on the base of operations has been the Orient. E.D. Sassoon & Co. of Bombay were organised in 1920 to take over the original merchant firm of the same name. Through control of Arnhold & Co., they operate extensively in China. David Sassoon & Co., with headquarters in Shanghai, were organised in 1901 to succeed the merchant firm of the same name that had its roots in China when China was known as the "Flowery Kingdom". The names of some of the members of the Sassoon family may be found in Burke's Peerage; their fame as merchant princes and bankers of the Orient is legendary. But to believe that the family fortunes have remained unscathed throughout the Depression while bankers elsewhere have taken their share of the licking is to accept as gospel The Arabian Nights.'

London's predatory economic policies meanwhile worsened an already deteriorating relationship between India and Britain. A fresh surge of nationalism coursed through the country. Jawaharlal Nehru unfurled the Indian flag and declared that the goal of the Indian National Congress would be complete independence from Britain. The Salt Satyagraha was undertaken as a response to Britain's heavy taxation imposed on Indians.

A major shift in the balance of India-British trade had taken place in 1930. The basic structure of trade between the two countries made it easier for India to replace imports. Indian mills could readily weave more cotton while Britain could not suddenly grow tea or jute. India's traditional deficit in its merchandise trade was, therefore, reduced considerably. For a few years it stabilised at a relatively low level.

With little textile imports from Lancashire and Japan during the Second World War, the industry in India flourished, even though it operated in a sheltered market. The mill consumption of Indian cotton rose from three million bales in 1937-38 to 4.3 million bales in 1942-43 and stayed around that figure till the end of the war. The cotton market boomed because there was no access to Egyptian cotton. American long staple was also scarce as all ships were utilised for the war. India produced short staple. When General Rommel arrived in North Africa, the supply of long staple Egyptian cotton was in the hands of the Germans. This resulted in a prolonged surge in prices.

The Second World War transformed the economy of the empire. By the end of the 1940s, not only had India achieved freedom but a new nation, Israel, had been founded in 1948 and the People's Republic of China was formed in 1949. Along the way Germany created the first programmable computer in 1941, using it to calculate wing clutter on their aircraft. The Americans followed with a computer of their own in 1942. The Bretton Woods conference created the World Bank and the International Monetary Fund (IMF) in 1944 in an attempt to avoid another Great Depression. In 1949, to counter Soviet expansionism, the West formed the North Atlantic Treaty Organisation (NATO).

All these developments would fundamentally alter the geopolitical and financial landscape. Karl Haushofer, the foremost German geopolitical thinker, observed after the signing of the Nazi-Soviet pact in 1939: 'Now finally, the collaboration of the Axis powers, and of the Far East, stands distinctly before the German soul. At last, there is the hope of survival against the Anaconda policy [the strangling encirclement] of the Western democracies.'

Haushofer had served as an adviser to Adolf Hitler. Many of his ideas, including his treatment of *lebensraum* or living space, were adopted by Hitler and incorporated into *Mein Kampf.* British imperialism was for Haushofer the greatest threat to German power. The alliance with Japan, he believed, as did Hitler, would counter British and American naval power in the Pacific.

As the war began to sweep across Europe, India's Governor-General and Viceroy Victor Hope, the second Marquess of Linlithgow, announced on 3rd September, 1939 India's entry into the Second World War. A product of imperialist ideology, he had done so without consulting India's 11 provincial governments, seven of which were ruled by the Congress.

The Congress had been growing in credibility and confidence following the previous decade's civil disobedience movement. In a show of strength, it now asked its elected representatives to resign from government. Yet despite this initial protest the British Indian Army would go on to become the largest volunteer force in the war, numbering 2,500,000 men in 1945. Several Indian Princely states not only donated generously to the allied war effort but provided 2,50,000 men for service. Indians fought all over the world, from Europe to North Africa and from South and Southeast Asia to West Africa. At the end of the war, as many as 87,000 Indian soldiers had died. Indian soldiers earned 30 Victoria Crosses.

In 1940, as the Battle of Britain, the German *Luftschlacht um England* ravaged England, Gandhi was besieged with suggestions and pleas from nationalists to take advantage of Britain's vulnerability and call once more for a massive Civil Disobedience movement. Gandhi however remained firm, insisting that India would not gain self-rule out of the ashes of a destroyed Britain. As the war wore on and the freedom movement gathered momentum, the rumblings grew louder in India. Dissatisfaction among Indian troops fighting in Europe rose alarmingly.

The British government knew it needed the commitment and sheer numbers of the Indian army in its war effort. Strong measures were taken to ensure this. A mission headed by Sir Stafford Cripps, a senior left-wing politician and government minister in the War Cabinet of Prime Minister Winston Churchill, was sent to India in March 1942. His goal: to negotiate a deal with the Indian National Congress under which, in exchange for the party's total cooperation during the war, there would be progressive devolution and distribution of power from the Crown and the Viceroy to an elected Indian legislature.

However, despite Cripps' unabashed sympathy for the Indian cause and his declaration that the aim of British policy in India was 'the earliest possible realisation of self-government in India', the Cripps Mission, as it came to be called, failed. The Congress' demand for the immediate transfer of effective power to Indians was anathema to the British government and especially, to Churchill. Promises for the future had been made and broken by the British in the past. India was, therefore, unwilling to accept Cripps' terms. Gandhi described Cripps' offer of Dominion status after the war as a 'post-dated cheque drawn on a crashing bank.'

Gandhi and other senior Congress leaders like Nehru and Patel realised it was time to force the British to meet their demands and obtain a definitive commitment on total self-rule. On 8th August, 1942, the Quit India resolution was passed at the Bombay session of the All-India Congress Committee (AICC). The resolution proposed a non-violent struggle under Gandhi's leadership. It declared that 'the immediate end of British rule in India is an urgent necessity, both for the sake of India and for the success of the cause of the United Nations. India, the classic land of modern imperialism, has become the crux of the question, for by the freedom of India will Britain and the United Nations be judged, and the people of Asia and Africa be filled with hope and enthusiasm. The ending of British rule in this country is thus a vital and immediate issue on which depends the future of the war and the success of freedom and democracy. A free India will assure this success by throwing all her great resources in the struggle for freedom and against the aggression of nazism, fascism and imperialism.'

Seksaria continued to play an important but often behind-the-scenes role in the freedom movement. He made generous donations to various political organisations. He gave a substantial donation to Thakker Bappa's Rajasthan Sevak Sangh organised on the lines of Servants of India Society. It was at Gandhi's and Jamnalal Bajaj's request that he gave donations for three educational institutions at Wardha, Jabalpur and Nagpur.

Abhaysingh Bharkatiya, son of Chandansingh Bharkatiya, who was one of Seksaria's managers, says: 'My father Chandansinghji was involved in the freedom movement and was known to national leaders. Later on, he also became a trustee of the Kasturba Foundation. Chandansinghji was instrumental in Govindramji giving a substantial donation of Rs. 1.5 lakh to Thakker Bappa's Rajasthan Sevak Sangh which was organised on the lines of Servants of India Society. I remember my father telling me that once Kudilalji expressed a desire to Govindramji to meet Gandhiji. When Bapu was next in Bombay, Govindramji Seth told my father to take Kudilalji to meet Gandhiji and gave him a package of Rs. 5 lakh to be offered to Gandhiji.'

Seksaria's grandnephew, Gaurishankar Modi (Bholaram's daughter's son) recalls having heard that, 'Gandhiji used to tell Govindramji that he should donate all his wealth to the Congress and join the nationalist freedom movement. Govindramji replied smilingly that he has the privilege to sit amongst Gandhiji and others because of his donations to the cause of freedom and if he did not have the money to do so, who would entertain him! He told Gandhiji that he will continue to earn and give to the freedom struggle spearheaded by Gandhiji as long as he lived.'

Seksaria had been seated next to Sardar Vallabhbhai Patel when he hosted the Congress Working Committee members at his home during the AICC Congress session at Poona on 27th-28th July, 1940. The seating arrangement points to his importance as it followed a certain protocol. The president of the meeting was Maulana Abul Kalam Azad. It would prove to be an important meeting. Several key decisions were taken on the future strategy of the freedom movement.

Azad and Gandhiji had sharp differences over whether total non-violence, which the Mahatma favoured, was pragmatic or not. In the event two resolutions were adopted at the July

1940 meeting which Gandhiji skipped. The first reiterated the Congress' steadfast commitment to non-violence; the second declared that the country's 'rightful place was in the democratic camp' following Independence.

Seksaria, now 52 and at the apogee of his career and wealth, increased both donations and personal encouragement to the Congress as the freedom movement entered its decisive phase. Seksaria's participation in the freedom struggle was, however, not restricted to donations. He was an enthusiastic and committed supporter.

In 1938-1939, Seksaria had been present with Netaji Subhash Chandra Bose at a public function. This showed that Seksaria had the courage of his convictions at a time when many did not attend public meetings with Bose because of dissent within the Congress of which Bose was then President.

The Times of India meanwhile reported on 1st September, 1940: 'A public meeting was held this evening at Congress House in protest against the Viceregal declaration of 8th August. Mr. N.V. Gadgil, president of the MPCC, addressing the meeting said that it is necessary in the interest not only of India but also of England and world peace that India should become independent. Whatever the reactionaries may say or do India is bound to be free as a result of this war. Mr. Shankarrao Deo, member of the Congress Working Committee, explained that the attitude of the British Government amounted to an attack on the very basis of nationalism by inciting the minorities. He asked the people to be ready for a struggle which he said was inevitable.'

The Quit India movement or the *Bharat Chhodo Andolan* was now launched. In his speech at Gowalia Tank Maidan in Bombay on the night of 8th August, 1942, the Mahatma said: 'I, therefore, want freedom immediately, this very night, before dawn, if it can be had . . . . Fraud and untruth today are stalking the world. You may take it from me that I am not going to strike a bargain with the viceroy. I am not going to be satisfied with anything short of complete freedom. Here is a mantra, a short one that

I give you. You may imprint it on your hearts and let every breath of yours give expression to it. The mantra is: Do or Die. We shall either free India or die in the attempt; we shall not live to see the perpetuation of our slavery . . . .'

It was stirring stuff. And India arose as one, suffused with patriotic fervour. The British, already alarmed by the presence of the Japanese army on the India-Burma border, responded by imprisoning Gandhi at the Aga Khan Palace in Poona the very next day. He didn't get the rough treatment in an Andaman prison earlier that freedom fighters like Bhagat Singh had received. The Congress Party's Working Committee was arrested and imprisoned at Ahmednagar Fort. Over 60,000 Congress leaders from all over the country were jailed. Many of the party's key office-bearers would languish in prison till the end of the war, although, Gandhi was released in May 1944 due to his deteriorating health. Concerned about the Mahatma's health, and as freedom loomed over the horizon, Seksaria visited Gandhiji in 'Gandhigram' in Bombay's suburban Juhu on 10th June, 1944.

When people first heard of the mass arrests of their leaders, they reacted with violence. Hartals took place in factories, schools and colleges and large demonstrations were held. Symbols of British authority such as police stations, post offices and railway stations were attacked. Telegraph and telephone wires were cut, railway lines destroyed and government buildings burnt.

The government's retaliation echoed the brutality it had used to quell the revolt of 1857—India's first war of independence. Demonstrators were machine-gunned and even bombed from the air. Villagers were flogged. The military took over control of strategic towns and cities. The press was muzzled. Prisoners were tortured so they would provide strategic information. The secret police unleashed a reign of terror. It is estimated that over 10,000 Indians died in this short period. The revolt of 1942, as it has been dubbed, was short-lived. But it demonstrated the depth of nationalist anger in the country.

It was during this crucial period in India's freedom struggle that Seksaria enlarged his own role. He met Gandhi, Nehru, Patel and Bose and donated liberally to the Congress. Congress leaders frequented his Marine Drive home.

In 1943, Bengal was plunged into famine. Within a few months over three million people died of starvation or malnutrition. A confluence of factors led to the catastrophe: the Japanese occupation of Burma stymied the supply of food and other essentials to the region; the local rice crop was damaged due to tidal waves; and a fungal epidemic caused havoc. Ever-increasing financial and material resources diverted to the war effort played a role as did mismanagement by Indian regional governments. An increase in demand for food as a result of refugees pouring in from Burma and Bengal worsened an already critical situation.

Dr. Gideon Polya, an Australian biochemist, has called the Bengal famine a man-made holocaust. 'The British brought an unsympathetic and ruthless economic agenda to India,' he wrote. Though Leopold Amery, the Indian secretary of state, and Archibald Wavell, the viceroy of India, requested the British government to stop exports of food from Bengal so that it could be used for famine relief. The request was ignored. When Churchill first received a telegram about the rising toll of famine deaths in Bengal, he was reported to have said that he regretted that Gandhi was not one of the victims. Later, at a War Cabinet meeting, Churchill blamed Indians themselves for the famine, saying that they 'breed like rabbits'. His attitude toward Indians was best summed up in his statement to Amery: 'I hate Indians. They are a beastly people with a beastly religion.'

Churchill's role in the 1943 Bengal famine was exposed in Madhusree Mukerjee's brilliant book, *Churchill's Secret War: The British Empire and the Ravaging of India*. Based on original sources and newly declassified British documents, the book is a grim indictment of colonial policy: 'On 27th May, 1943, Linlithgow advised Amery that he was unable to guarantee the stability of the Indian economy. Every necessity of life—food, fuel, drugs, cloth was approaching the scarcity limit. The manifold causes included the lack of shipping for imports and the diversion of every industry to war production, which had left a dearth of products for civilian use. As a result, all the cash in the economy was being used to buy up grain, the only commodity at hand.' 'Thus far,' the viceroy continued, 'the Government of India had succeeded in producing the men and material needed for the war and in keeping the vast majority of the population quiescent.' But the real resources of the country are already strained almost to breaking point: on the psychological side, we are 'within sight of a collective refusal to accept further paper currency.' The time had come when the United Kingdom needed to choose between 'utilising India as a base for operations and utilising India as a source of supply for overseas theatres and countries.'

'Bengal is rapidly approaching starvation,' the governor of Bengal wrote to the viceroy on 2nd July. Unless he received immediate help, Herbert could not 'guarantee two indispensable requirements of the war effort, internal security and war production.' (At no recorded instance did either the governor or the viceroy express concern for their subjects: their every request for grain would be phrased in terms of the war effort. Contemporaries attested that Herbert did care about the starvation in Bengal; so prioritising the war effort may reflect his and Linlithgow's estimation of which concerns might possibly have moved their superiors.) Hunger was widespread in the districts, Herbert wrote three weeks later, and masses of ticketless beggars were boarding trains in the hope of finding food in the towns. The US Board of Economic Warfare reported in July: 'Famine has been a real and ever present threat and it is now reliably estimated that unless substantial quantities of food-stuffs are forthcoming from outside sources, hundreds of thousands of deaths from starvation will occur in India during the current year.'

'In London on 30th July, the War Cabinet's shipping committee considered Viceroy Linlithgow's request for grain. An India office representative stated that famine conditions were appearing in Bengal and in parts of the south and relayed Auchinlek's opinion that India might not be usable as a base until the food problem was solved. The committee was divided in its response. Some members argued that meeting the colony's need could hardly do more than involve some degree of interference with the re-establishment of stocks in the United Kingdom, unless some large military need showed up in 1943. The minister of war transport objected, however, that providing the ships to lift any more than 30,000 tonnes of grain a month from Australia would involve a serious dislocation of our plans. In the end, the shipping committee noted a wide divergence of opinion as to the part which the import of cereals should or could play in solving the Indian economic problem and left the decision to the War Cabinet.'

Mukerjee writes in her book: The prime minister 'hates India and everything to do with it.' Wavell observed in his diary on 27th July, after witnessing an outburst in the War Cabinet: 'Winston drew harrowing picture of British workmen in rags struggling to pay rich Indian mill-owners; and wanted to charge India the equivalent of our debt to her for saving her from Japanese invasion.' The Field Marshal pointed out that India had 'defended us in the Middle East for the first two years of war' rather than the other way around. Amery, for his part, noted that it was not a good idea 'when driving to catch a train for life or death, to lean through the window and tell the taximan that you do not mean to pay the fare at the station because you have a moral counter-claim against him.' Because it was patently counter-productive to seek a revision of the financial agreement at that juncture, the prime minister had been frustrated in his resolve to abolish the balance owed to India.

The Bengal famine of 1943 claimed over three million Indian lives. 'Rich Indian mill-owners,' whom Churchill had disdainfully referred to in the War Cabinet, were outraged. The whole of India seethed. The die was cast. Britain's hold on India had irretrievably slipped.

The freedom movement found new expression in the rise of the Azad Hind led by Subhash Chandra Bose. 'Give me blood and I shall give you freedom,' was his ringing declaration as he urged the people of India to join him in his armed freedom struggle. India's entry into the Second World War had been strongly opposed by Bose who was president of the Congress in 1938 and 1939. He differed with Gandhi on several counts over the conduct of the nationalist movement. Bose eventually resigned from the Congress to start a separate political party, the All India Forward Bloc. Several Congressmen with socialist views left to join him.

The British placed Bose under house arrest in Calcutta. He escaped and made his way through Afghanistan to Germany. Bose sought Hitler and Mussolini's help in raising an army to fight the British. The Free India Legion comprising Erwin Rommel's Indian POWs was formed. Japan helped Bose set up the Indian National Army (INA) which fought alongside the Japanese, mostly in Burma. Bose also headed the provisional government of free India, a government-in-exile based in Singapore.

As the war progressed and Germany's fortunes faltered, a German land invasion of India became untenable. Hitler advised Bose to go to Japan. Bose was ferried to Japanese-controlled Southeast Asia, where he formed the Azad Hind Government and reorganised the Indian National Army composed of both Indian POWs and Indian expatriates in Southeast Asia. Its aim was to reach India as a fighting force; it would be bolstered by Indian volunteer-soldiers along the way to defeat the British Raj.

Bose's plan was not entirely unrealistic. There had already been two mutinies within the armed forces which strained relations between Indian soldiers and their British officers. After the Japanese attacks on Christmas Island in 1942, Indian troops assisted by Sikh policemen mutinied, killing five British soldiers and imprisoning the remaining 21 Europeans on the island. The Royal Indian Navy mutiny began in Bombay and spread throughout British India. It involved 78 ships, 20 shore establishments and 20,000 sailors. But again, it was suppressed before it could do real damage to the British occupation of India.

After the end of the Second World War, India's struggle for independence entered its final phase. The war had changed the balance of global power. The United States and the Soviet Union emerged as the world's new superpowers. There was a change of government in Britain. The Conservatives were replaced by the Labour party, many of whose members supported the Congress demand for independence. British soldiers were weary of war, having fought for over six years against Germany, Italy and Japan. The British Indian Government could no longer rely on Indian personnel in its civil administration and the army to suppress the freedom movement. The Indian police were also showing signs of rebellion. They too could no longer be relied upon to quell an uprising. The cost of maintaining the Empire had begun to outweigh its benefits. Britain was in retreat.

In 1946, the year Govindram Seksaria passed away, India was in deep turmoil. The peasant movement, reacting to high rents and a paucity of available land, became more assertive. Students took a leading role in implementing strikes. The British government sent a Cabinet Mission to India to negotiate the transfer of power to Indians. Though numerous hurdles needed to be overcome, by September 1946 an interim cabinet headed by Nehru was formed by the Congress. The Muslim League reluctantly joined the cabinet. On 20th February, 1947 Prime Minister Clement Attlee declared that the British would quit India. Riots soon broke out between Hindus and Muslims as Partition loomed. Lord Louis Mountbatten, the last viceroy of India, accelerated the process of Partition, leading to even more bloodshed.

India had crossed the bridge from colonialism to Independence. With Independence came Partition which deeply affected the cotton industry. Most weavers were Muslim. They migrated to Pakistan. Of India's 394 cotton mills, 14 went to Pakistan. More importantly, 40 per cent of undivided India's cotton producing area was located in newly formed Pakistan. India was forced to import raw cotton to keep its mills spinning.

Govindram Seksaria died the year before India won Independence. But his legacy would live on. It was a legacy tethered to centuries of Marwari history, culture and entrepreneurship.

Chapter Eight

An Entrepreneurial Ecosystem

To understand the milieu in which Govindram Seksaria and his peers would make their fortunes in trade and industry, it is important to trace the events in the era that preceded them. British India was run by a small number of officials. In 1805, there were only 31,000 Britons in India. Though this figure rose after the uprising of 1857, even in 1911 - the height of Empire - there were only 1,64,000 Britons in the subcontinent. In 1931, the number peaked at approximately 1,68,000, hovering around that figure till Independence.

A large percentage of the income of the ruling elite was repatriated to Britain. The drain began at the advent of the British Indian Empire. Robert Clive, commander-in-chief of British India in the mid-1700s, for example, took a quarter of a million pounds for himself as well as a *jagir* worth 27,000 pounds annually. British salaries were usuriously high. The viceroy received 25,000 pounds and the governors 10,000 pounds. An engineer earned 420 pounds, sixty times the average income of the Indian labour force. At today's prices that would constitute a fortune. Besides this there were reimbursements for long home leave in Britain, early retirement and lavish amenities in the form of subsidised housing, utilities, rest houses and hill station bungalows. By the 1930s, the official transfer of funds to Britain by the Indian colonial government (euphemistically called home charges) was in the range of 50 million pounds annually.

The total drain amounted to around 1.5 per cent of India's GDP from 1921 to 1938. By 1939, foreign assets in India totalled $42.8 billion of which $1.5 billion was government bonded debt. The rest represented direct investment. Net investment was about five per cent of GDP by 1947. India did not reduce its foreign debt during the First World War as many other developing countries did. It had been forced to make two voluntary war gifts to Britain totalling 150 million pounds. Indian troops were also financed by the Indian budget. Britain fought the war with Indian men and Indian money.

The drain of resources continued through the 1920s and 1930s. The Second World War, however, changed India's financial position. Britain financed military expenditure in India by borrowing rather than taxation. India was able to liquidate $1.2 billion of pre-war debt and acquire sterling balances of more than $5 billion. At the end of the war, India was a large net creditor. These assets and the end of the colonial drain gave the country a much needed boost to its post-war development.

Paradoxically, certain regions in India benefitted during the early years of British colonial rule. Settled law and order drew migrants to these British-controlled areas. Govindram Seksaria's family came from the barren Jhunjhunu district in Rajputana. With increasing influence of British rule in Rajputana during the last few decades of the nineteenth century and the early-twentieth century, there was a transformative change in the region's economic, social and political condition. The business environment in many districts of Rajputana became adverse compared to British-controlled regions. This led to migration of a large number of Marwaris in search of a livelihood in Bombay, Calcutta, Assam and other parts of the country.

Besides doing business across India, many Marwaris also

participated in the freedom movement. During the 1890s, most small towns in Rajputana were connected by commercial roads to facilitate import and export of goods from other business centres. This boosted business opportunities for traders in Rajputana.

The main mode of transport was the camel. The principal connecting roads through the region were Delhi to Pali, Multan to Kota, Ujjain to Kota, Indore to Jaipur, Agra to Ujjain, Gwalior to Jodhpur and Jaipur to Ahmedabad. A new rail network was under construction in Rajputana. The nearest railway stations were Delhi, Indore and Ahmedabad. Reaching these destinations by camel was tiresome and risky. The journeys were, therefore, undertaken in groups. These commercial routes though soon became unsafe. Incidents of loot increased. The British government started imposing heavy tolls on the routes under its territory. As a result, most routes were abandoned. The traditional business structure of Rajputana was disrupted. Businessmen began to search for new avenues of employment and livelihood, mainly in areas under British control.

During this period geographical conditions in Rajputana underwent a change. Due to poor rains, the region had faced many droughts during the last few decades of the nineteenth century. Business activities suffered. Exploitation of businessmen by the powerful lobby of 'Samants' rose alarmingly. They would borrow money at low rates of interest and not pay back. Law and order deteriorated. These proved the trigger points for the migration of Marwaris from Rajputana.

The main products of Rajputana – salt, opium and cotton came under the control of the British. They managed all international trade activities. This accelerated the migration of Marwari traders to British-controlled areas. Marwaris started earning significant incomes around the turn of the nineteenth century. The British needed local businessmen as agents to sell goods produced in England and to procure raw material in India. The community's influence grew steadily. The British government realised their potential. It encouraged them and provided protection to their businesses. The British government also helped them recover their dues from kings and jagirdars and provided them special privileges. They were given various honorific titles: Seth, Raja and Rai Bahadur.

The British government helped traders and businessmen recover dues of Rs. 40 lakh from Bikaner kingdom in 1872. Whenever there was a dispute between rajas and businessmen, the British government supported the businessmen. That was another reason why traders preferred to do business in British-controlled areas. Between 1870 and 1900, nearly 80 per cent of Marwari businessmen became *'banias'* of British companies.

In 1899, Marwaris started establishing 'sabha societies' and formed Marwari associations. The changing political environment in the country compelled Marwari youth to form such societies and run them with new, progressive ideas that were in the interest of common people. Many enthusiastic youths came forward to run the sabha societies. Besides dealing with social and business issues, the societies started participating in political affairs. They began communicating with government officers.

Initially, all income groups participated in these societies. Subsequently, powerful individuals began to advance personal agendas. Differences between the rich and poor became visible. People were soon disillusioned and perceived societies as a means for a select group of powerful individuals to get titles from British government officials.

In 1900, the policies of the British government started changing. Adverse steps taken by the viceroy, Lord Curzon, triggered political awareness and caused dissatisfaction amongst local people. During this period a revolution began around a swathe of social, economic and educational issues throughout the country. Marwaris were an integral part of this movement.

Govindram, then 11, lived with his family in Nawalgarh. He was an inquisitive but quiet child. His father Gordhandas continued to run a small trading operation. The family lived in an old haveli. The Seksarias looked towards Bombay to expand their business. It would be left to young Govindram to make a decisive move to Bombay after his parents' death in 1905.

According to the economist and researcher D.R. Gadgil, unlike other business communities, Marwaris moved in large numbers across the entire country. This boosted the economy of various remote regions like Assam and Bengal. Going to Assam was extremely difficult. It took almost three months, involving travel by foot, camel and boat to cross the Brahmaputra against the stream. Former Assam Governor Sri Prakasa[48] had observed that Marwaris showed great courage and tenacity to travel through difficult terrain, crossing hills and rivers to reach remote areas.

In Calcutta conditions were equally bad. An entire family would stay in one room, cooking and washing within the room. After migration from Rajputana, Marwari businessmen established Calcutta as their base. Initially, they started working as cashiers (munims) with established Marwari firms. Diligent and meticulous, they soon became *banias* in British firms. They then began establishing themselves in Calcutta's financial community and developed a strong social structure.

The Marwari Association was formed in 1898. It started educational institutions and gave new direction to social change in the early years of the twentieth century. It contributed significantly to public health and helped people who suffered due to floods, earthquakes and famines. To provide succour during natural disasters, the Marwari Relief Society was established in 1913. Mahatma Gandhi lauded its contribution: 'The society is service-oriented countrywide for human welfare having resources and committed workers.' Subsequently, many

[48]Sri Prakasa, governor of Assam from 1949-1950, was a politician, freedom fighter and administrator. He served as India's first high commissioner to Pakistan from 1947 to 1949, governor of Assam from 1949 to 1950, governor of Madras from 1952 to 1956 and governor of Bombay from 1956 to 1962.

social organisations like Kashi Vishvanath Seva Samiti were created to undertake social reforms and overcome traditions which hindered the community's progress.

Marwaris earned copiously through speculation and commissions in opium, jute, cotton and silver. But many businesses closed down as well due to heavy losses in speculative trading. In Calcutta, Marwaris had a monopoly in speculation of opium and patsan. By 1905, the volume of such speculative business had increased substantially. Contrary to the general perception that Marwaris were active only in business and commerce, they participated enthusiastically in political activities. Marwari youth took part in the freedom struggle in several ways. They openly pleaded the cases of freedom fighters and attended their secret meetings. Their names were registered in police records. Marwaris also helped freedom fighters with funds. Many used the homes of Marwaris as hideouts and even for storing bombs. They published literature and made the general public increasingly aware of the freedom struggle.

In 1915, Jamnalal Bajaj met Gandhi for the first time and was greatly influenced by him. He decided to involve Marwari businessmen in the freedom movement. He appealed to Marwari youth to actively participate. This had a significant impact in Calcutta. More and more Marwari businessmen started joining the freedom struggle. In 1920, Jamnalal Bajaj was made treasurer of the Congress.

He started collecting funds in the name of the Tilak Swaraj Fund with his own contribution of two lakh rupees. The target for the Tilak fund was kept at one crore rupees. Jamnalal Bajaj travelled across India and also to Burma to generate funds. The Marwaris of Bada Bazaar in Calcutta collected Rs. 10 lakh. In the next two decades, Seksaria would emerge as one of the largest donors to the Congress.

Before Gandhi began the *Swadeshi andolan*, an important business component of Marwaris was foreign trade. Gandhi's appeal to boycott foreign goods adversely affected their business but Marwari youth sacrificed profits in the interest of the freedom struggle. Jamnalal Bajaj pleaded with businessmen that importing foreign goods was detrimental to the country as a large amount of Indian funds were repatriated out of India. He asked them to follow simple living and use *khadi*. Impressed by the commitment of Marwaris to the freedom struggle, Gandhi remarked: 'This community is liberal in charity, honest and can serve the country.'

Many Marwari businessmen in Mumbai who opposed foreign goods were put in jail. Ladies also participated in large numbers to boycott foreign material. Jankidevi Bajaj and Indumati Goenka sat on a *dharna* in front of shops selling foreign goods. Bhagwandevi Seksaria (not a relative) went door to door to sell khadi cloth and participated in the dharna and picketing. Marwari ladies donated cash and jewellery and took a pledge not to use any foreign products. The Marwari Chamber of Commerce participated actively in the Non-Cooperation movement by boycotting foreign goods and clothes.

In 1921, Gandhi established the District Congress Office at the *gaddi* of Jamnalal Bajaj in Calcutta's Bada Bazar area to coordinate fund-raising. Gandhi and Jamnalal Bajaj visited Bombay on 30th July, 1921. They were felicitated in the office of Hindustani Merchant and Commission Agents Association. Generous donations were given to the Tilak Swaraj Fund by Marwaris present at the meeting. Seksaria promised to contribute to the fund every month. Gandhi was pleased with the liberal donations by members of the association. He remarked that Marwaris were adaptable.

Several wealthy Marwaris withdrew their deposits from British banks. Deposits given by Marwaris were of the order of Rs. 15-20 crore. The entire expenses of the Congress in Bengal and Bihar were financed by Marwaris. When Gandhi visited various parts of the country to gather support for the *andolan*, he frequently stayed at the house of Marwari businessmen.

Dr. D.K. Taknet, one of the foremost chroniclers of the Marwari ethos, sheds more light on how the community overcame adversity to emerge as India's most enterprising business class: 'The Shekhawati region of Rajasthan, also known as the Scotland of India, is the heart of Marwari entrepreneurship,' he says. 'It was one of the largest Nizamat of the old Princely state of Jaipur and was named after Rao Shekha and his ancestors. Endowed with rich historical, geographical, social and cultural traditions, Shekhawati has become a symbol of courage, sacrifice and fortitude. Besides its legendary warriors, Shekhawati has a reputation as the home of wealthy merchants and industrialists who have won laurels and scaled heights of business success at home and abroad.'

'In this region, Nawalgarh is an important town which was founded by Nawal Singh, the fifth son of Thakur Shardul Singh. During the second half of the nineteenth century, the migration of Marwaris increased by leaps and bounds from Rajputana. By 1850, prominent Marwari firms had opened their branches all over the country. These included the firms of Saujiram Hardayal, Tarachand Ghanshyamdas, Sevaram Khushalchand and Bansilal Abirchand Daga.'

Dr. Taknet's analysis of Seksaria in the context of his peers furnishes useful insights: 'Govindramji Seksaria, a progressive and visionary entrepreneur, invested in industry. After huge profits in speculation, he turned his attention to manufacturing in the late-1920s. He focused primarily on innovation, customer satisfaction and optimal utilisation of resources, both human and material, woven around the concept of the welfare of the community. Seksaria's whole philosophy of life was based on the dictum – "Keep on earning and keep on spending for good causes." A Sanskrit maxim quotes that a man's birth can only be said to be justified if he promotes the glory of his family. Govindramji perfectly exemplified it. He brought credit and honour to the family of Seksarias both nationally and internationally.'

A stockily built, erudite scholar based in Jaipur, Dr. Taknet says: 'Marwari industrial entrepreneurship is based on geo-socio-politico factors. Born and bred in an area where nature taxes the very soul and spirit of a human being, where the struggle for existence is a continuous battle, Marwaris braved heavy odds and set out to distant places to earn a livelihood. The adverse geographical conditions in the land of their origin also helped them to develop the virtues of patience, endurance, perseverance and resourcefulness. Diligent by nature, it is no surprise that their business ventures became profitable right from the beginning. However, the most commendable and intrinsic quality was their ability to utilise every opportunity and capitalise on it. Where another businessman would hesitate, wait, analyse and calculate, a Marwari would immediately assess the pros and cons and act. Perhaps this ability to judge quickly and take calculated risks could be attributed to the inherent culture and hardiness of the Marwari mind and body to deal with the trials and tribulations of being bred in a desert land.'

An important factor in the success of Marwari businessmen like Govindram Seksaria was the support system provided by fellow Marwaris. Strong communities helped them work at the grassroots with other businessmen in different regions, imparting to them fundamental community knowledge. Sharing this sense of brotherhood, they often engaged in business partnerships which helped them obtain capital. It also spread their risk. Their personal relationships usually lasted a lifetime.

'They set up *basas* to enable younger migrants to settle down in a new city and establish their business without financial pressure,' adds Dr. Taknet. 'The experienced businessmen among them shared business strategies and insights with the newcomers. Imbued with a strong community spirit, they preferred to employ relatives to ensure trust and loyalty. A deep-seated sense of religious and spiritual belief ensured their personal lives were free from excesses. Leading simple, austere lives, they preferred to keep business expenses to the minimum and spent frugally on themselves and their joint families.'

According to Dr. Taknet, Marwaris have not compromised their 'essential core values of creditworthiness, excellence of execution, a risk-taking attitude, simplified business procedures, efficiency, dynamism, creativity and innovation through learning and entrepreneurship.' To what other key qualities does he attribute their success? 'Their passion for a global vision, being socially responsible corporate citizens, transparency, flexibility, respect for stakeholders, self-confidence, a keen sense of observation, dignity of labour and a humane approach to management. All of these are augmented by quick decision-making, decentralisation of power, effective accounting systems, diversification in business, quality products, efforts to enrich society, result orientation, teamwork, winning trust internally and externally, integrity, customer focus and satisfaction. This has underpinned their success.'

In his book *Marwari Heritage,* Dr. Taknet explores the Marwari way of doing business: '*Gaddi* literally means seat or cushion, but linguistically it became an accepted colloquialism for a Marwari business firm. Since the 1850s, traders and other *banias* were conducting crores of rupees of business as agents and brokers for European managing agencies. Simultaneously perched comfortably on their *gaddis,* they dealt in wholesale and retail trade in cloth, thread, utensils and many other local and international commodities. The *gaddis* traditionally consisted of large ten-by-ten feet white cushions placed on the floor with bolsters for back support. During the day, merchants would sit on the *gaddi* cross-legged, with their wooden cashbox, large accounting books open, and a constantly ringing telephone (or more than one, depending on the traders in question). Traditionally, accounts were maintained in large, red, cloth ledgers. These, along with the *gaddi* cushions, were changed every Diwali with the blessings of Lakshmi. The *bahi* was maintained through a system known as *parta,* in which daily accounts of cash and credit were counted and recorded at the end of every business day. This method of closely monitoring cash flow was recognised as the secret of their enduring success.'

'The *seths* would sit surrounded by *munims* who were experts at money lending. The *munims* and *gumastas* at the Marwari traders' *gaddis* also specialised in book-keeping and maintaining files. They even handled purchases and sales of commodities bearing in mind falling or rising market prices. These men managed other details as well, from the loading of goods and loan recovery to making forward deals. In many of the larger firms such as Calcutta's famous Tarachand Ghanshyamdas, established in the early-eighteenth century, the *munims* were so loyal and experienced that they practically ran the firms themselves. Even the owners rarely went against their advice.

'Business transactions would often go on late into the night, in which case the *gaddi* would double as a bed for both the *munims* and *seths*. The small *gaddis* enacting business transactions worth crores of rupees became the legacies bequeathed to modern Marwari industrialists by their ancestors. It is said that many Marwaris started their careers from *gaddis*. Most young Marwaris began their commercial careers as clerks with one or the other Marwari *gaddi*. Every day, after morning prayers, clad in their traditional dress of turbans, *kamaris* and *dhotis*, they sat on their respective *gaddis*, surrounded by *munims* who were experts in trade and business.'

In the midst of political and economic turbulence, Marwari businessmen went about their business with calm resolve. Marwaris had cultivated a strongly traditional identity based on close family ties and tight-knit trading circles from Rajputana as well as long-standing local connections to princely households as moneylenders and bankers. Nevertheless, any definition of Marwari identity as merely traditional risk-takers stereotypes the community as isolated and out-of-touch with modern social reality. This stereotype is illusory because it excludes the way in which Marwaris were highly adaptive to new conditions emerging in twentieth-century India. These included the growth of industrial capitalism alongside a new international stock market trading system in increasingly abstract commodities (futures, bonds, shares) and communications technology (the telegraphic cable).

Moreover, to categorise Marwari identity as merely 'traditional' would be like ignoring the important role this community played in shaping and defining a modern nation. Paradoxically, Marwari businessmen combined traditional business practices with highly evolved financial book-keeping. This modern-traditional amalgam lies at the heart of Marwari commercial success in Seksaria's era and beyond.

After 1870, trading had taken a new turn with the development of long distance telegraph routes that connected imperial metropolitan centres to their colonial possessions. These outposts became increasingly folded into international trade. Commercial networks were located well beyond the old networks of the Marwaris of Rajputana. A significant trait of nineteenth-century Marwari pioneers was their ability to assess and even predict the potential impact of international developments on local and regional trading. In particular, they developed a sophisticated understanding of the financial impact of global crises—for example, dips in the availability and supply of raw cotton. This profoundly affected the economic fortunes of the British following the 1860s cotton boom, heralding new opportunities for Indian cotton and the imminent decline not only of English textile manufacturing, but of the British Empire itself.

Another example of this aptitude for exploiting crises in favour of Indian business interests is the Marwari response to the outbreak of the First World War in 1914 when, as Kudaisya M. Medha[49] has noted, Marwaris began refining a unique multi-layered system of investment that took advantage of economic

---

[49]Medha and Ng. Chin-Keong, eds, *Chinese and Indian Business, p 91. Also Kochanek, Business and Politics in India,* 133-137; and Rity Birla. *Stages of Capital: Law, Culture, and Market governance in Late Colonial India,* Duke University Press 2009, p 152.

opportunities in manufacturing. This was spawned by global warfare on a hitherto unimaginable scale. Alongside lay the use of speculation to fuel the growth of Indian industries that had previously been controlled exclusively by Europeans, particularly jute and coal. The war economy built many Marwari fortunes. With their enormous appetite for risk, Marwaris controlled much of India's inland trade by the end of the First World War. They turned to industry after the war.

Though, a major share of most Marwari businessmen's commercial interests lay in trading and moneylending, the fall in profit margins of these traditional activities catalysed a shift of capital towards industry. The move was impelled by the sugar boom that offered high returns on investment. It created an opportunity to invest large amounts of accumulated capital obtained through trading.

The profits accrued allowed many traders to plough funds into industries like paper, oil, textiles and cement. By the 1940s, in popular parlance, just as Govindram Seksaria was known as India's cotton king, Ramgopal Mohta was Karachi's iron king, Bansidhar Jalan was Calcutta's jute king, Baldeodas Dudhawala was the stock market king and Motiram Jhunjhunwala the silver king.

Most industrialists in pre-Independence India were self-made men. Karamshi Jethabhai Somaiya was born in 1902 in rural Maharashtra in Ahmednagar district in a village called Malunjar. Despite the difficulties of his childhood, he was an entrepreneur by nature. He came to Mumbai to make his fortune. Nandkumar Seksaria says, 'Karamshibhai was a doyen of the sugar industry. He was a contemporary of Govindramji. He used to live in our building at Marine Drive.' As with so many of his contemporaries Somaiya reportedly got his first opportunity from a Marwari family. They wanted to trade in sugar. He was soon offered a partnership and became one of the country's leading sugar traders.

Ramkrishna Dalmia was a speculator on the Calcutta Stock Exchange. He set up a sugar mill with a relative who owned land in Bihar. In 1937, he launched Dalmia Cement Co., openly challenging ACC's monopoly. Dalmia also bought Bharat Insurance, one of India's oldest insurance companies. G.D. Birla, who already had large interests in jute and cotton, added four sugar mills, one paper factory and new cotton and jute mills as well as numerous trading and real estate companies to his group's portfolio in the 1940s. More importantly, he pioneered the manufacture of textile machinery in India. Lala Padampat Singhania meanwhile enlarged his cotton mills and entered the jute, sugar and aluminium industries.

Among these illustrious contemporaries, Seksaria quietly set about building what in the 1940s would emerge as one of the largest and most profitable business groups in India.

Like Govindram Seksaria, Shiv Narayan Birla was a young man when he started trading following the death of his father. He had just turned twenty. Govindram was sixteen when his parents died. Like the teeming city of Calcutta, where Birla began his career, cosmopolitan Bombay, at the turn of the century, was an exciting business hub into which Seksaria was hurled at a tender age. He did not, though, encounter a void; instead, an émigré business community of Marwaris formed a support system. Seksaria, barely seventeen, was helped by members of his father's business network from whom he would have received modest starting capital for new ventures.

Mangtulal Seksaria emphasises: 'Juharmalji Roongta's brother's daughter married our cousin brother, so they were relatives. The Roongtas are one of the oldest Marwari families from Bagadh near Jhunjhunu. Baijnath Seksaria (Govindram uncle's son) was married to Roongta's daughter. These linkages proved very helpful to Govindramji when he arrived as a young boy in Mumbai.'

The Bombay Marwari diaspora was fast becoming enmeshed

with Gujarati speakers who had also migrated to the city. These groups had financial expertise in common, sharing backgrounds in moneylending and trading. As a new urban capitalist class, they saw a compelling future in the construction of a powerful business hub in Bombay that could serve the nation as a whole.

This diverse, lively, but also fiercely loyal business community comprising Gujaratis, Marwaris and Parsis would have had much to offer young Seksaria. He was an orphan, but also responsible for his wife and six siblings—three younger brothers and three younger sisters. Business communities in Bombay adhered to a strict code: mutual aid and support within which 'families' were literally indistinguishable from businesses. Families represented the tight units through which business practices and social solidarity could be effectively organised against competition and (British) protectionism.

Forming strong and trusted allegiances was more than a form of social support. It was the very means by which local business networks operated. In receiving social support from community elders in Bombay, Seksaria was privy to information across various areas of business and trade. Members of these diaspora communities formed strong and meaningful attachments to one another.

In Seksaria's case, they provided him with life-long allies and political role models. One such ally and inspirational teacher was the lawyer Bhulabhai Desai, a powerful Bombay Gujarati who advised Seksaria in legal actions against rivals. Desai was also an ardent nationalist. Though, only some records allude to Seksaria's business and legal dealings with the Bombay emigrant community, it is clear that young Govindram listened to the passionate debates around British rule generated by men like Desai in the years following his journey to Bombay in 1905. And yet politics was not uppermost in Govindram's mind. He was busy navigating the complex pathways of trading. Politics could wait.

Jamnalal Bajaj with his connections to Gandhi and the

Swadeshi movement would provide impetus decades later to Seksaria's interest in the freedom movement as both passive host to Congress meetings and active donor to the party. Men like Bajaj would also encourage Seksaria to develop cordial relations with the British while at the same time cultivating powerful alliances within Indian business networks through the rapidly expanding cosmopolitan chambers of commerce in Bombay. In this formative period, Seksaria learned first-hand a valuable lesson: while working with the British, be wary of them, for as one mentor said, they 'do not and cannot under present conditions share your business interests.'

The historian Aditya Mukherjee agrees, 'Beginning from 1882 to the start of the First World War, the tariff and excise policy of the colonial government gave Indian industry no protection whatsoever, whether direct or indirect.'[50] It was a policy of 'Non-Cooperation' that the British followed assiduously in India.

British protectionism would have reinforced in Seksaria the importance of cultivating informal business networks. Businessmen in Bombay, throughout the early years of Seksaria's career, increasingly voiced anti-British sentiment. They were deeply critical of British policy, in particular towards tariff restrictions on Indian industry and the wilful neglect of education.

As his business grew in size and geographical scale with factories in several parts of the country, it became increasingly important for Seksaria to maintain diplomatic relations with the British whilst supporting the freedom movement. Thomas A. Timberg suggests that, Marwaris had access to resources beyond the purview of the British: membership of powerful trade associations and networks. Moreover, Seksaria's cordial relations with British authorities, established on the basis of Britain's historic cooperation with Marwari business elites, permitted Seksaria and his associates to retain significant economic influence even as political relations between the British and Indian nationalists steadily deteriorated.

[50]Mukherjee, *Imperialism,* p 173.

Marwari dominance of commodities such as cotton as well as their powerful presence in the stock and bullion markets was not ostensibly threatening to colonial rule. The reason was simple: business was conducted, on the one hand, beyond the remit of colonial authorities and, on the other, within an established framework of harmonious Marwari relations with the British based on pragmatism. As in Calcutta, European agency houses assumed responsibility for industry and foreign trade. Marwari traders took responsibility, begrudgingly tolerated by the British, for internal trade.[51]

Seksaria's growing wealth enabled him to invest in a broad swathe of enterprises, including the Bank of Rajasthan, of which he was the founder and chairman. *The Economic Times*[52] reported the fascinating history of the bank and the region that gave it its name:

> 'Bank of Rajasthan will lose its identity after its merger with ICICI Bank, but its association with Rajasthan specifically, with the name of the state will remain forever. The bank was instrumental in the state being renamed Rajasthan, in January 1949, according to the archives of City Palace, Udaipur. In 1943, six years before the state was renamed, Bank of Rajasthan was set up with Udaipur as its registered office. It was the brainchild of late Rai Bahadur PC Chatterjee, the then finance minister of what used to be Mewar. Mr. Chatterjee roped in two mining businessmen from Bhilwara—Seth Pusa Lalji Mansinghka and Seth Damodar Lalji Mansinghka to set up a bank with an initial capital of Rs. 10 lakh. It was formed as a public company, with shares owned by investors, including Founder and Chairman Seth Govindram Seksaria, an eminent industrialist of his time.
>
> 'In line with common practice, the stakeholders suggested two names: Bank of Mewar and State Bank of Udaipur. But the promoters, especially Mr. Chatterjee, had other thoughts.

[51]Kochanak, *Business and Politics in India,* p 133.

[52]14th August, 2010.

Mr. Chatterjee felt that Rajputana—a union of nine princely states, of which Mewar was a part was the preserve of royalty, and the bank's name should reflect that exalted status. 'He proposed Rajasthan, or the "place of royals", the name symbolising the line of rajas and maharajas who had ruled there. The other promoters accepted it. And evidently, they did so with a clairvoyant eye on what that name could mean in the years to come, with India poised for independence and some form of regional consolidation. According to the Bank of Rajasthan website, the promoters felt the word "Rajasthan" will be more advantageous in the future to expand activities to other princely states as under the new Constitution, grouping of the local princely states was expected under one umbrella. "The cards fell the way they expected. India became independent in 1947. The painful process of consolidation began, with Home Minister Sardar Vallabhbhai Patel meeting rulers of princely states for their integration into India. Rajasthan was formed after a long process of integration, which began in March 1948 and ended in November 1956. When the integration started, the state was called Rajputana. It was renamed Rajasthan after a meeting on 14th January, 1949, between Sardar Patel and the Princely states of Rajputana. The meeting was convened by the then ruler of Udaipur, the late Maharana Bhupal Singh, who was also the Rajpramukh of Rajputana. At the meeting, the Maharana suggested renaming Rajputana as Rajasthan. He cited the example of Bank of Rajasthan and its wider identity. Sardar Patel accepted his suggestion. Rajputana was renamed Rajasthan and Bank of Rajasthan got its place in history."

As a founder of the Bank of Rajasthan and its chairman, Seksaria played a pivotal but, as ever, an unobtrusive role in nurturing the region's premier financial institution. It was a characteristic that would define him throughout his life.

Chapter Nine

Going For Gold

Through the 1930s and 1940s the political environment in India was increasingly charged. This had a knock-on effect on business. According to Gordon, Bombay was particularly affected with a high level of unemployment. The global economic crisis coincided with the civil disobedience movement, heightening its effects. As ever, the big industrialists refused to cooperate in the movement. The labour force, Gordon[53] argues, had been affected the most due to constant economic changes and the failure of local governments to address their concerns. As a result, they became volatile, introducing an element of violence in the Non-Cooperation movement. Moreover, major Indian industrialists felt increasingly that nationalist boycott movements were discouraging foreign capital and affecting their businesses.

They began to blame the movement for all the economic problems which were crippling Bombay, India's commercial centre. The views of traders and the Congress differed widely

[53]A.D. Gordon, p 202.

from the industrialists. They held the British colonial government's fiscal policy responsible for the escalating crisis.

The two opposing views were used as counter-propaganda tools by the two groups. Their interpretations of the economic crisis differed widely. The industrialists believed the end of the nationalist movement to be in their interest and assumed the role of intermediaries between the Congress and the British government. The industrialists and their quasi-official representatives (managing agents) were also divided in their attitudes. By 1930, industrialists who supported the nationalist movement were a minority. Subsequently, even they turned away from the movement.

Labour problems arose due to other reasons as well. By the early-1930s, for example, the Indore Malwa United Mills Ltd., then managed by the Currimbhoy group, was beset by agitations. Closure due to labour lockouts was only part of this crisis. Poor liquidity as a result of indifferent management was another. The unit was one of the largest textile mills in central India. It would emerge as the fulcrum of Seksaria's burgeoning industrial empire.

Seksaria meanwhile had kept a keen eye on developments in America. His trading operations in cotton had outgrown India. He sought a larger market. New York provided it. An example of Seksaria's finely honed business acumen and thirst for market knowledge lies in the various written communications he exchanged over his long-standing interest in gold and silver.

In 1933, the United States had adopted a new policy of dual silver prices. There were to be two silver prices; the government price of 64½ cents a fine ounce for all the silver produced domestically and the market price for any foreign silver.[54] The new policy intrigued Seksaria. He wrote a letter of inquiry about it in 1934. A reply to his letter was provided and documented as

---

[54] *The Wall Street Journal,* 23rd December, 1933.

the Hans A. Widenmann papers which came from the collections of the Seeley G. Mudd Manuscript Library, Princeton University in Princeton, New Jersey.

The Widenmann Papers (also known as the Mudd Report), published in 1934, a crucial and profitable year for Seksaria, show the level of detailed analysis that characterised Seksaria's trading strategy. He made a careful selection across a wide range of staple commodities for speculation and trading. The Mudd Report identified the value of US government purchases of gold and silver. It highlighted the openness of the market as early as 1934. It also took a broad view from a transnational perspective, accounting for 'payment from foreign governments' as well as assessing the amount of domestically mined silver over 1933-1934 when the Gold Reserve Act was passed in the US. This gave the Federal Reserve the title to all collected gold. It allowed them to change the price of gold from $20.67 per ounce to $35 per ounce.

This was just the sort of 'fixing' that would immediately capture the interest and watchful eye of Seksaria who was always looking to further diversify his portfolio. The element of risk involved in speculation in bullion was a permanent feature of the twentieth century—an era dramatically encapsulated by Britain's and America's abandonment of the gold standard in 1931 and 1933, respectively. But Seksaria was a Marwari. His community's ancestors had worked the bullion markets for centuries before the Great Depression, the two world wars and the fatal wounding of European imperial hegemony. He made and lost money in bullion trade but never abandoned his taste for it.

In 1933, when Seksaria was investing and trading in bullion, Bombay had attracted the attention of American media. *The Wall Street Journal* on 14th December, 1933 wrote: 'Support entered the local silver market Wednesday in the form of purchasing orders received from India. They were described as comparatively small but unusual interest attached to the transactions inasmuch as the New York price was above both the London and Bombay prices, making it apparent that the purchases did not represent arbitrage on New York. The incident, it was said, possibly reflected some Indian operations in sterling, but local silver circles could shed no light on the reason. Orders were received for both spot metal and future delivery.'

'It was not disclosed whether the Indian purchasers intended to hold the silver in local vaults or actually to withdraw the metal for shipment abroad. There have been no shipments of silver from New York to India this year, the last reported being 201,000 ounces in October 1932. Total shipments in 1932 amounted only to 652,000 fine ounces, compared with 20,609,000 in 1931 and 24,554,000 in 1930. At the same time that India was buying in New York, Shanghai was buying in London, but there was no evidence of Chinese activities in this market. London was said to show little interest in local trading.

'Unusual interest attaches to any purchases of silver in New York by the Orient because in the past China and India have taken the bulk of the world's supply of new silver each year. Of late, however, speculative enthusiasm for silver in the United States has kept the New York price at a premium above world prices. At times, the premium has been sufficiently large to permit foreign countries to sell silver to New York on an arbitrage basis. This was especially marked last spring when receipts of metal from London and the Orient for this purpose were large.'

By 1934, when Seksaria had begun to transform his relatively modest fortune into one of India's largest industrial enterprises, the Indian maverick in 'modern dress', as American newspapers dubbed him, had gained plenty of experience trading in cotton, silver and gold. In an article in *The New York Times,* on 17th November, 1935, Edward J. Condlon remarked testily about India's appetite for gold: 'Since the advent of the present flow of gold to the United States on September 9, few weeks have passed without shipments from India, a fact which brings up the old question: Where does it all come from? (India has exported gold worth more than a billion dollars since 1931.) The bullion dealers of the Indian bazaars have organised a system of scouts who scour the country for gold much after the fashion of our dealers in antiques; the gathering consists of old coins, bars and great quantities of jewelry. The supply of gold in India defies estimate; a fact which should be taken into consideration by those economists who argue that there is insufficient gold above ground to meet world requirements for currency backing.'

When Seksaria began trading heavily in bullion in the late 1920s, the price of gold was Rs. 18.75 for 10 gms (1925). In 1946, when he passed away, the price was Rs. 83.87—an increase of nearly 400 per cent in 20 years. That, of course, pales in comparison with the increase 70 years later to around Rs. 30,000 in 2016—a more than 300-fold rise. The bullion and share markets had their own arcane terminologies, many based in traditional Indian trading parlance. In a series of articles in 1935, critics pointed out how the practice of '*anka*' and '*fadak*' in cotton futures speculation was driving away genuine investors from the market.

In a report published in *The Times of India* on 21st January, 1935, the paper's commercial correspondent highlighted in particular the stratospheric rise in Tata Steel's deferred shares: 'The speculative fever which has seized the Bombay Stock Exchange is reminiscent of a war-time speculative boom. The bullish feeling prevalent is indicative of the return of confidence and better times ahead and is welcome on that account but investors are unloading their shares which are carried over by speculators on payment of a very high rates of interest. There is a plethora of cheap money available in Bombay which has given a fillip to speculation. It is possible to get any amount of money at five per cent per annum, but on the Stock Exchange the interest realised is 10 to 12 per cent per annum. As there is a very large appreciation in the values of certain scrips every week and even every day, speculators do not mind paying a heavy rate of interest. The result is that the rapid and almost daily rise in speculative counters is frightening away genuine investors.'

'It is true that the Tata Iron and Steel Company is doing exceedingly well and that the gross profit will come to nearly two crores and eighty lakhs of rupees. There is, therefore, justification for a fair rise in the value of the shares. But when a deferred share of Rs. 30 is pushed up to Rs. 600, cautious men may well begin to shake their heads. Opinions vary. On the one hand, it is calculated that in 1937 the company will declare a dividend of Rs. 78 to Rs. 80 on the deferred shares, while on the other it is maintained that there will be no dividend on deferred shares till 1939 or 1940.' One authority in *The Times of India Illustrated Weekly* states: 'Even assuming that profits from now onwards can be maintained at last year's level it will be 1938 before the ordinary shares can look forward to a return.' It is too big an assumption that profits will be maintained on the present scale, especially in view of the Damocles sword hanging over the head of the company in the shape of increased excise duty if and when the profits exceed two crores of rupees. There may be unforeseen contingencies.

Puranmal recalls one of Seksaria's lucrative stock market trades in Tata Deferred shares: 'At one juncture, around 1943, Sethji had short sold a very large quantity of Tata Deferred shares and had to pay *"oondha badla"* (backwardation charges) on about six occasions. When the price of Tata Deferred became Rs. 1,600, he decided to reverse his entire position and became a buyer and continuously kept buying. He did this on the strength of the large sums of money lying in First National City Bank of New York. These funds were from the profits generated by his trading activities in America. Govindramji then demanded high *badla* charges from the short sellers. And from those who were willing to give delivery of Tata Deferred shares he was willing to accept it. Govindramji was a shrewd man. The moment the market sensed that Sethji was in a position to accept delivery from money that has come from America and was purportedly lying in First National City Bank, the whole market mood changed! Sethji earned high *badla* charges on several occasions. Eventually, Sethji sold the shares at around Rs. 2,200-2,400 and earned a huge profit just by showing that he had the power to buy! This whole arrangement was done by letters exchanged between him and the bank's branches at Bombay and New York, that's it.'

The British Raj meanwhile intensified its imperialistic economic policies through the 1930s. While these policies helped protect Britain's economy, they threatened to damage India's. International trade dropped. Imports fell by over 47 per cent and exports by 49 per cent. Between 1928–29 and 1933–34, Indian exports due to seaborne trade decreased by 55.75 per cent to Rs. 125 crore while imports decreased by 55.51 per cent to Rs. 202 crore.

Farmers who had been forced to move to cash crops to meet the demand of the Liverpool mills were the most severely affected. With prices soaring they were unable to sell either domestically or export to Britain due to the latter's protective policy prohibiting imports from India. Rebellions and riots broke out. Between 1930 and 1932, the decline in exports and imports led to a decrease of Rs. 15 crore in railway revenues. Expenses in these years had to be paid from the Railway Reserve Fund.

Like Dhirubhai Ambani would 50 years later, Govindram Seksaria continued amidst the turbulence to play the stock and commodities markets with a firm hand.

During British rule, gold and silver were imported into India – particularly Bombay, a major hub of the bullion trade – through ships. At the beginning of the 1920s, the time was ripe to set up formal bullion trade associations since the bullion forwards market in Bombay was one of the largest in the world. On 24th January, 1923, the Bombay Bullion Exchange was registered. Seksaria was a member. This later led to the formation of the Bombay Bullion Association Ltd. (BBA) in 1948, the apex body for bullion trade in India. Even today, it is the BBA that gives the opening and closing rates for bullion across India, rates which are followed by the Reserve Bank of India (RBI) as well.

H.T. Parekh in *The Bombay Money Market* expounded on this: 'Bombay's bullion market forms a sector of the money market in its wider sense. Its importance is derived from its being the largest organised bullion market in India and probably the largest free market in the world. In India, tradition confers so high a social value on gold and silver that the existence of an organised free market has come to be regarded as indispensable to normal life. Because of its position as a principal centre as a port and, in recent years, as the seat of the Reserve Bank of India, Bombay has been the main bullion market on which the numerous small markets all over the country are dependent. The war and post-war years have shown the capacity of the Bombay market in handling an enormous volume of business in gold and silver.'

'Gold in India is valued for its non-monetary uses, and this accounts for the existence of a large free market. Like any other commodity it is an article of free trade. The internal market is so large that it functions actively irrespective of any restrictions on exports and imports which may be imposed. The gold market in India is in some ways distinct because of the special characteristics of the demand for and supply of gold in this country. Since September 1939, imports and exports of gold have been prohibited except on licence from the Reserve Bank of India. For a short period during 1946 its import was freely allowed but the ban was re-imposed. This has isolated the Indian market from the rest of the world. But within the country the existence of large private stocks and the universal popularity of gold for ornaments, jewellery and as a traditional form of investment makes for an active and continuous market.'

Parekh emphasises that the bullion market in gold and silver functions under the auspices of the Bombay Bullion Association, formed as a limited liability company. 'Business is transacted either for ready delivery or for forward delivery with monthly settlements,' he writes. 'Transactions for three monthly settlements are allowed simultaneously. Although, at present, dealings are permitted in two following monthly settlements. The business for ready delivery takes place over the counter against payment usually received in cash. The rules of the Association made for forward transactions may now be examined in detail. The monthly settlements are according to the Hindu calendar months from *Kartik* to *Asod* and end on every Punam. Forward transactions in gold bars and sovereign are deemed to have been effected for each month and at the end of each month deliveries are completed. Where deliveries have not been effected transactions are carried over to the new settlement by *badla*. *Badla* or carry-over takes place by squaring one's position in the current settlement and simultaneously opening a new position in the next settlement so that an outstanding purchase or sale is carried over to the next month as a purchase or sale. Usually the quotation for the new settlement is slightly higher than that for the settlement which is ending, the difference between the two reflecting the charges incurred by way of interest, storage, insurance, etc., for holding gold for one month.'

Bullion formed an important part of Seksaria's trading portfolio. And he was not averse to using mild subterfuge to profit from the fluctuating price of gold as an incident in 1931 illustrates. Mangtulal Seksaria recalls having heard this account: 'Govindramji went to meet the governor[55] in Bombay to find out whether the sterling pound was going off the gold standard. Apparently the Governor was busy and Govindramji met his wife. The wife asked him, "I am told, Mr. Seksaria, that you are a very big speculator. If the gold standard goes off, what do you think will happen to gold?" On hearing this, Govindramji feigned a stomach ache and told his aide: "Let's go, we don't need to meet the Governor, we have got the information we wanted." He went back and bought a lot of gold, and the gold standard did go off. And then he made such good money that

[55]Mumbai didn't have a governor-general and the governor-general of India was not based in the city. At the time, Bombay had governors. In 1931, the year Britain went off the gold standard, the governor was John Ernest Buttery Hotson, who remained on the post for that year alone.

he became a crorepati for the first time. This was in 1931 when a crore was a lot of money.'

Seksaria bought the gold at the rate of Rs. 20/25. Once Britain announced it was abandoning the gold standard, he sold it at an inflated price of Rs. 40.

Although, Seksaria made his mark in cotton speculation, associates concede his first big break came through gold when Britain abandoned the gold standard in 1931. 'From there on it was a continuous climb up with normal trading setbacks in between,' says a veteran trader. After initial successes in bullion, Seksaria continued to trade in bullion but never struck it big again. Market players recall that there were times when he lost heavily in bullion trading. However, as an investment he continued to hold large quantities of gold and silver as a strategic reserve. It proved a ready resource for him to tide over temporary difficulties.

Suresh Kotak emphasises the point that 'Britain going off the gold standard was a monetary revolution. It was epoch-making and Govindramji understood that. Which is how, when the value of gold started going up, he made a lot of money. But he was very clear in his understanding. People may call him a speculator, but I would say he was an investor. He invested in gold, so why call him only a speculator? He understood the value gold would have in the future.'

Chapter Ten

A Nation In Ferment

Claude Markovits observed that despite the economic impact of the Depression in India, industrial expansion continued through the 1930s. The negative fallout was felt mostly by traders and not industrialists. Due to the fall in food prices, the real income of urban dwellers began to increase. This led to a shift in demand from necessities to luxuries. Industries expanded to meet this demand. Moreover, the reduction of cotton and steel imports benefitted these two industries in India but had negative consequences for Britain.

Several mills meanwhile closed down in the early 1930s as the Depression began to bite. Problems were also experienced in the bullion trade which suffered constantly from closures due to nationalist boycotts. The price of silver had fallen to its lowest during 1930, coinciding with its purchase by the government. The export of 'distress gold' worsened matters as those affected by riots sold their gold in desperation to fund liquidity. The Congress viewed this with growing alarm. It advocated an embargo against gold exports. The lack of firm guidelines and the nationalist boycott movement led to an atmosphere of uncertainty. This affected small manufacturers the most. All these events together contributed to the industrialists renewing their call to seek an end to the civil disobedience movement.[56]

Markovits raises an interesting point when he writes that the 1930s in fact benefitted certain communities who saw opportunities in unsettled internal and external conditions during turbulent times. A fall in profits from traditional activities led to a shift in focus to industries. Profits which were earned during the sugar boom were reinvested in other industries such as paper and cement. Government tariffs on sugar aided this development.

Markovits notes: 'Marwari enterprise was burgeoning and sought to exploit opportunities in other fields. The strength of kinship and caste ties among Marwaris provided them with a pool of resources upon which no other community was able to draw. Marwari credit networks thus compensated for the lack of a well-developed modern banking system but, as credit was extended strictly within the community, the Marwaris started to establish a real domination in some fields.'[57]

According to Gordon, the period after the Depression was one of industrial consolidation and diversification despite the casualties suffered by several industrialists. Seksaria's business expansion in the 1930s underscores Markovits's analysis. The decade witnessed a sharp rise in Seksaria's industrial activity as he diversified rapidly across sectors: textiles, sugar, vegetable oils, mining and banking.

The turmoil caused by the freedom struggle sparked a financial crisis in India. It affected three major sources of internal revenue. Customs duties were hit by the fall in imports. Income-tax fell due to the overall drop in income. And railway revenue plunged owing to a slowdown in the movement of goods. As a result

[56]Gordon, pp 205-217.

[57]Markovits, pp 62-66.

of the Gandhi-Irwin Pact signed by Mahatma Gandhi and the viceroy of India on 5th March, 1931, Gandhi finally agreed to end the campaign of Civil Disobedience in exchange for Irwin accepting the participation of the Indian National Congress in Round table talks in London on British colonial policy in India.

In January that year, Gandhi and other members of the Congress Working Committee (CWC) had been released from prison as the Viceroy was keen to hold talks with Gandhi. Many conservatives in England and India viewed these talks with loathing. Winston Churchill famously expressed his disgust '. . . at the nauseating and humiliating spectacle of this one-time Inner Temple lawyer, now seditious fakir, striding half-naked up the steps of the viceroy's palace, there to negotiate and parley on equal terms with the representative of the King Emperor.'

The Gandhi-Irwin Pact was approved by the Congress at its annual session in Karachi in March 1931. The execution of Bhagat Singh, Rajguru and Sukhdev (in connection with the Lahore conspiracy case) cast a shadow over the proceedings but Sardar Vallabhbhai Patel, the president of the session, authorised Gandhi to attend the Round Table Conference in London.

Unfortunately, Lord Irwin was succeeded by the Marquess of Willingdon who ignored many of the primary provisions of the Gandhi-Irwin Pact. When Gandhi returned from the Round Table Conference he was dismayed to see repression in full swing. Harsh ordinances were still part of the vocabulary of the colonial government. Lord Willingdon was said to have been afraid of the influence wielded by Jawaharlal Nehru and Khan Abdul Ghaffar Khan. Nehru had no faith in anything except complete independence and Khan had raised a force of Pathan volunteers on the frontier, the Khudai Khidmatgars, a body that later became a part of the Congress.

Lord Willingdon was merciless in his efforts to quell the unrest in the country. Thousands of freedom fighters languished in jail. By 1934, the Civil Disobedience movement had officially ended. The movement, despite its limited success, served an important purpose. It showed both India and Britain that all sections of India could come together against oppression. The mass movement lent the Congress new status and prestige. Seksaria too was entering the most productive phase of his career. He was beginning to take an interest in politics. Over the next few years he would emerge as one of the Congress party's most important donors.

Despite the blood the new decade was soaked in, there were bursts of creativity through the 1940s. A proliferation of innovative technologies revolutionised intercontinental aviation, radio and film. It was to prove a defining period for Seksaria. He had emerged as one of India's leading businessmen with a vast portfolio of industrial assets as well as philanthropic and educational institutions.

Around him global innovation exploded. Despite the economic slowdown, some of the world's most arresting developments coincided with Seksaria's decade of rapid growth. The Empire State building was completed and the monument of Christ erected in Rio, the atom was split and the helicopter invented, the cheeseburger was created and Superman appeared in comic books and iconic movies, *Gone with the Wind* and the *Wizard of Oz* were released, Penguin's first paperback hit book shelves and the Volkswagen Beetle was produced.

Seksaria's empire had expanded significantly since the mid-1930s. His industrial interests now comprised vegetable oil mills, cotton ginning factories, cotton seed oil extraction plants, textile mills, sugar mills, printing presses, mining, banking, motion pictures and real estate. He exerted influence over the activities of foreign cotton exchanges (in New York and Liverpool), as well as over British and American copper, sugar and wheat markets. 'His industrial undertakings dotted over half of the country and his commercial network was spread over three continents,' one report in *The Free Press Journal*[58] said after his death in 1946.

[58] 14th June, 1946.

Seksaria's empire seemed to indicate a palpable turning of the tide whereby it was Bombay calling the shots rather than London, Liverpool or New York. *The Free Press Journal* added, 'The great business houses of America learnt to watch Seksaria's moves as a guide to their own operations.'

Seksaria's daily business operations took him from Bombay's Khattar Galli to Zaveri Bazaar where the Cotton Exchange was situated. A Chrysler conveyed him from one to another. He 'commanded the *satta*', as his contemporaries described it, from Khattar Galli (today's Thakurdwar Road) as well as Kalbadevi (also known as Marwari Bazaar), having moved there from Chandanwadi.

Seksaria's rented office in Kalbadevi was on the second floor of a building next to the cotton exchange situated at 18/22 Marwari Bazaar, Sheikh Menon Street. The building belonged to Seth Ramnath Daga of the firm Rai Bahadur Bansilal Abirchand. The Roongtas had a *Pedi* on the ground floor of the building and Govindram invariably used to go and sit there.

As business continued to boom, Seksaria bought Seksaria Chambers in 1937 in Bombay's central business district, moving the offices of Govindram Brothers there. The fourth and fifth floors housed the group's offices while Indore Malwa Mills operated from the second floor. Ramchandra T. Shetty, now aged 94, who completed 75 years of service in Govindram Brothers in 2016, reminisces: 'Seksaria Chambers was a five-story building. Govindram Seth used to come to Seksaria Chambers daily. I remember that he used to come to the fourth floor hall and sit on a chair which was near the desk I used to sit at. He would make a few phone calls and leave thereafter.'

Seksaria had meanwhile also become a member of the Liverpool Cotton Exchange, a prestigious membership at the time. The Liverpool exchange was established by cotton merchants in protest against the fact that those who dealt in futures could only operate through a broker. This meant they were effectively being charged for brokerage twice. Though the end of the First World War had led to a post-war boom, it was short-lived. The Liverpool Cotton Association had been able to continue to operate, albeit with a struggle, during the First World War. Unfortunately, it was dealt a death blow by the Second World War. German U-boats destroyed merchant ships in the Atlantic as well as near major ports and cities in the UK. Cotton supplies became increasingly vulnerable.

The British government took responsibility for the purchase and distribution of all cotton supplies. It revived the cotton control which had operated in the previous war. At noon on 31st March, 1941 the last prices were made in the ring at the Liverpool Cotton Exchange. The cotton world presumed that the market would re-open after the war. It was, however, the end of an era.

In 1937, Seksaria along with a peer group of businessmen had proposed the formation of the Indian Stock Exchange. According to a report published in *The Times of India* on 30th October, 1937, 'The promoters of the new stock exchange, named the Indian Stock Exchange Ltd., have received about 200 applications for membership. The company is limited by guarantee, each member having undertaken to pay Rs. 100 towards the losses, if any, to the company. Besides the guarantee, the member is also required to pay Rs. 10,000 as entrance fee. The rules and regulations governing the business of the exchange, it is understood, are based on most of the recommendations of the Morrison Committee. The exchange proposes to have the system of fortnightly clearing, though the settlement will be once a month. Business will be transacted in a spacious building where arrangements will be made for a visitors' gallery to enable investors personally to watch the execution of their transactions. The organisers of the exchange will shortly apply to the Bombay government for recognition under the Bombay Securities Contracts Control Act. It is likely that the new exchange will provide a platform for transacting business in scrips of companies in Bombay as well as those in other provinces.'

The report confirmed that Govindram Seksaria would be on the ISE's board of directors and that the exchange also has 'on its directorate Mr. Chunilal B. Mehta, Mr. Hoosenbhoy A. Lalljee, Mr. B.N. Karanjia, Mr. Ramdeo Anandilal Podar, Mr. Mulraj Karsandas, Mr. Hemraj Anandilal, Mr. Juthalal Motilal, Mr. Maneklal Chunilal Shah, Mr. Ramanlal Dahyabhai Choksi, Mr. Piramal Chaturbhuj, Mr. Premchand Chaturbhuj Bhayani, and Mr. Bishwambharlal Maheshwari.'

In February 1938, the Indian Stock Exchange commenced business. Its office was located in Laxmi Building in South Bombay's Fort business district. The Indian Stock Exchange had appealed to the British colonial government for recognition under the Bombay Securities Contracts Control Act but had not been provided this even after a year. The recognition was necessary in order to conduct forward trading. This was perhaps one of the reasons the Stock Exchange closed down after a few years.

Trading on modern stock markets are credited to practices Marwari traders developed in the late-nineteenth and early-twentieth centuries. Just as L.C. Gupta's analysis of the *badla* system highlights its efficacy as a borrowing and lending mechanism, these traditional trading techniques demonstrate why Seksaria had an intuitive sensibility for futures trading. In an article in *The Hindu,* Harish Damodaran explains the 'Marwari business model':

> 'In 1905, six Marwaris introduced *fatka* or futures trading in raw jute that registered meteoric growth at the *baras* (informal exchanges) of Kolkata's *Burra Bazaar* market. These contracts, rarely resulting in delivery of the underlying goods, since most purchases and sales got cancelled against each other before maturity date weren't taken kindly to by entrenched European interests. Used only to spot buying, they saw their supply-and-demand calculations and produce

> flows disrupted by the rampant speculation engendered by such trades, which extended to cotton, opium and grain as well. No wonder, one of their (European) representatives claimed *fatka* to have been invented by Marwaris deprived of the pleasures of rain gambling, and only able to satisfy their craving for the gains of chance in a system of contracts purporting to evidence the purchase and sale of jute, but where in no single instance has jute ever been delivered! That view, in a sense, echoes those of many who even *today* harbour a suspicious attitude toward futures transactions, which they contrast to legitimate business.'[59]

Damodaran suggests that the extensive business networks Marwaris used profitably in moneylending and trading across different parts of India meant that they were able to draw on a wealth of sources for information to use in their business calculations. Like many Marwari businessmen of his day, Seksaria deployed his network to further his industrial and trading activities within India.

Despite the fact that he never travelled outside India and did not speak English, Seksaria was able to apply an inborn talent to succeed at speculating on foreign cotton exchanges as well as the Bombay Exchange. In this sense, Seksaria represented a continuity with the business practices of Marwari traders and merchants from the mid-nineteenth century. However, Seksaria also departed from this history by employing these techniques in the complex international market in cotton futures.

Damodaran's account is also interesting in the way it explains why Europeans resented even these early forms of futures trading undertaken by Indian businessmen. British firms recognised the financial benefits of working with Indian traders because of the latter's extensive hinterland networks. Marwaris became intermediaries in the distribution of raw jute and raw cotton. They also played an important role in financing such

---

[59]*The Hindu,* 8th April, 2013.

operations. However, the language Damodaran quotes in his analysis reveals a level of frustration among the British at what seemed like an illegitimate advantage Marwaris enjoyed because of their gift for futures speculation.

Futures trading was characterised as an inferior way of doing business. In fact, the argument was not unlike the one put forward against Seksaria in the American press. Europeans placed futures trading in the realm of gambling—a pejorative categorisation from which speculators regularly differentiate themselves. Gambling was decadent, anti-social and did not involve intellectual analysis.[60] American commentators in 1938 had described Indian practices like short-selling as something Americans had left behind. They used language that suggested an immorality to the practice.

Seksaria absorbed the criticism with characteristic calm and ignored the epithets directed at him by both the US media and several members of the NYCE. He continued, relentlessly, to trade and profit in New York, in Liverpool and in Bombay.

---

[60]Dickson G. Watts, *Speculation as a Fine Art and Thoughts on Life,* reprinted in 1965 and Madan Gaur, *King of Cotton: Camaraderie with Cohorts,* 1994.

Chapter Eleven

Towards A New World Order

As far as speculators in New York were concerned, Seksaria's 'cold' and 'manipulative' dealings[61] were clinically planned. They seemed to be paying off handsomely and American speculators didn't like that. Who was this enigmatic figure from Bombay whose invisible presence was enough to create mild panic amongst the most experienced of New York's market speculators? From where did he get his confidence, resources and financial acumen? Why was he such a threat to financial traders in the world's most powerful countries of the time?

In 1938, the world was on the brink of yet another war. America, and much of the rest of the world, was still reeling from the long-term effects of the financial crash of 1929. This had resulted not only in a sharp economic decline across America's domestic industrial sectors but also led to a loss of faith in the national banking sector. Storied banks experienced wave after wave of panic and disruption.

[61]Louis M. Schneider, *Oakland Tribune,* 8th May, 1938.

In stark contrast to the 1920s, when financial speculation gained its reputation for risk-taking and gambling, America in the 1930s witnessed the emergence of a new public-spirited political culture. This was overlaid by fears over continuing high unemployment and social deprivation as well as an outpouring of contempt for banks, seen as avaricious, callous and a national liability. Hindering industrial and economic progress and contributing to the impoverishment of the general population, the financial sector of the United States was subjected to intense state scrutiny. President Franklin Roosevelt was driven to warn businessmen and bankers before Congress in 1935:

> 'Let him, who, for speculative profit or partisan purpose, without just warrant would seek to disturb or dispel this assurance, take heed before he assumes responsibility for any act which slows our onward steps.'

Business and capital were under assault from the government. American trade unions agitated in support of workers' rights and a new, fairer social contract. This helped deepen a cultural perception that capital was not only at war with the state but with the whole of organised labour. Labour and capital were presented as politically and ideologically irreconcilable. In a sense, both sides could see themselves as potentially weak, vulnerable, and the victims of cultural and media bias. The idea that capital and labour could form alliances with each other and build the country to mutual advantage was anathema to the political orthodoxy of the day. This was true not only in the United States but also in older industrialised economies such as Britain where factory workers had become used to fighting bitterly for political rights and improved working conditions.

In addition to this political climate of hostility between labour and business, there were strong winds of geopolitical change blowing across the world. This was not confined to impending war in Europe in 1939 and the growing threat from Germany's imperial aspirations within continental Europe. There was a general sense among traditional centres of global power (Britain,

America and Western Europe) that the established world order was at an inflection point. Organised along a colonial and Western axis, this global order was being radically undermined. President Roosevelt put it succinctly in his annual message to Congress (his second State of the Union address) on 4th January, 1935:

> 'Throughout the world, change is the order of the day. In every nation economic problems, long in the making, have brought crises of many kinds for which the masters of old practice and theory were unprepared. In most nations social justice, no longer a distant ideal, has become a definite goal, and ancient governments are beginning to heed the call. Thus, the American people do not stand alone in the world in their desire for change.'

The economic chaos in both America and Britain in the 1930s played a key role in defining how an 'outsider' like Govindram Seksaria was received in those countries. What the west saw in Seksaria was someone who seemed to flourish in contrarian market conditions. Whereas, Western capitalists were under attack from socialist labour movements in industry and state regulations in the financial sector, here was an Indian businessman - Seksaria - who appeared unperturbed by organised workers and peasant movements in his own country. Indeed, such agitations formed a strong backbone of a broader national independence movement to make India an economically viable and self-sufficient sovereign entity.

This was a goal the capitalist but intensely nationalist Seksaria fully supported. He didn't even seem to be distracted by the volatile global economic environment of the 1930s. Roosevelt referred to the debilitating financial straits the west found itself in as '*crises*'. World events dominating the news in the 1930s were unwelcome in the Euro-American capitalist philosophy: the abandonment of the gold standard, the economic slowdown, and the rise of anti-colonial independence movements worldwide. All of these subverted the principle of order versus chaos. They disrupted the rules of colonialism that had been sacrosanct for two centuries. And they threatened to transform the world's economic pecking order.

Such thoughts did not worry Seksaria. He saw in the first four decades of a turbulent twentieth century, wracked by world wars and economic Armageddon, an unpredictability of markets. This contained rare opportunities for the generation of extraordinary wealth for those with the skill and gumption to take calculated risks. To American and European businessmen, the financial and geopolitical churn represented a threat to the established way of doing things. The old order had served bankers, industrialists and speculators in Europe and America well for centuries. It derived its strength from the notion that the industrial and commercial nerve-centres of Europe and America would remain the economic pivots of the future.

The west took comfort from the idea that the rules of manufacturing and trading were fixed. They suited the strongest players. Since the rules of trade always operated in the interests of wealthier nations, it was imperative that those rules did not change. For Seksaria, however, fixed expectations surrounding markets were barriers to real economic opportunity. Rather, it was Roosevelt's notion of *crises,* war and systemic change that were critical and necessary conditions for significant economic leverage. War enabled both a loosening of the rules and a seizing of financial and trading advantage.

According to Benedict Anderson, author of *Imagined Communities,* capital raised by merchants and bankers was to be the 'instrument of Indian nationalism. It could be used to sponsor a version of home-grown industrialisation in India compatible with modern technology and focused on cotton above all other industries.' Anderson added, 'India of course had dominated world cotton production prior to the Industrial Revolution in England and the rise of British imperial hegemony.'

The financial global transformation, of which Seksaria and

his business contemporaries with Gandhi, Nehru, Patel and Bose as inspirations were an integral part, helped them leverage crises to advance the cause of both Indian political freedom and their own businesses. 'Thematically, the Independence movement as an all-encompassing struggle against Empire focused primarily on the plight of the poorest, most vulnerable people in Indian society,' writes Anderson. 'These encompassed the rural poor and those at the bottom of a punishing and rigid caste system, as well as women, minorities, and tribal or ethnic groups who were able to take advantage of the political mobilisation sweeping India to demand civil and political rights as part of a wholly new "imagined community"'.[62]

The beginning of the Second World War ironically caused Seksaria a financial setback. Before the war broke out, Seksaria was short on various commodities. With prices spiralling following the outbreak of war, he incurred significant losses. Interestingly, archival records speak of his firm Messrs Govindram Seksaria borrowing 25,000 tolas of gold from Gordhandas Govindram HUF. Presumably, part of these losses were made good by pledging the gold with banks and the balance must have been made up from other sources. The firm shortly returned the gold to his family HUF which shows that Seksaria was able to tide over the crisis and was soon back in the saddle.

Seksaria's industrial, trading and speculative activities were now giving him huge returns. A flipside was constant attention from the income-tax department even over routine matters. Puranmal recalled an incident in which Seksaria challenged the income-tax officer to take him to jail. He had cleared all his *tijoris* (safes). He told the income-tax officers, 'Look, mine is a rented office. If you want, take all the chairs, tables, everything . . . take this *gadda* if you want.'

[62]Anderson, Benedict, 1991. *Imagined Communities.* London: Verso.

Seksaria's wealth, however, remained firmly in the crosshairs of the income-tax authorities. Seksaria presumably believed that rather than paying taxes to the British government it would be far more expedient to donate money to charitable causes. This is borne out by the fact that he founded large charities during his life, including creating charitable trusts totalling Rs. 1.25 crore—an extremely large sum for that time. Even the tax department at one point commented, 'While on the one hand, members of this community (Marwaris) may be credited with the desire to keep their undisclosed income beyond the possibility of detection as far as possible, they are equally known for their anxiety to make the best use of their money that the circumstances may permit.'

It is well known that before Independence and until the Benami Abolition Act, 1988 was passed by Parliament, businessmen traded and held assets in the name of other trusted persons for various reasons, including circumventing the draconian laws of the time. As a result, British tax authorities were continuously targeting business houses. Seksaria was not an exception and also conducted significant business on trust. During the early 1940s, Seksaria was continuously at loggerheads with the tax authorities. A settlement of his tax returns for the years 1936-37, 1937-38, 1938-39 and 1940-41 resulted into an assessment of his income at Rs. 1.42 crore on which additional taxes of Rs. 52 lakh were paid.

How did Seksaria's wealth compare with his peers? Nandkumar recalls, 'It is said, after Govindramji's demise, his contemporaries would remark that the wealth his widow has under her lock and key itself constituted a fortune. It was also said that he ranked amongst the top Indian Business houses pre-Independence.'

Interestingly even during the 1930s, Seksaria used various tax planning strategies to mitigate his taxes. He channelled his income from various sources through entities located in Indore and Jaipur which were outside the ambit of income-tax laws in British India. As Puranmal Jiwarajka observes, 'It is without doubt that, but for his tax woes, Govindramji's business growth would have been substantially higher.' Prafulbhai Hirji adds, 'In spite of the tax problems he faced, it is said that he was at his zenith during the Second World War.'

Nationalist sentiment actually favoured avoiding British-imposed tax. This led Seksaria to give large amounts of money on trust to several people and invest in businesses which were on other peoples' names. Upon his death, several of these trusted associates betrayed him. This resulted in a considerable fortune, estimated in crores, being written off: real estate, advances to trusted aides and several businesses.

Chapter Twelve

The Anatomy of Risk

In order to set Seksaria's achievements in a historical context, it is important to analyse risk. Today it is taken for granted that risk is reduced through diversification. Without diversification, there is only risk with no benefits. This approach is of course ahistorical. It does not take into account the fact that diversification itself was only made possible in recent years by globalisation and decolonisation. The creation of multiple global markets was contingent to dismantling systems of financial monopoly. Seksaria displayed remarkable foresight, far ahead of his contemporaries, to use diversification from trading to industry, and then deploy forward integration, to mitigate risk.

Risk is, thus, the central theme in the story of Seksaria. It requires a different explanation though from the one offered by his competitors on Wall Street. They called him cold and manipulative—a plunger. This term is both ironic and untrue. A plunger is a derogatory term for Wall Street traders, the 'good old, bad old days' of the era before the New Deal when men could risk large amounts of capital on a single trade without stops or exit strategies, *plunging* in with very little investment of their own. This kind of risk-taking has often been treated as an unhealthy and self-destructive addiction.

The opposite of a plunger, in today's world, is one who diversifies his investment portfolio, deriving long-term profits from many different trades and accumulating profits in excess of losses by a consistent margin. To call Seksaria a plunger in the 1930s, as Wall Streeters frequently did, overlooks the farsighted manner in which he de-risked his business empire by diversifying assets across India's industrial manufacturing sectors. Colonial India did not offer a climate for Indian entrepreneurs in which diversification through industry was an easy option, much less a strategic option for risk-reduction. How did Seksaria acquire the self-confidence to invest and diversify across industries under such circumstances?

There are two explanations. One, Seksaria was in the throes of an unhealthy addiction to speculation, unable to control himself. Beholden to no one, Seksaria invested his surplus funds from speculation like no other industrialist of the period, throwing himself into newly emerging industries in India during the 1930s without paying heed to inherent risks and immune to clear monopolies still enjoyed by the British. He saw clearly, and before most others, opportunities thrown up by failing markets in the West, in particular cotton markets, and by economic recession across parts of Europe and North America.

The other, more sober hypothesis, and one which is less reliant on the imperial prejudice of commentators on the American stock market in the 1930s, is that Seksaria had attained a very high level of confidence in his own financial ability to merge speculation and industry in ways where one complemented the other. Speculation not only enabled Seksaria to invest in industry, it enabled him to diversify broadly across industries at a time when this was virtually unheard of in the colonial world. Conventional wisdom would have regarded it as risky rather than risk-averse, which in fact it was.

Speculation gave Seksaria a level of capital, security and confidence in the markets. It allowed him to dive head first, without restraint, into wholly novel areas of investment in India. The inherent risks would have finished (and did finish) other industrialists. Seksaria emerged unscathed even in the aftermath of a number of reverses. His approach was contrarian. But it was predicated on a shrewd calculation of risk and reward. Success was a direct result not only of Seksaria's former years as a young maverick speculator but of his ongoing career as a mature, experienced trader in global commodities. Few players felt equipped to navigate these choppy waters with the same measure of assurance.

What else did Seksaria count on to ensure risk-proof capital guarantees for his investments in the post-Depression era—an era of brewing military conflict, flux and uncertainty across the world's financial markets? Seksaria's self-belief derived from his historical experience in trading, his ability to commandeer multiple commodity markets, and most significantly, his location in Bombay. This might have seemed to many at the time as a constraint given the conditions imposed by British rule. Nevertheless, the unregulated markets of Bombay had their advantages compared with the regulated markets in London and New York in the 1930s. Bombay too sat on a convenient time zone between New York and Tokyo, both key commodities markets.

Does it matter that Seksaria ventured into manufacturing largely through acquisitions to expand his industrial empire? It matters because such levels of sectoral diversification following unprecedented success in speculation was unique in the 1930s. Diversification across these two financial domains involved calibrated risk. And risk was the leitmotif of Seksaria's extraordinary life and work.

The geopolitical climate though the first half of the twentieth century was changing in ways that encouraged homegrown Indian businessmen. Aditya Mukherjee has shown that with the outbreak of the First World War, which 'marked a watershed in British tariff policy', opportunities gradually arose that had not existed under nineteenth-century colonial rule: an export surplus for India, declining British competitiveness in the face of other industrialised economies, and the growth of a powerful lobby in the form of an indigenous Indian business class. The Second World War laid bare these contradictions at the heart of the British Empire. Indian businessmen were quick to seize advantage of conditions that were ripe for launching 'a process of rapid industrialisation.'[63]

However, industrialisation was not the sugar pill the national movement had hoped it would be. In place of the spirit of optimism that should have characterised the last phase of British rule (1939-1947), a cynical spirit prevailed. This was because, as Mukherjee wrote, 'of the use made by the colonial government of the instruments of state policy, whether monetary or fiscal or any other, to buttress imperial interests at the cost of India.'

The Second World War, which was seen as an opportunity for rapid economic development, turned out to be yet another occasion when Indian interests were subordinated to those of British imperialism.[64] Yet during this period of subordination and financial cynicism, Seksaria built a sizeable industrial empire. He had little regard for the inevitable risks that diversification might hold for someone in his position. In colonial India especially, it might even have been considered foolhardy. Bold contrarianism thus, lay alongside calibrated risk, at the heart of Seksaria's success.

Diversification among traders and businessmen in Asia was rare. Imperial nations wielded ideological and material power; their financial models were presented internationally as templates. Anything deviating from those models was seen as atavistic and unworthy. Trade monopolies, using the strong arm of states and armies, sought to subjugate seemingly chaotic jurisdictions that characterised territories of the colonial world.

---

[63]Aditya Mukherjee, *Imperialism,* pp 176-177.

[64]Mukherjee, p 299.

India was not yet a country during Seksaria's entire career. It was 'becoming national', to use Geoff Eley's well-worn phrase.[65] Becoming a nation-state meant that India should be heavily involved in a convoluted process of negotiations and compromises leading up to the final deal with the British government. And though the country was, during this period, edging towards a settlement, it was derailed at every step by a heavy-handed colonial and regulatory structure. That structure had secured British control of economic development in India and favoured British interests at the expense of India's.

To diversify across industries in such a context was hardly plausible for an Indian businessman like Seksaria who did not speak English and who had never left his home country. Yet Seksaria did just that and ploughed his profits into philanthropy.

The life of a man exists in a complex landscape in which business ethics, family values, artistic aesthetics, and culture combine to produce a habitus uniquely equipped to trade, to speculate, to invest, and to diversify across financial ventures.[66] Seksaria's business ethics were intertwined with his cultural milieu. The community's deeply ingrained historical approach to doing business revolves around the organisation of trade through informal but well established regional power networks. It is an approach that was and still is a natural vocation for many Marwari businessmen.

The religious and ethnic sub-castes that made up the diverse

[65]Geoff Eley is an author and the Karl Pohrt Distinguished University professor of Contemporary History at University of Michigan.

[66]*Aditya Vikram Birla. A Biography,* Viking (Penguin Books) 1997, p 24. The concept of 'habitus' is the idea that an individual's development, mentality, attitudes, mannerisms, decision-making practices, habits, and skills and resources are shaped by their particular socio-cultural milieu: that is their social status, family mores, religious and ethnic group identity, education, occupational opportunities, etc. See for example Pierre Bourdieu, *The Logic of Practice*, Polity Press, 1990.

body of Rajputana trading communities worked together with their own association which in 1903 referred to itself as 'the Parliament of the Marwari *jati*.'[67] This was a powerful economic and (later) political lobby working in tandem with Marwari *Swadeshi* nationalists such as Anandilal Podar and Jamnalal Bajaj in the 1930s.

Marwaris were seen by the British as inward-looking for their seeming resistance to English as the dominant language of business and their rejection of British cultural values and attitudes to education. Marwari families favoured values based on honour and business ethics as well as close-knit community ties and trust. However, Marwaris were not a community out of touch with the realities of modern, twentieth-century capitalism. In the west, the spirit of corporatism—the organisation of professions and industries into corporations based on collectively shared interests was only a set of theoretical projects that had not yet taken off. It did so only in the 1920s. Yet in late nineteenth-century India, Marwaris, perhaps more than any other Indian community, developed and practised a model of community organisation that was wholly modern. It radically reshaped traditional definitions of community. Marwari families were organised across traditional religious and caste lines on the basis of an entrepreneurial trading identity that transcended regional cliques and affiliations.

Marwaris were able to 'subordinate various intra-class (or caste) conflicts in order to arrive at a common class position', fulfilling the criteria set out by author Aditya Mukherjee for a mature Indian business class that could become a strong basis of Indian nationalism even though late nineteenth-century India was still only a 'nation in the making.'[68] As historians of the period like Stanley A. Kochanek have pointed out, Marwari

---

[67]*Chinese and Indian Business: Historical Antecedents*, Brill Press, Netherlands, 2009, p 91, Kudaisya M. Medha and Ng. Chin-Keong, eds.

[68]Aditya Mukherjee, *Imperialism, Nationalism and the Making of the Indian Capitalist Class 1920-1947*, Sage 2002, p 19.

businessmen were among 'the first to speak out for purely Indian economic interests and to attack British economic policy in India.' This was 'very closely allied with the (Indian National) Congress movement.'[69]

More than simply a tale of individual success, Seksaria's career also offers us a window to an important historical moment that served as an unparalleled opportunity for Seksaria's business operations. The first thirty-five years of the twentieth century were a moment of transformation in international financial markets and regulation. Seksaria absorbed the significance of the shift of economic and political power towards Asia. And yet, during his lifetime, while the contours of a new world order were discernible, it was less certain how long the transformation would take. Seksaria spent his entire life as a British subject in India. It is a matter of speculation what additional success he would have enjoyed had he not died in 1946 at 58, while contemporaries such as G.D. Birla multiplied their wealth for several decades after Independence.

Prof. Dwijendra Tripathi began his career in 1954. One of India's most respected business historians, Prof. Tripathi lives in a compact bungalow in Ahmedabad. Speaking softly but in strong, distinct tones, Professor Tripathi places Seksaria's success in the context of colonial India: 'By the 1900s, the British were moving from free trade in the Empire to protectionism and discrimination. It was tough for Indians to set up industries in India. The Tatas were exceptions. Marwari families moved from speculation and trading to industry—jute, cotton, sugar, oil. The possibility of raising money in the stock market did not exist before the 1940s. So most industrialists sourced investment into their manufacturing plants from trading profits. Apart from being a speculator, trader and industrialist, Govindram Seksaria was

[69]Stanley A. Kochanek, *Business and Politics in India*, University of California Press, 1974, p 142.

a great philanthropist and educationist, especially with regard to women's education.'

Professor Tripathi adds reflectively: 'Marwaris in the freedom movement took the middle path. They supported the freedom struggle with donations, not so much by agitation. The Tatas stayed largely aloof. The Godrejs were the big donors among the Parsis. Seksaria was a big donor too.'

Hidden in the minutiae of Seksaria's work and life lies a key insight: he was a precursor to the international trader and hedge fund manager – a figure of increasing fascination to contemporary scholars of India's business history. While today's international trader is an elite member of global capital and finance, in the 1930s Seksaria was an unlikely pioneer. Financial commentators struggled to make sense of his ability to read markets across national boundaries and time zones. It suggests that he was operating at a high level of competence and knowledge before many in the United States or India had fully grasped the complex warp and woof of international commodities trading.

While Seksaria knew what financial uncertainty and loss entailed from the time the markets went against him in his early days of trading, his triumphs far outstripped his financial failures. It was acumen and a measure of luck, in his trading on the Bombay and New York Cotton Exchanges that made his fortune and enhanced his influence.

Seksaria's textile, sugar and oil mills expanded rapidly through the 1930s and 1940s. He had begun to fund a hospital, promote a bank and set up educational institutions. Philanthropy engaged him deeply. All this renders him a significant figure in India's business history. The manner in which Seksaria earned global recognition points to an important turning point in India's relationship with the world. Many Indian businessmen would follow in his footsteps, making strategic choices by setting up or acquiring global assets after Independence. Seksaria's trading decisions internationally, especially in cotton, underline how he assessed risk and pursued opportunities provided by international commodities and security markets that were regulated unevenly by national bodies.

Seksaria was regarded as an extraordinarily successful individual in this second phase of his life. This is underscored by the international attention he received from the late 1930s to well after his death. He was admitted to the New York Cotton Exchange at a time when Indian members on global exchanges were rare. Seksaria's gift for identifying opportunities within India's nascent industrialisation in the 1930s is clearly a remarkable quality. One long-term business associate in the United States, Orvis Brothers, who worked with Seksaria for several years up until his death, recalled his 'initiative in establishing a cotton extraction and crushing plant' and his 'prominent place in the cotton business.'

In a letter to an associate written in 1968, over twenty years after Seksaria's death, Rudolph G. Wetter of Orvis Brothers and Co. wrote (somewhat emotionally for the mores of the time): 'The memory of this really great merchant and industrialist is still vivid in my mind.'[70]

The formal tributes paid to Seksaria as a successful Indian industrialist, both during his lifetime and posthumously, demonstrated international recognition of India as an independent sovereign nation-in-the-making. Such tributes acknowledged a radically changed global environment that characterised the 1930s and 1940s: the growth of industrial nationalism across Asia which prioritised indigenous manufacturing—homespun cotton and khadi, for example. It was, thus, as much as an industrialist as a speculator that Seksaria was recognised and will be remembered.

What then explains the difference in attitudes towards 'Seksaria, the speculator' and 'Seksaria, the industrialist'? One

[70]Letter from Rudolph G. Wetter of New York (Orvis Brothers and Co) to Mr. Ratanlal C. Dalal (Cincinnati, Ohio), dated 27th October, 1968. Family archives.

reason is that commentators during Seksaria's own lifetime, and chroniclers subsequently, have all insisted on compartmentalising his life into two phases: the speculation phase followed by the industrial phase. Seksaria's industrial career was intricately linked to his laser-like focus on trading and speculation throughout his career. Even when he was at the apex of his industry-acquisition phase in the 1930s and 1940s, Seksaria never stopped trading and speculating across a swathe of commodities and securities.

Seksaria's real talent lay in seizing opportunities during times of global restructuring and military crises. For someone of his background, it was natural to vigorously explore new opportunities in Indian industry over the years leading up to, and after, the First World War. Like other Indian businessmen, Seksaria was well positioned to leverage profits made from the country's commodities trade between 1920 and 1930, the decade during which Seksaria was building his cotton trading empire.[71]

Seksaria's most productive period was during an era of imperial dismemberment: formerly large and powerful empires, such as the Ottomans were in disarray. The geopolitical stability of Europe and the Middle East was endangered. Britain and other world powers saw in the collapse of the Ottoman Empire an opportunity. But even British hegemony was no longer guaranteed. Anti-imperialism breathed life into diverse social causes. All of them invested in having a voice in the new state, India, that would inevitably replace British colonial rule. At the onset of the Second World War, Seksaria, now 50, had lost heavily in trading but recovered quickly. During the war years his group prospered. The early and mid-1940s were his finest moments.

It was not lost on Seksaria that Indian nationalism and the rise of the Khilafat movement in the immediate aftermath of the First World War would further undermine British control across the Indian subcontinent. The two World Wars, coupled

[71]Rajat Roy, ed, *Entrepreneurship and Industry in India 1800-1917*, Oxford University Press, 1992, p 234.

with the tectonic shift in the balance of global economic power, had taught Seksaria three lessons:

One, powerful industries such as Britain's cotton manufacturing sector were not stable, and therefore the foundation of the British economic empire was not stable either.

Two, new nations can gain economic power and global influence by strengthening their ethno-cultural identities and building a powerful industrial base.

Three, war creates business opportunities in both manufacturing and trading.

Sven Beckert has renamed mercantile capitalism 'war capitalism' because he sees the development of trade as heavily reliant upon military expansion. Through integration of labour, resources, markets, raw materials and capital, new markets were being created. Revolution, war and economic boom-bust cycles were the signposts signalling where, and when, to invest. Knowledge then, as now, was a potent tool. Manufacturing techniques in the 1920s and 1930s were rudimentary. Establishment costs were not high. Land was cheap. What remained to be proved was that profits from manufacturing could be as substantial as those from trade, commerce and moneylending.[72]

Despite his lack of education, Seksaria had a sharp memory and a systematic method of recording trades. The moment he did a trade he would inform his accountants to make a note of it. He could nevertheless recall from memory, without referring to notes, the exact date and details of each trade. Seksaria believed in brokers. He used to say to his associates: 'If any broker comes, give him business, because they are the people who give us information.'

Abhay Singh Bharkatiya recalls his father telling him: 'Once Seth Govindramji asked my father to stock large quantities of cotton in the Khandesh area and ensure that cotton shipments are

---

[72]*Empire of Cotton. A New History of Global Capitalism*, Sven Beckert, Random House, 2014, xvi.

not made to Bombay. Chandan Singhji was able to ensure that cotton was not loaded onto the railway wagons, and as a priority food grains were transported instead through rail to Bombay. With cotton supplies not arriving at Bombay, the market was starved of cotton and prices began to rise. Govindramji thus benefited on his holdings. While food grain supplies increased.'

Seksaria understood the value of information. Prafulbhai Hirji says, 'Govindramji's network of informers was very strong. Once when some high denomination notes were going to be cancelled he got the information the previous day after bank closing hours. He was able to fill gunny bags with currency and deposit them in the bank.'

Information, allied with intuition, was to prove Seksaria's greatest asset.

Chapter Thirteen

WEALTH FOR CHARITY

Seksaria's charitable and philanthropic work gathered pace every year. He had displayed an early interest in philanthropy. On 22nd February, 1927, when still just 38 years old, the Baldeodas Gordhandas Charity Trust was formed, which set up a girls' school in Nawalgarh, it presaged his future philanthropic undertakings, especially in education.

Seksaria donated money to set up several educational institutions and other organizations. In July 1940, at the request of Mahatma Gandhi and Jamnalal Bajaj, Seksaria donated a substantial sum for three colleges to be set up at Wardha, Nagpur and Jabalpur. The college in Wardha is called Govindram Seksaria College of Commerce and was the first of its kind in the Central Provinces and Berar. The college was inaugurated by Sardar Vallabhbhai Patel. Soon after on 9th August, 1945, Gandhi inaugurated Hindi-medium teaching of commerce in the college. The college in Nagpur is called Govindram Seksaria College of Commerce and Economics (1945) and the other in Jabalpur is called Govindram Seksaria College of Commerce and Economics (1946). These colleges are presently run by Shiksha Mandal,

Wardha, under the leadership of the Bajaj family. Seksaria was the president of Shiksha Mandal from September 1944 until his death in 1946. Subsequently, his younger brother Makhanlal Seksaria succeeded him as the president until 1951.

According to retired Justice Padma Bhushan Chandrashekar S. Dharmadhikari, 'Govindramji Seksaria was an exemplary visionary in the field of education. He started the commerce college in Wardha with a view to offer a place of learning not just to young people of the Marwari community, but also to all the youth who could benefit from this education. You would be surprised to know that people like Viren Shah (who became the governor of Bengal) had also come to study in this college. Another outstanding feature of the college was that during summer, its students would go to train as interns in the firms of various Marwaris so that they could better understand the practical aspects of business. A similar college was then started in Jabalpur too. Thus Govindramji made a tremendous contribution to the study of Commerce in India.'

'The second thing you may have realised is that Govindramji never did business in charity. In today's day and age, people do business in charity. What this means is that businesses do charity because they save on tax. This is where Govindramji differed. His faith and belief in Jamnalalji is also a fact that shouldn't be overlooked. A lot of credit for Jamnalalji's efforts and contributions in the field of education should be given to Govindramji. Their love and affection for each other was such that the two colleges in Jabalpur and Nagpur were also named for Govindramji by Jamnalalji. Govindramji could engender respect and affection in many such people, and this was one of his strengths.'

'Another noteworthy aspect was that Govindramji never wanted to be at the forefront of these activities. He never chased fame. He never published any advertisement about his altruistic ventures. One of the reasons he chose Wardha as the location for his college was his interest and involvement in Gandhiji's cotton to khadi movement. By then the manufacturing process of making cotton to *khadi* and then into cloth was prevalent and Govindramji was deeply interested in this industry. And of course, he also chose Wardha because of his friend Jamnalalji.'

'These are the two things about Govindramji's life that I find very important. He had a lot of industrial ventures, of course, but even in his work and his business, he had the heart for charity. Today also people do charity, but want a concession in tax because of it. Moreover, they want to gain recognition because of their social work and because of this recognition expand their business. This was something that Govindramji didn't believe in and this separated him from his contemporaries. These are the few things that I hold in really high regard and believe that when such a person does charity, it transforms it from mere alms to a virtue (*dan se punya dan*).'

A lot is said about Seksaria's lack of knowledge of English and the fact that he never travelled abroad.[73] While these facts are significant, they are rarely linked to his business strategies and nationalist sympathies. Seksaria never had the opportunity to study English. This explains his keenness to invest in educational institutes from his profits in business. Seksaria's lack of English language skills and unwillingness to leave his country are important elements in his 'genetic jigsaw'. Clearly Marwaris were not afraid of travel under difficult conditions. As the ex-governor of Assam, Shri Prakasa, observed, Marwaris were prepared to travel through difficult terrain within India, crossing hills to remote places and enduring harsh living conditions (one family to a room). Travelling on foot, by camel, and even by boat was common. Commercial routes were unsafe due to frequent ambushes and looting, which helped these vulnerable migrant groups develop a sense of close kinship.

While Marwaris were open to opportunities, they were a deeply conservative clan with a powerful sense of obligation

[73]Obituary of Seksaria in *The Indian Textile Journal*.

to family and kin. They were also involved in nourishing a moderate political critique of British colonial authority. This was especially true in the commercial centres of Calcutta and Bombay where an economic basis for a new Indian industrialist class was emerging. A significant part of the process by which Marwaris nurtured not only their identity but also their informal networks was through a conscious rejection of the English language. This was accompanied by a fervent rejection of British cultural norms in business, education and government, over the significant years of Indian nation-building in the first half of the twentieth century.

Seksaria resisted English because he did not need to speak the language of colonial overlords. His communities and networks guaranteed him the resources, capital and knowledge to command a domestic and international empire from within the nation and within his own language, assisted by trusted English-speaking aides and confidants where necessary. Such a rejectionist approach, contextualised in terms of a Marwari cultural milieu, also explains Seksaria's personal attitude to philanthropy and to the various national causes that he supported financially with extraordinary generosity.

And yet Seksaria would have readily embraced English had he been able to study it in his youth. He held no dogmas: if English helped, he would have deployed it. Seksaria's resistance to the English-speaking world could only have encouraged him to value a nation being built independently of British colonial rule: new India. This mindset encouraged him later in life, after building his business empire, to pour the profits into philanthropic causes. These included setting up various charitable trusts in his name, generous donations to medical institutions such as Bombay Hospital, the establishment of specialised medical centres (Govindram Seksaria Cardiology Ward), as well as centres for the specific medical needs of women and girls (Smt. Basantibai Govindram Seksaria Maternity Ward, occupying an entire floor in Bombay Hospital).

The donors first wanted to call it Marwari Hospital but Sardar

Vallabhbhai Patel said it should be called Bombay Hospital. The Birlas were the leading figures in the whole project. The largest donation was by the Shri Puranmal Singhania family. Newspaper reports of the time carried photos of Singhania, R.D. Birla and Seksaria. The three principal families—Birlas, Singhanias and Seksarias were the leading donors of Bombay Hospital. A newspaper article in Bharat-Bombay Hospital Trust Supplement dated 22nd May, 1950 carried a photograph of Govindram Seksaria under the caption 'princely donor'.

Bombay Hospital was inaugurated by Deputy Prime Minister Sardar Vallabhbhai Patel in 1950, four years after Seksaria's death. And yet it was Seksaria's contribution of Rs. 7.50 lakh, along with a similar donation by the Birlas and a larger one by the Singhanias, that allowed the construction to proceed.

Seksaria's charitable activities grew significantly in the 1940s. At the instance of Bhulabhai Desai, Seksaria donated Rs. 50,000 to Manav Sena Sangh Bal Niketan, Sion for constructing a building. In March 1941, the Gordhandas Govindram Charity Trust was founded with a corpus of Rs. 11 lakh. A year later, the Vidya Bhavan Govindram Seksaria Teachers Training College was established in Udaipur.

On 14th October, 1942, Maharana Bhupal Singh inaugurated the building of Fateh Singh School in Udaipur for which Seksaria donated Rs. 1 lakh. In July 1945, Seksaria formed the Shri Govindram Seksaria Charity Trust in Indore with a corpus of Rs. 50 lakh, which was later increased to Rs. 1 crore. The Trust went on to promote the Govindram Seksaria Institute of Technology and Science at Indore.

At the time of Seksaria's death there was a plan to donate Rs. 5 lakh to start an engineering college in Greater Bombay which did not materialise. However, the opportunity for that arose when Prime Minister Jawaharlal Nehru expressed a desire to a group of leading industrialists of Indore for establishing of a technical institute in Indore. Kudilal responded by donating an amount (Rs. 5 lakh) for starting the institution in the name of his late father. When established, it was known as Shri Govindram Seksaria Kala Bhavan. The institute's 50th year celebration was held on 22nd December, 2002, which is now called SGSITS Day. The President of India, Dr. A.P.J. Abdul Kalam, was the chief guest.

Grandson Nandkumar reminisces, 'The annual day slogan of the institute is *Seksaria Maharaj ki jai!* I didn't know of it until I was a guest at the Golden Jubilee function where I heard it for the first time. It filled me with a sense of great pride that his legacy continues to live on in people's hearts even today, seventy years after he has gone.'

A month before he passed away in May 1946, Seksaria donated Rs. 1.5 lakh towards Govindram Seksaria Science College at Sawantwadi which later shifted its campus to Belgaum and is now called GSISC. It falls under the aegis of South Konkan Education Society (SKES). Rani Parwati Devi, the late Rajmata of Sawantwadi, was its first patron-member. B.G. Kher, chief minister of Bombay, inaugurated the college in June 1948.

The philanthropic cause closest to Seksaria's heart was girls' education. Seksaria's commitment to female education was unprecedented in an era where women had few rights and fewer opportunities. Seksaria Saraswati Kanya Pathshala was set up in Nawalgarh in 1927 when Seksaria was just 38 years old and had not yet hit the big time. 'Wherever Govindramji had a factory, schools and Inter colleges were set up in those places,' says Nandkumar.

For Seksaria, education was a tool for people, especially women, to develop the skills and resources they needed to be economically and politically independent. Older, wealthier European nations were adjusting themselves to the radical idea that education should include women and girls. It was difficult at the time for women in the West to attend schools or acquire a university degree. They even struggled to be allowed to vote through universal suffrage. In this pre-feminist era, Seksaria showed extraordinary vision. He believed educating girls would make them more effective contributors to nation building and economic growth. This demonstrated an unusually evolved and progressive mind.

At the beginning of the twentieth century, female literacy in India was below one per cent in every province of British India and in nearly every Princely state.[74] In *History of Modern India, 1707 AD to 2000 AD,* Radhey Shyam Chaurasia writes: 'In 1873, there were only 1,640 girls' schools of all kinds in British India. In 1883, the Education Commission finally began to focus on the backward condition of female education. Government grants for girls' schools became more liberal. In 1901-02, there were twelve female colleges: six in the United Provinces, three in Bengal, and three in Madras.'

Gauri Srivastava in *Women's Higher Education in the 19th Century* writes in similar vein: 'Early in the 1900s, compulsory education for boys under 12 and girls under seven was introduced, boosting literacy rates, especially those of girls. As a result of this Act, the total number of girls studying in (all-girls) schools in 1911-12 was 28,045. The total number of girls studying in these, as well as co-ed schools, was 60,541.'

Missionary and state efforts aside, Chaurasia credits social and religious associations such as the Brahmo Samaj and Arya Samaj for encouraging girls' education. Despite this, the state of female education remained dismal during British rule.

One of the first educational institutes Seksaria set up, a girls' school in Nawalgarh, was the first ever school for girls in his ancestral village. Called the Seksaria Saraswati Kanya Pathshala when it opened, it is now the Shri Seksaria Saraswati Girls Senior Secondary School. 'Girl's education was very important to my grandfather,' says grandson Rajkumar Seksaria. 'When he first made money, he started the first girls' school in Nawalgarh.'

Rajkumar sheds light on another facet of Seksaria's

---

[74]*India: Development and Participation* by Jean Dreze, Amartya Sen.

philanthropy. 'Any poor person who would go to him for money would get it without question. But what I'll narrate now shows the sensitive way in which he would give this money. Suppose someone came asking for some money for his daughter's wedding. Govindramji would listen and then say, "Go meet my employee, Murlidhar Shah, at my Kalbadevi office tomorrow morning at 10:30. He will give you the money." From the cotton bales he had speculated with, he would tell his manager to keep, say, 100 aside for the man, so the next day, the manager would tell him, "Sethji has done some speculation of some bales, and that 100 bales have been kept in your name. So the profit from these 100 bales is yours." What was in his mind, I think, is that the person who has asked for money shouldn't feel he has taken a loan or charity to marry off his daughter. He had gotten money by way of speculation profit. Govindramji would do this to preserve the person's self-respect and dignity.'

Nandkumar Seksaria adds, 'Charity was the hallmark of his career. He was always giving to others in so many different ways. Since the time he started making money he was donating to charity. And the real charity in that period was done by him in the field of education.'

There was pragmatism and patriotism as well to Seksaria's philanthropy—education in national languages of instruction other than English would build confidence in the concept of self-rule. Had not the British constantly reiterated throughout the era of the Raj that Indians were incapable of self-determination? Education was, in Seksaria's philanthropic mission, an important part of asserting intellectual independence.

The schools, hospitals and other charitable institutions Seksaria established or funded were organised on the basis of local knowledge, addressing local issues and employing local professionals. The vision was of a new Indian middle-class able to rise to the challenges of remaking a nation.

Chapter Fourteen

SPARTAN LIFE, ROYAL COMPANY

Seksaria's relationships with the royalty of Rajputana and the Holkars of Indore were abiding. Arvind Singh Mewar of Udaipur reflects on Seksaria's contribution to Mewar, as told to Dr. D.K. Taknet: 'Marwaris are popular around the globe for their entrepreneurship and philanthropy. Seth Govindram Seksaria was the leading personality among Marwaris. When most of the Marwaris were taking interest only in the Shekhawati area, the philanthropic activities of Seth Govindram Seksaria were based throughout Rajputana. It is mentioned in our old records that he took interest in socio-economic development of Mewar. Therefore, Maharana Bhupal Singh granted him the right of wearing gold on 10th February, 1943. He was authorized to wear gold while attending the durbar of Udaipur. In those days, it was deemed a big honour to Seth Govindram Seksaria for his services for Mewar.'

Archival records[75] confirm that on 27th February, 1940 Seksaria visited the court of Maharana Bhupal Singhji of Mewar. He was given permission to wear gold and also offered a chair to sit on

---

[75]Maharana Mewar Reserve Institute, Archives, Udaipur.

in the durbar. In return, Seksaria gave the Maharana Nazarana. On 14th October, 1942, the Maharana Sahib inaugurated the building of Maharana Fateh Singh School in Udaipur for which Seksaria had donated one lakh rupees. Maharana Sahib also attended the inauguration ceremony of the Bank of Rajasthan on 8th May, 1943.

Seksaria was 42 when his only son Kudilal was born in 1930. 'He was married at the age of 12 into the Nemani family,' says Nandkumar. They were stalwarts in the cotton trade. 'Shivnarayanji Nemani, my mother's great-grandfather, was reputed to be one of the earliest Marwari crorepatis of Bombay. To honour him, his bust was installed in the East India Cotton Exchange building at Kalbadevi. Apart from many others Sir Hukumchand, who was very friendly with Govindramji, came for the wedding. Sir Hukumchand was another big businessman, a big speculator who made huge amounts of money. He used to live and dress like a Maharaja with all the *sarpech* and *kanthas* etc. I have heard that he had a gold-plated car. He lived in Indore and had set up large industries: Hukumchand Jute Mills, Hukumchand Insurance and several textile mills. Govindramji, after he took over Indore Malwa Mills, used to go once a year to Indore. That was the time when His Highness, Sir Hukumchand and Govindramji used to meet.'

Mangtulal fondly remembers, 'It is customary for the *dulha* (bridegroom) to go to his in-law's house for breakfast the day after the wedding. This ceremony is called *kuvar kaleva* (the bridegroom is invited for breakfast). Those younger than the groom would also go. Kudilalji was called to go for the ceremony, while Govindramji and my father were at the gate. Govindramji told me to go as well. I went a little further and then stopped, so Govindramji called me and said, "Why are you not going, why have you stopped?" I was a year older than Kudilal. I said, "I am elder to him so I will not go!" While I was trying to resist, Govindramji ordered me to go, turned to my father and said, "See what a *gaddha* (donkey) he is, even when I've told him to go with Kudilal, he won't go!"'

A month before son Kudilal's marriage in 1942, Seksaria went to Jaipur to invite Maharaja Man Singhji for the wedding. He stayed there for a few days but could not meet the Maharaja since he was busy. After some time, the Maharaja came to Bombay. He stayed at the Taj Mahal Hotel. Most of the big seths of Rajasthan went to pay their respects to him. However, Seksaria did not go. The Maharaja inquired about this. It was brought to his notice that Seksaria had come to meet him in Jaipur but was not given an appointment. The Maharaja promptly invited Govindram to the Taj.

Mangtulal recounts the background to the incident: 'Kudilalji's marriage in 1942 had been a grand affair. There was a *howdah* made of silver. Many people came. Silver coins were distributed. There was cinema, theatre, *goth* (general dinners). The Nemanis (Kudilalji's in-laws) stayed at Govindramji's new haveli during the wedding. A big gate was made. Musicians sat at the gate and played the *shehnai*. All functions took place at the haveli. Films were shown for 21 days. The family had opened up the haveli to all the guests. The films were shown in the *nohra* (property) next to the haveli. They screened three movies every day. Now before Kudilalji's wedding, Govindramji had gone to Jaipur. He was there for 3-4 days. He wanted to invite Maharaja Man Singhji for the wedding. The person he took with him, Mahadev, was known to the Maharaja. Mahadev used to talk often to the Maharaja and he told Govindramji that he would be able to get the Maharaja to come to Nawalgarh for Kudilalji's wedding. Unfortunately, the Maharaja's secretary had all appointments booked for those days in which Govindramji was in Jaipur. After waiting for a few days Govindramji decided to leave.'

'So anyway, the wedding got over. After some time, the Maharaja of Jaipur came to Bombay and stayed at the Taj hotel. All the big *seths* of Rajasthan used to pay him a visit. They would ask him whether Govindramji had come to meet him and arouse his curiosity about Govindramji. His Highness lamented to Mahadev that Govindramji had never met him. Mahadev said, "When he had come to Jaipur just to meet you, you did not meet him for several days." So the Maharaja rang for his secretary and asked him what had happened. The secretary said, "But sir, you were very busy." HH then expressed a desire to meet Govindramji. Mahadev was in a dilemma. He told HH he cannot promise that. HH said if he does not come I will go to meet him. Mahadev arranged for Govindramji to speak on phone with HH who expressed a desire to meet him. Govindramji said he would present himself. Mahadev had however cautioned HH Jaipur that if Govindramji were to invite him to the Cotton Exchange to do *satta* (speculation), he should politely refuse because Govindramji's luck is so strong that the Maharaja is likely to lose money.'

'Govindramji went to the Taj Mahal Hotel in Bombay where one of the lifts was reserved for HH's expected guest. He was accompanied by Mahadev. But when Govindramji reached the Taj and said he had come to meet the Maharaja, the liftman must have been expecting to see some finely dressed, rich man who was important enough to have a lift reserved for him. What he saw instead was Govindramji in his khadi! The liftman said, "The lift has been reserved for Govindram Seksaria." Even when Govindramji said that he *was* that man, the liftman wouldn't budge. So Govindramji said, "Come on, Mahadev, we'll take the stairs!" Govindramji paid his respects to HH and HH in turn explained the misunderstanding that took place in Jaipur. After the pleasantries were exchanged Govindramji said *"Maharaj, kabhie cotton exchange padhariye."* (Please visit the cotton exchange sometime). HH politely declined.'

By now philanthropy had come to occupy a central role in Seksaria's life. Great-grandson Harsh Seksaria recalls having heard a particularly touching episode: 'When my grandfather Kudilalji was getting married, Thakur Bagh Singhji a good friend of Kanhaiyalalji, had come to the wedding. He was sitting in Kanhaiyalalji's haveli and said to him, "Govindramji's son is getting married. So, I request you to ask Govindramji to donate two lakh rupees for my village, for a water tank because there is no water available. Water is being fetched from miles away. Every morning, villagers spend two hours getting water for washing, cooking, and drinking. If you get two lakh rupees from Govindramji, we can begin work on a *taalaab*. I don't have much command over Govindramji, but I have command over you, and you are his cousin brother. Will you make this request for me?"'

'Kanhaiyalalji asked, "How much will it cost?" Thakur Bagh Singhji replied that the project required four lakh rupees in total. Kanhaiyalalji agreed to speak with Govindramji. He said, "My brother will definitely say yes. He is in a very good mood right now." So Kanhaiyalalji took Baghsinghji to Govindramji's haveli, where he was warmly welcomed. In fact, he asked Kanhaiyalalji, "*Bhaisabhji, Baghsinghji ko hum koo maan kare?*" (How can we honour and welcome him?) That was the perfect opportunity for Kanhaiyalalji, so he said, "*Baghsinghji ke gaon me pani nahi hai.* There is no water in Baghsinghji's village, so you can make a tank." "*Banaa denge!*" Govindramji said, without hesitation. When Baghsinghji heard this, he said, "Sethji, you have agreed, but you don't know how much money we require!" Govindramji replied, "Whatever it takes! Here, where cattle, women and children have to walk miles a day for water, what better use of my money can there be? This is the most pleasing day."

'The tank took three years to complete. It was done in 1945, a year before Govindramji's death and it cost four lakh rupees which was a large sum in those days.'

Rajkumar Seksaria says, 'My grandfather had many interests: from textiles to sugar to oil to mining, and so on. He even ventured into the film industry. Along with Maneklal Chunilal, he took over majority shareholding of Bombay Talkies in his lifetime and subsequently we acquired the negative rights of some of the popular films produced by Bombay Talkies. Bombay Talkies was started by Devika Rani, who later sold her shares to Shiraz Ali Hakim. Shiraz Ali Hakim borrowed money from Govindramji as he had an ambition to make Hollywood in Bollywood. Shiraz Ali Hakim started Famous Studios at Mahalaxmi[76] in Bombay with an air-conditioned shooting stage as well as air-conditioned offices for film producers. He also had Famous Cine Laboratory in Tardeo from the early 1940s. So he thought, with the studio and the cine laboratory, he would have the entire film operations under his roof. He took off, but landed himself in a financial mess and had to start borrowing money.'

'Unfortunately, when Shiraz Ali realised that things had got out of hand and he wouldn't be able to pay up the debts, he fled to Pakistan.[77] All his properties got attached by the court.'

Rajkumar is animated as he describes the unfolding saga: 'In 1947 we got the laboratory. When we first got Famous Cine Laboratory, Tardeo it was handed over to Prahladraiji, our associate, to manage. In 1948, our managers thought it would be good to have a recording studio as well. We opened Famous Recording Studio in 1948, affiliated to the Famous Cine Lab, with Minoo Katrak as the recordist. I understand that the first film which recorded its music there was *Mela* with music director Naushad. That was a superhit film and later all the top music directors started coming to the studio. I'm talking particularly about Famous Recording Studio at Tardeo and its history.

'More than 13,000 songs have been recorded here. The three most famous music director *jodis* – Shankar-Jaikishan, Kalyanji-Anandji, Laxmikant-Pyarelal – all three started their careers at Famous Recording Studio and have recorded maximum songs at our studios. Lataji (Mangeshkar), who is the greatest singer today, has gone on record to say: "*Mere* career *ke sabse prasidh gaane inn chaar dewariyon mein* record *hue hain.*"

Raj Kapoor, the only name which spelt music from his first film till he died, recorded all his songs at our recording studio.

---

[76]Famous Studios was started in 1946, according to their website and according to the MCA listing.

[77]Shiraz Ali Hakim left for Pakistan in 1947 shortly after Partition, according to multiple web sources.

Even his black and white films—from *Aag*, his first film, to *Jis Desh Mein Ganga Behti Hai* were all processed at our laboratory.'

'The greatest epic of our film industry, *Mughal-e-Azam*, was also processed at our laboratory. In the same way, Dev Anand, Filmistan, Rajshri, L.V. Prasad, to name a few, all the top producers were getting their films processed at our laboratory. So we thought, we have a recording studio and we have a laboratory, why not start a film/motion picture studio as well? That's when we started Modern Studio at Andheri. We bought it. We started with one shooting stage, and then we bought some land nearby and developed three more stages. Stage number 4 was the largest stage in Bombay. There were outdoor shooting facilities like waterfalls, tennis courts, etc.'

In contrast to his otherwise simple tastes, Govindram Seksaria had developed a fondness for horse racing. He was a member of the Royal Western India Turf Club (RWITC) and regularly attended important race days. He was a big punter but always bet on place rather than outright win. The strategy brought him large winnings. 'He used to go to Poona in the racing season at the Turf club,' says Nandkumar. 'During the period of the late 1930s to early 1940s, around six lakh rupees was his earnings through horse racing. One of his associates was a person named Rao Saheb Parker. He was a horse owner. Govindramji did not own horses directly. It is said that he had an interest in Parker's horses. His visits to the race course also enabled him to meet important people there. He met a wide spectrum of people.' 'All evidence, however, suggests he was not otherwise social. But he used to love betting and hence went to the race course. Govindramji used to never play a horse on win, always on place. Whether 1st, 2nd, 3rd—whereby some winnings would come.'

Apart from his love for horse racing, Seksaria lived a spartan life. He did not believe in leisure except in the pleasure hard work gave him. He and his wife never visited the cinema or the theatre or ever hosted or attended a party. Seksaria was not overtly religious either. Though he would do his Mala Jaap once a day at home, he would not accompany his wife when she visited temples or set off on *teerth yatras* to Rameshwar. Seksaria would tell his wife, 'I have planted enough trees in the garden, now it's up to those after me to pluck and enjoy their fruits.'

Seksaria looked upon the entire family, brothers and sisters, nephews and nieces, as a single unit. He would spend a considerable amount of his time looking after not only immediate family but distant relatives and friends as well.

Rajkumar Seksaria was eight months old when Seksaria passed away. When Rajkumar (his first grandson) was born and people went to give Seksaria the good tidings he said, 'I already have grandchildren. You go and tell Basantibai the news, she will be happy to hear it and will reward you.'

Seksaria was against wasteful expenditure. Once Kudilal went to Tansa Lake without informing Seksaria. When he came to know, he was very angry and sat and waited in the hall for Kudilal to return. When he did, Seksaria said: 'What did you go so far for? What was there to look at? Water? There is plenty right in front of you, why are you burning petrol to see water?' Basantibai tried to reason with Seksaria, saying Kudilal was just a young boy, but the father refused to listen.

Seksaria meanwhile continued his philanthropic work. According to Puranmal, Govindram had no pride in his wealth and was always ready to help the downtrodden. He would go to them first and offer money. Generosity was a deeply ingrained trait. Despite his wealth, Seksaria dressed simply at work and at home, and showed no opulence.

Seksaria faced terrible personal tragedies in the last few years of his life. The first was the death of his close associate Nagarmal Dharnidharka and five of his family members in a train accident on 15th May, 1940. The family was on their way to Nawalgarh in the Frontier Mail for Nagarmal's elder son's marriage. Only three children of the family survived. The injured were taken to a hospital in Dohad[78]. Seksaria flew down to Dohad to offer his help.[79] Four years later, in 1944, the deaths of his brother Ramnath and his nephew Kesardeo was another blow and affected him greatly. These tragedies seem to have impacted his health which deteriorated steadily.

Nagarmal Dharnidharka passed away in 1940. He was both a key aide of Seksaria and related to him. Dharnidharka was moreover a partner in Messrs Govindram Seksaria. According to Mangtulal Seksaria, 'Nagarmalji was the only one who could act upon Govindramji's trades if Govindramji was unavailable for any reason.'

Seksaria's nephew Kesardeo died at the age of 21. He was looking after Indore Malwa Mills at the time. 'Kesardeo was considered a very competent young man before death snatched him away,' says an associate. 'Seksaria needed an able person to look after Indore Malwa Mills. Kesardeo's death thus, left a big void. So deep was Seksaria's affection for family that these deaths shattered his health. He never fully recovered again.'

Seksaria suffered a heart attack in 1945. Despite this he refused to stop working. His wife requested the family physician, Dr. Vakil, to explain to him that he needed to rest. Govindram refused, telling the doctor that his heart was like steel and if he could not speculate he would die anyway.

Nephew Mangtulal Seksaria recalls that when Govindram had a heart attack, he was confined to the house all the time but continued *satta* from home. '*Chachi* (Basantibai) sent a message to my father, Kanhaiyalalji, because Govindramji used to listen to him. She asked Kanhaiyalalji to tell Govindramji, "*Bahut paise kama liya,* stop using the telephone!" But Kanhaiyalalji said, "He is not going to listen." Govindramji had suffered a serious heart attack and Dr. Vakil said to him, "Sethji, you've had a heart attack, now stop using the telephone!" Even *chachi* came and said, "Doctor, make him understand that for a month or two

---

[78]*The Times of India* archive, 16th May, 1940.

[79]Dharnidharka family blogs.

he should stop using the telephone." Govindramji said, "Doctor *sahib,* she does not understand. *Mere saamne sone ke eet padi hui hai* – there are bricks of gold in front of me. If I don't pick them up, someone else will. I can't stop *satta.* I can see the gold bricks waiting for me. If I die, it will be on the telephone doing *satta.* If I stop *satta,* I shall die." He refused to listen. He said, "Doctor, if I don't speculate I won't get sleep. This is a sleeping dose for me." So Dr. Vakil told my *chachi,* "*Sethaniji,* he will not listen to me, let him do his *satta.*" Again, Govindramji said, "Doctor, you go. Nothing is going to happen to me. My heart is like steel".'

Pushpabai says that Seksaria had been unwell for three years before he passed away. He suffered his first heart attack in August 1939 when he was 50. He had his second heart attack in late 1944. Seksaria's health deteriorated because of his long and relentless working hours and frugal diet. He would be awake till late at night to follow the US markets which were open at that time. This led to erratic and deprived sleep. However, Seksaria continued to work, ignoring the pleas of family members to take it easy.

Late on the night of 21st May, 1946, Seksaria's heart began to give way. He died peacefully at 6.45 am on 22nd May, 1946. In his last few moments, he told his son, Kudilal, aged 16, to look after the family, continue his charities and that the businesses would be divided equally among his brothers.

Nandkumar Seksaria remembers his father Kudilal telling him what Govindram said to him: 'The night before he passed away, he called me and said, "Whoever has come into this world must eventually leave it. After my death, my business interest will be divided four ways. I am leaving you enough wealth, so please take good care of your two sisters and take care of my trusts. Now you take my blessings and go to sleep.'

Savitribai Nathani recalls emotionally: 'This is similar to what Govindramji Tauji's mother had told him before she passed away. Govindramji Tauji lived up to the promise he had made to his dying mother.'

Following Seksaria's death, according to the *Morning Standard* (22nd May, 1946), all city markets, including the stock exchange and the cotton, bullion and seeds markets, remained closed on 22nd May, 1946 as a mark of respect. Several commodities markets, including steel, did not trade for the next three days.

A month after Seksaria's death, *The Free Press Journal* in June 1946 published this tribute: 'Born at Nawalgarh in the Jaipur State on 19th October, 1888, Govindram Seksaria was marked by fate to face life at an early age. In 1903, a lad of fifteen, he accompanied his father Gordhandasji to Bombay. Early marriages were the custom in those days and little Govindram had already been married. It is difficult to visualise what shape his career would have taken had the family been left to carry on its normal existence. Death, however, bought down its fell hand, and Govindram lost his father as well as his mother at an interval of but a few days. An orphaned lad, Govindram was faced with the problem of looking after not only himself and his little wife, but a large family of young ones, including his brothers Bholaramji, Ramnathji and Makhanlalji, and three sisters. He was also faced with the task of running a none-too-prosperous business.'

'Govindramji hardly made a public appearance. He sought no titles, no place on public committees, no headlines. His political leanings were sound, but he kept scrupulously away from politics. He would play the host to public men, would finance public causes, but would not make a public statement or a public appearance. For a man of his position, entry into public life would have been easy. To be sure, the temptations must have been great. But it was sound instinct that led him to reject those temptations. His gifts were of a different stamp, though it is true that he could make his own environment.'

'And so, at the comparatively early age of 58, this giant

among men reached the end of a hard-fought worldly life. Apart from the host of friends and businessmen who had learned to rely on him, he leaves behind him a large family to mourn his untimely end - his widow, who has been a faithful and inspiring companion in life, son Kudilalji and grandson Rajkumar, brothers Bholaramji and Makhanlalji, two daughters, both happily married and nephews including Subhkaranji, Radheshyamji and Jagdishprasadji.'

On 24th May, 1946 two days after Seksaria's death, the East India Cotton Association Ltd. held a meeting of its board of directors. The recorded minutes (circular dated 22nd May, 1946) stated: 'Re: Closing of the forward market and the association's rooms at the Cotton Green building on that day as a mark of respect to the memory of the late Seth Govindram Gordhandas Seksaria. The chairman made a deeply-felt reference to the sad death of Seth Govindram Gordhandas Seksaria and said that he had earned for himself a very high reputation not only in the cotton market of Bombay but also in other forward markets in India and abroad. He said that a letter be addressed to the firm as well as to his family on behalf of the board conveying their sincere condolences in the great loss sustained by them by his death. The resolution was passed unanimously, all members standing.'

The flamboyant editor of *Blitz*, Russi Karanjia, paid his own fulsome tribute on June 1946: 'To begin with, I consider it my duty to pay my humble respects to the sacred memory of the late Mr. Govindram Seksaria, who dominated practically each and every important market in the city for over a decade. The present generation at least will remember him for his shrewd judgement and market operations, which extended from shares, cotton and bullion to iron and charcoal. Some years at least will perhaps elapse before we get an opportunity to have another Govindram.'

Other tributes poured in. The Bombay Municipal Corporation (BMC) met on Monday, after an interval of nearly a month, and adjourned 'as a mark of respect to the memory of Mr. Govindram Seksaria, a prominent businessman, who died on 22nd May. Mr. Ramnath A. Podar moved a resolution placing on record the sense of sorrow of the Corporation at the death of Mr. Seksaria. Mr. Podar eulogised the services rendered to the country by Mr. Seksaria as a great businessman and as a public-spirited citizen. He said that Mr. Seksaria had made munificent donations towards social and educational causes. Mr. S.K. Patil seconded and Mr. Jamnadas Dwarkadas supported the condolence resolution which was carried.'

According to newspaper reports in *Janmabhoomi* and *Mumbai Samachar* dated 22nd and 23rd May, 1946 respectively, 'Seksaria's body was wrapped in the national flag and national flags were flying around his *arthi* (pier). *Mumbai Samachar* reported on 24th May, 1946 that the total amount donated by Seksaria in his lifetime would add up to almost Rs. 2 crore, a very large sum in the mid-1940s.' The report also confirmed large donations made by Seksaria to the Congress. Such large charitable donations at the time, compared to his Indian and global contemporaries, set Seksaria apart.

Not all the tributes were entirely complimentary. According to *Capital* (26th May, 1946), 'Rarely does the death of a leading operator cause so much depression in the market as happened in the raw cotton market during the week when the leading long passed away. The July contract dropped precipitately to Rs. 435/-, almost on par with the maturing May contract on Friday last. This was mainly due to the uncertainty about the fate of the enormously large commitments of the deceased operator who had hitherto provided the main inspiration for uptrend in cotton prices. The decline is a measure both at the size of its operations and lack of the intricate justification for the appreciation in prices which has been seen lately.'

'The precise total of the bales which the bulls have had to take delivery of the May contract is not known but it is surmised that it may be well over the two lakh mark. So large a commitment undertaken by a few speculators cannot but be without its reaction on the other futures contracts. In a way, there, it is surprising that the July contract was marked down to Rs. 440/-.'

'A few thousand bales changed hands on Friday and Saturday last at favourable prices to the mills, who have great reason to welcome the decline in raw cotton prices. It is a well-known fact that the sharp upswing in raw cotton prices in the last three months had cut into their profit margin so much that many spinning sections have had to close down. With the exit of the chief of the bulls, it is expected that the market will be relatively free of speculative ramps and that any rise in prices will be more orderly than in the past and justified by facts rather than fancies. Post his death, the bull syndicate disintegrated.'

The funeral procession left Seksaria's Marine Drive home at 10.15 am on 22nd May, 1946. Bombay's elite accompanied the cortege: K.S. Firodia, Speaker of Bombay Legislative Assembly, Hon. G.S. Motilal, R.D. Birla, Ramdeo Anandilal Podar, Rai Bahadur Govindlal, Shivlal Motilal, Sardar Chandulal Shah, Kantilal Ishwarlal, Anandilal Hemraj, Swarupchand Prithviraj Roongta, Bajranglal Birla, Ramji Juvalka, Ganeshnarayan Onkarmal, Surajmal Nemani, Umadutt Nemani and many other businessmen and friends.

Janmabhoomi reported: 'The procession wound itself from Marine Drive to Churchgate, Queens Road, Dhobi Talao, Kalbadevi and Princess Street to Zaveri Bazar. Flowers and money were thrown, *shankhnaado* was done to give felicitation to one of the wealthiest persons in Mumbai. *Harkaho, Harkaho, Raam Naam Satya Hai* was chanted. There was a big gathering of people all along the route to see the procession. Many people were joining the procession en route. Trams, buses and cars were stopped for some time. The body was decorated with flowers, the tri-colour national flag was flying on the four corners of the *arthi* and silver coins were thrown.'

Puranmal Jiwarajka recalls: 'I was the person throwing silver coins during the procession. I threw thousands of them. My hands started to pain.'

'When the procession passed through Zaveri Bazar, it arrived at the East India Cotton Exchange and stopped for a few minutes. Each and every window, balcony and terrace, all the shops on every street were full of people. Some were bowing to the body by lying on the road (*sashtang danvat pranam*). From Kalbadevi via Dadi Sheth Agiary Lane and Girgaum, the procession reached the crematorium. At 12:15 pm, Govindram Seksaria's body was lit with fire on sandal wood.'

An era had ended. The legacy though, would endure.

APPENDIX 1

THE JAMNALAL BAJAJ DIARIES:

Selected excerpts from Jamnalal Bajaj's diary show the close relationship between Bajaj and Seksaria during the freedom movement:

JUHU, BOMBAY

21st JANUARY, 1937

Met Shri Piramalji Chaturbhujji, Vishwambhar Maheshwari, Surajmal Nemani, Juharmalji, Shrinarayanji Roongta, Govindramji Seksaria for Bombay election fund, satisfactory conduct.

JUHU, BOMBAY

30th JUNE, 1940

Had lunch at the residence of Shri Rameshwardas Birla and exchanged views.

Shri Govindramji Seksaria has agreed to donate Rs. 1,25,000/- for Govindram Seksaria Commerce College at Wardha to Marwari Shikshan Mandal on the condition that no objections are raised by the Nagpur University. Shri Rameshwardas Birla was also together then. All the points were also clarified in front of Sardar Vallabhbhai and Bhulabhai. He will send a cheque tomorrow.

1st JULY, 1940

Spoke to Rameshwardasji Birla over the phone regarding the assistance of Shri Govindramji.

Was to go to meet Shri Govindramji Seksaria. The terms and conditions of Shri Govindramji's offers were prepared. Shri Govindramji came to Shri Rameshwardas Birla's house and he signed the terms and gave a cheque of Rs. 1,25,000/-. Rs. 25,000/- would be paid later. It was a satisfactory outcome.

NEW DELHI

2nd JULY, 1940

Shri Jamnalal Bajaj got down at New Delhi station and proceeded to Birla House and reported to Bapu, who was staying in the upper floor room, that Govindramji Seksaria has given Rs. 1.25 lakh for the college and has further assured of Rs. 25,000/-. He was happy to hear that, Shri Ghanshyamdasji was surprised and also happy.

14th JULY, 1940

On 14th July, 1940 Govindram Seksaria Commerce College was inaugurated by Shri Sardar Vallabhbhai Patel in the presence of many friends.

22nd July, 1940 Shri Jamnalalji Bajaj had a prolonged discussion about the Govindram Seksaria Commerce College, Wardha, with Shri Govindramji and Shri Makhanlalji Seksaria.

BOMBAY-PUNE

24th JULY, 1940

Stayed at Shri Govindram Seksaria's bungalow in Koregaon Park.

BOMBAY-PUNE

28th JULY, 1940

Discussed with Govindramji regarding Wardha Commerce College.

2nd AUGUST, 1940

Met Shri Govindramji and Shri Makhanlalji and discussed about the G.S. Commerce College from 8.45 to 10.45 a.m. and came to the conclusion that the said college should be at Wardha. Even if the college is required to be made in Nagpur for the benefit of the people, then they have no objection. He gave the names of Shri Makhanlal Seksaria and Shri Sitaram Poddar for the College Management Committee.

NAWALGARH - SIKAR

22nd SEPTEMBER, 1940

In Nawalgarh, among other institutions, visited Govindramji Seksaria's Kanya Pathshala. Also met Govindramji's brother.

22nd SEPTEMBER, 1940

Discussed with Govindramji & Makhanlalji about Shiksha Mandal, Vanasthali and their differences with Prithviraj Juharmal. In the afternoon, Govindramji, Juharmalji, Brijlal, Ramdeo and others came to the office and for more than two hours tried to understand all their problems.

NAGPUR JAIL

12th APRIL, 1941

Keshavdeoji Nevatia, Kamalnayan, Rukmani (from Nimach) came to meet, went back soon. They talked about the marriage at Ramkishan Dalmia's and also narrated Govindram Seksaria's income tax disputes.

BOMBAY-JUHU

11th OCTOBER, 1941

Met Shri Govindram Seksaria and had brief discussion.

24th JANUARY, 1942

Tried calling Govindramji Seksaria to talk about G.S. College, could not speak to him.

GOPURA

31st JANUARY, 1942

Govindramji Seksaria came from Bombay.

Appendix 2

Mukul Goyal, a Jaipur-based architect, speaks eloquently about how havelis, including the Seksaria Haveli define the unique character and culture of the Marwari heartland.

The Indian haveli is similar to the English 'bungalow' or the French 'casa'—a large house in which the rich and famous live. Rajasthan has its share of havelis sprinkled over the state, mingling amongst large forts and palaces. These were the homes of businessmen, nobles, and other courtiers who were not allowed to build bigger homes than the next door palace. Therefore, it was the city palace that governed the size of the havelis around it.

But there was one region in Rajasthan which was devoid of palaces and forts. This belt was the Shekhawati region with Nawalgarh at its centre. Due to the absence of palaces, the size and status of the havelis went unnoticed by the royals. The region's harsh climatic conditions and its proximity to the desert provided it natural security from an attacking army. Thus Shekhawati enjoyed a peaceful existence.

Despite harsh living conditions, peace allowed this belt to convert itself into a popular trade route to Afghanistan and the surrounding areas. Many traders started relocating their business along the source and destinations of this trade route. As trading increased, so did wealth and power. Many of the Shekhawati traders shifted to Calcutta, the seat of power during British rule, and also to Bombay, which was the main shipping port to Europe. It was not long before even the famous tea gardens of Assam had the Marwari traders settling there.

As the traders and their families shifted to all the major business hubs in India, they longed for their native land. Their roots were deeply planted in their home towns where they sent back money to their extended family and friends. Visiting home needed a purpose and a statement. Havelis provided the statement: it announced the prosperity which each trader had achieved. The schools, colleges and temples which they built for charity provided the purpose for returning to their home town twice or thrice a year. These havelis exhibited their own language and stature.

A typical haveli would have a high plinth with an outer verandah, then the pouli, or lobby, which further opened into the chowk or courtyard. This courtyard would be surrounded by a colonnade which led to various rooms. Somewhere in this series of rooms there would be gateways leading to other chowks and stairs. There were no formal bedrooms, drawing rooms or dining rooms. They all evolved with the family structure and living habits around the courtyard.

The size of the haveli would depend on the prosperity of the owner and the size of his family. A small trader had a single chowk (courtyard) haveli. A medium-level trader had a two chowk Haveli. A more prosperous businessman would build three, four and five chowk havelis.

Seksaria built a magnificent haveli in his home town. This was a huge two-storied, five chowk haveli. It is the largest haveli of the Shekhawati region. Placed on a three-meter-high plinth in front of a large forecourt, the grand structure can be discerned from the front gates. With gardens on both sides, the approach is by a carved ramp. This leads to a colonnaded outer verandah and the main gates. A notable feature of the front garden is the original cast iron lamp posts imported from England. They are single piece hollowed structures and have stood the test of time.

The haveli has no opening on the outer face except for the gates in the external courtyard and small shuttered windows all around the facade to allow fresh air. The introvert nature of the building speaks volumes of the purdah system that existed in the social milieu of the first half of the 1900s. Once inside, the haveli consists of four small and one large courtyard, with well ventilated rooms around it. The covered area is around 47,000 sq ft and has a total of 66 rooms and units placed in the two floors. There is a basement level as well, which houses all the stores and service rooms.

The Tudor-like arches of the colonnade have often made historians wonder about its origins because the British had brought along with them the Roman style of architecture, known as the Renaissance style, in which the shape of the arch was a true half circle. The Rajput arches were nothing but variants of the four-pointed arch of the Mughal period. The only explanation for the typical Shekhawati arch would be that they wanted to be different. It is highly unlikely that Tudor/Persian artisans travelled from Eastern Europe to create these arches.

The Seksaria haveli has a multitude of carved sandstone arches placed on stone pillars along all five courtyards on both floors. There are glimpses of Renaissance architecture with some round columns holding up the roof in the middle family spaces on the first floor. It is interesting to see the drainage systems which allow rainwater to flow freely out of the haveli through a series of drains around each chowk. The electrical wiring came late in those days and therefore has been done externally. Not many havelis in those days had the luxury of electricity.

The high ceilings are typical of Rajasthani buildings, as they create cooler rooms through natural flow of hot air which rises allowing cooler air to enter through the lower windows. In Seksaria's time a special grass mat would be hung on the windows and sprinkled with water in intervals to keep it wet. This way air entering the rooms would be naturally cooled keeping out the heat. The thick lime roofs added to the insulation to the sun. All doors and windows were placed in exact opposite sides to one another to allow cross ventilation.

Though materials were limited in those days, lime mortar was used as a finishing material. These lime works are so smooth that not even an ant can climb on the surface. The intricate paintings on the ceilings and colourful borders which decorate the walls are another riveting feature. The carved wooden doors and main gates can scarcely be replicated by carpenters of today. The main gate is further clad in a metal sheet which ensured the wood inside was protected from external elements. The imposing haveli is a tribute to the talent of the artisans and craftsmen who worked on various facets of the structure.

Govindram Seksaria built a magnificent haveli in his hometown of Nawalgarh. The two-storeyed, five chowk haveli is the largest haveli of the Shekhawati region

The grandeur of the structure can be discerned from the front gates

The haveli is placed on a three meter high plinth in front of a large forecourt with gardens on both sides. A notable feature of the front garden is the original cast iron lamp posts imported from England. They are single piece hollowed structures and have stood the test of time. The approach is by a carved ramp, which leads to a colonnaded outer verandah

The outer face of the haveli has small shuttered windows all around the façade to allow fresh air. The introvert nature of the building speaks volumes of the purdah system that existed in the social milieu of the early 1900's

The main gate of the haveli which leads to the central courtyard

Once inside, the haveli consists of one large courtyard and four small courtyards, with well ventilated rooms around it

The covered area is around 47,000 square feet and has a total of 66 rooms and units over two floors. There is a basement level as well, which houses all the stores and service rooms

The haveli has a multitude of carved sandstone arches placed on stone pillars along all five courtyards on both floors

The Tudor-like arches of the colonnade are slightly different from the Roman style of architecture, commonly known as the Renaissance style. The Shekhawati arch is more reminiscent of the four pointed arch of the Mughal period

There are glimpses of Renaissance architecture with some round columns holding up the roof in the middle of family spaces on the first floor

There was a drainage system which allowed rainwater to flow freely out of the haveli through a series of drains around each chowk

The high ceilings are typical of Rajasthani buildings, as they create cooler rooms through natural flow of hot air which rises allowing cooler air to enter through the lower windows

All doors and windows were placed in exact opposite sides to one another to allow cross ventilation

The intricate paintings on the ceilings and colorful borders which decorate the walls are another riveting feature. Though materials were limited in those days, lime mortar was used as a finishing material

The carved wooden doors and main gates can scarcely be replicated today. The gates are further clad in a metal sheet which ensured the wood inside was protected from external elements

The imposing haveli is a tribute to the talent of the artisans and craftsmen who worked on various facets of the structure

APPENDIX 3

Chronological list of Industrial and Business Undertakings which formed part of Govindram Seksaria Group in 1946:

1920s

Shree Krishna Rice and Oil Mills Ltd., Masaurhi, Bihar

1930s

Bharat Vanaspati Products Ltd., Pachora, Maharashtra
Bharat Vanaspati Products Ltd., Akola, Maharashtra
Govindram Brothers Pvt. Ltd., Bombay, Maharashtra
Indore Malwa Mills Ltd., Indore, Madhya Pradesh
Messrs Govindram Seksaria, Bombay, Maharashtra
Shree Mahalaxmi Oil Mills Ltd., Agra, Uttar Pradesh
Seksaria Sugar Mills Ltd., Babhnan, Uttar Pradesh
Seksaria Cotton Mills Ltd., Bombay, Maharashtra
Seksaria Oil Mills, Hyderabad, Sindh
Seksaria Biswan Sugar Factory Ltd., Biswan, Uttar Pradesh

1940-1946

Bank of Rajasthan Ltd., Udaipur, Rajasthan
Bombay Talkies, Bombay, Maharashtra

Bhavnagar Oil Mills Pvt. Ltd., Bhavnagar, Gujarat
Diamond Pictures Ltd., Indore, Madhya Pradesh
Jamuna Hosiery Mills Pvt. Ltd., Delhi
Mysore Art and Wood Works Ltd., Mysore, Karnataka
New Jack Printing Works Ltd., Bombay, Maharashtra
Premier Cotton Mills, Bombay, Maharashtra (was known as Seksaria Cotton Mill No. 2)
Shree Bijay Cotton Mills Ltd., Ajmer, Rajasthan
Seksaria Trading Co. Ltd., Delhi
Shree Mahadeo Cotton Mills Ltd., Bhilwara, Rajasthan
Sawantwadi Minerals and Trading Co. Ltd., Sawantwadi, Maharashtra
Seksaria Cotton Ginning and Pressing Factory, Mathura, Uttar Pradesh
Seksaria Pressing Company, Bhavnagar, Gujarat
The Estate Investment Company Pvt. Ltd., Bombay, Maharashtra

Govindram also had a partnership in the following concerns:

India United Mills Ltd., Bombay, Maharashtra
Anand Sugar Mills Ltd., Khalilabad, Uttar Pradesh

Pre-Independence Map of India showing locations of Industrial Units of Govidram Seksaria

APPENDIX 4

Chronological list of Education Institutions and Healthcare facilities which benefited from Govindram Seksaria's Philanthropy.

1920s

Seksaria Saraswati Kanya Pathshala, Nawalgarh, Rajasthan

1930s

Govindram Seksaria High School, Pachora, Maharashtra
Shree Nawalgarh Senior Secondary School, Nawalgarh, Rajasthan

1940–1946

Govindram Seksaria College of Commerce, Wardha, Maharashtra
Govindram Seksaria College of Commerce and Economics, Nagpur, Maharashtra
Govindram Seksaria College of Commerce and Economics, Jabalpur, Madhya Pradesh
Govindram Seksaria Teachers' Training College, Vidya Bhawan, Udaipur, Rajasthan

Seksaria School, Masaurhi, Bihar
Hindu Deendayal Sangh, Bombay, Maharashtra (now known as Shree Manav Seva Sangh)
Seksaria Kanya Pathshala High School, Gonda, Uttar Pradesh
Govindram Seksaria Science College, Savantwadi (later shifted to Belgaum, Karnataka)
Govindram Seksaria Science College, Khamgaon, Maharashtra
Govindram Seksaria Inter College, Basti, Uttar Pradesh
Seksaria School, Babhnan, Uttar Pradesh
Seksaria Theosophical Girls' College, Sitapur, Uttar Pradesh
Gordhandas Govindram Seksaria Ayurvedic College, Nawalgarh, Rajasthan
Seksaria Education Society, Bhilwara, Rajasthan
Govindram Seksaria High School, Bhilwara, Rajasthan
Seksaria School, Sawai Madhopur, Rajasthan
Free Kitchen and Dharamshala at Lakshman Jhula near Hardwar

Donations have been made to the following:

Bombay Hospital, Bombay, Maharashtra
Marwari Vidhyalaya High School, Bombay, Maharashtra
Marwari Commercial High School, Bombay, Maharashtra
Maharana Fateh High School, Udaipur, Rajasthan
Rajasthan Sevak Sangh
Willingdon Hospital, Udaipur, Rajasthan

Seth Govindram Seksaria also founded the following charitable trusts:

Baldeodas Gordhandas Charity Trust, 1927 - Rs. 1 Lakh
Gordhandas Govindram Charity Trust, 1941 - Rs. 11 Lakh
Gordhandas Govindram Family Charity Trust, 1941 - Rs. 11 Lakh
Shri Govindram Seksaria Charity Trust, 1945 - Rs. 1 Crore

These Trusts along with Shri Kudilal Govindram Seksaria Foundation (Established 1997) have promoted the following endeavours:

Govindram Seksaria Scouts Pavilion, Shivaji Park, Bombay, Maharashtra

Shree Govindram Seksaria Institute of Technology and Science, Indore, Madhya Pradesh

Shri Govindram Seksaria Girls Hostel, Indore

Cardiology Wing, M Y Hospital, Indore

Shri Manav Ashram, Vidyapeet, Jaipur

Govindram Seksaria Institute of Management and Research, Indore

Kudilal Govindram Seksaria Sarvodaya School, Rajasthani Sammelan Education Trust, Mumbai

Kudilal Govindram Seksaria English School, Rajasthani Sammelan Education Trust, Mumbai

Shri Govindram Seksaria Advanced Cataract Surgery Centre, Indore Eye Hospital, Indore

Shri Kudilal Govindram Seksaria Emergency Services Centre, LV Prasad Eye Institute, Hyderabad

Shri Govindram Seksaria Institute of Dacryology, LV Prasad Eye Institute, Hyderabad

Pre-Independence Map of India showing locations of Educational Institutions and Healthcare facilities which benefited from Govindram Seksaria's philanthropy

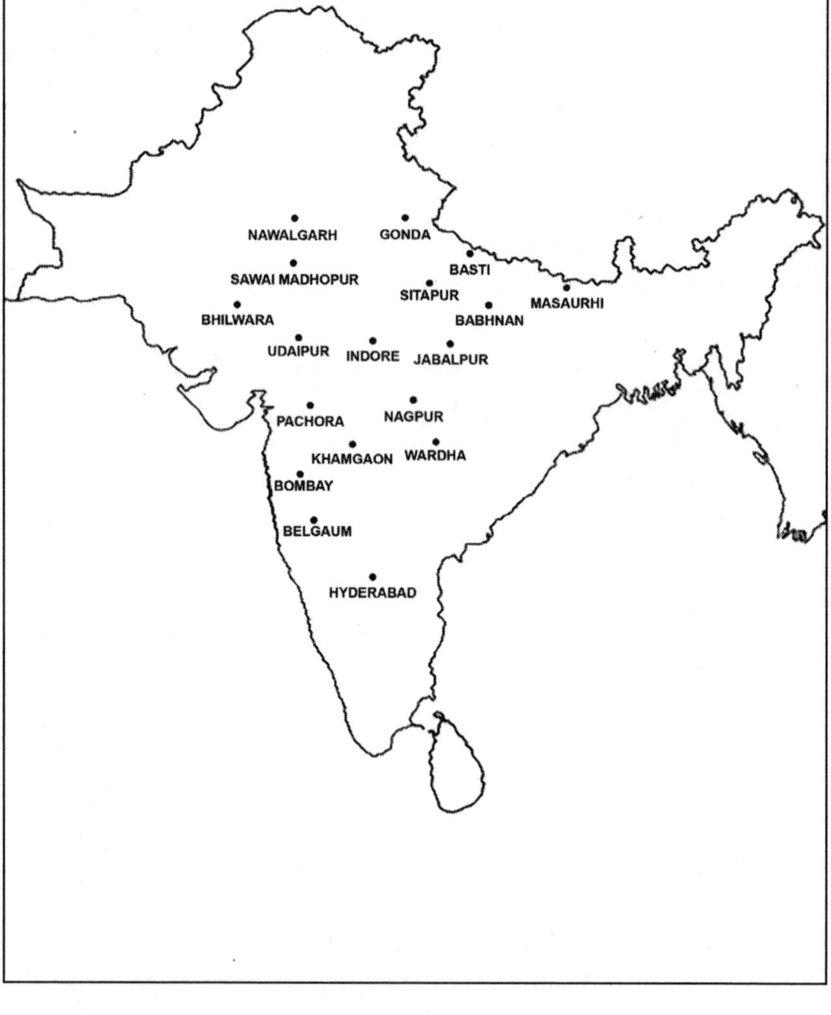

Bibliography

The History of Indian Business: A Complete Account of Trade Exchanges from 3000BC to the present date, by P.N. Agarwal; Vikas Publishing House Pvt. Ltd., India, 1978

The Origins Of Industrial Capitalism In India: Business Strategies And The Working Classes In Bombay, 1900-1940, by Rajnarayan Chandavarkar; Cambridge University Press, 1994

Problems and Prospects of Sugar Industry in India, by Rakesh Chandra Tyagi; Mittal Publications, 1995

Empire of Cotton A New History of Global Capitalism, by Sven Beckert; Allan Lane by Penguin Random House, 2014

A Centenary History of the Indian National Congress (1885-1985), general editor B.N. Pande, All India Congress Committee (I), 1985

Maharaja, by Diwan Jarmani Dass, Hindi Pocket Books Pvt. Ltd., 2008

Three Merchants of Bombay, by Lakshmi Subramanian; Allan Lane by Penguin Books India, 2012

Cities of Empire: The British Colonies and the Creation of the Urban World, by Tristram Hunt; Metropolitan Books, 2014

Premchand Roychand (1831-1906): His Life and Times, by Sharada Dwivedi; Eminence Designs Pvt. Ltd., 2006

Industrial Entrepreneurship of Shekhawati Marwaris, by Dr. D.K. Taknet; EDI Press, 1986

King Cotton: Camaraderie with Cohorts, by Madan Gaur; Press Publicity Syndicate of India, 1994

The Marwaris: From Traders to Industrialists, by Thomas A. Timberg; Vikas Publishing House Pvt. Ltd., 1978

The Indian Cotton Textile Industry, by M.P. Gandhi; The Book Company Limited, 1930 – 2013 reprint

Temples of Nawalgarh, by C.P. Bhatnagar

Indian Business and Nationalist Politics 1931-39: The Indigenous Capitalist Class and the Rise of the Congress Party, by Claude Markovits; Cambridge University Press (1985), First Paperback Edition, 2002

Business and Politics: Rising Nationalism and a Modernising Economy in Bombay, 1918-33, by A.D. Gordon; Manohar Publications, New Delhi, 1978

The Marwaris: From Jagat Seth to the Birlas, by Thomas Timberg; Penguin Books Limited, 2014

The Bombay Money Market, by H.T. Parekh; Oxford University Press, 1953

Saga of the Cotton Exchange, by Madhoo Pavaskar; Published for the Cotton Association of India, Second Edition, 2014

Cost of Marketing Cotton, by Madhoo Pavaskar; New Apollo Printing Works, 1970

Towards Development of Commodity Exchanges, by Madhoo Pavaskar; Allwyn Prints for the East India Cotton Association, 2002

Economics of Hedging, by Madhoo Pavaskar; Popular Prakashan Pvt. Ltd., 1976

Jaipur: Gem of India, Dr. D.K. Taknet; International Institute of Management Entrepreneurship, Jaipur

Business Houses in Western India: A Study In Entrepreneurial Response, 1850-1956, by Dwijendra Tripathi and Makrand Mehta; Jaya Books, 1990

India Industrialists Vol I, by Gita Piramal and Margeret Herdeck, Three Continents Press, First Edition, Second Printing, Revised, 1986

Congress Ka Itihaas, by Madhusudan Tripathi - Hindi; Radha Publication, 2007

A Hundred Years of Indian Cotton, by M.L. Dantwala; Orient Longmans for East India Cotton Association Ltd., Bombay, 1948

Marwadi Samaj, Dr. D.K. Taknet; International Institute of Management Entrepreneurship, 1990

Indian Cotton Annual, 2011-12, No. 92

The Portfolio Book of Great Indian Business Stories; Penguin Books India, 2015

Impediments to the Growth of Commodity Futures, by Madhoo Pavaskar

Private Investment in India 1900-1930, by A.K. Bagchi; Cambridge University Press, 1972

Studies in Economic Policy and Development of India, 1848-1939, by S.K. Sen; Progressive Publishers, 1972

Cotton Exchange Marches Ahead, Madhoo Pavaskar and Rama Pavaskar, Replica for East India Cotton Association, 2002

Marwari Heritage, by Dr. D.K. Taknet; International Institute of Management Entrepreneurship, Jaipur, 2016

Entrepreneurship and Industry in India, by Rajat Ray; OUP India, 1992

Cotton Production in India, by Henry W. Spielman; published by Office of Foreign Agricultural Relations, United States Dept. of Agriculture (1950)

B.M. Birla - A Great Visionary, by Dr. D.K. Taknet; Indus - An imprint of HarperCollins Publishers India, New Delhi, 1996

Desh Ke Itihaas Mein Marwadi Jati ka Sthaan, by Balchandra Modi; Raghunath Prasad Singhania, at New Rajasthan Press, Calcutta, 1996

Aditya Vikram Birla, A Biography, by Minhaz Merchant; Viking, Penguin Books India, 1997

Narendra Modi: A Political Biography, by Andy Marino; HarperCollins Publishers India, 2014

The New Clash of Civilizations: How the Contest Between America, China, India and Islam will Shape Our Century, by Minhaz Merchant; Rupa Publications Pvt. Ltd., 2013

Cotton Association of India Publications

National Cotton Board of India
Cotton - Miles to Go
Indian Cotton - Today and Tomorrow
Glimpses of World Cotton

Glossary of Terms

Anka and Fadak	:	speculation on the last digit of the price of cotton
Bahi	:	ledger
Bania	:	trader or merchant
Basa	:	a boarding house or lodging run by marwari traders
Bhabhi	:	brother's wife, sister-in-law
Bhaiji	:	brother
Chachi	:	aunt
Dharmashala	:	a charitable or religious rest house for travellers
Dhoti	:	a long loincloth worn by Hindu men in India
Gadda	:	mattress
Gaddi	:	the seat of business or a business office
Gumastas	:	a native Indian clerk or steward
Raam Naam Satya Hai	:	the name of Lord Rama is the truth. A chant while carrying a dead body to the crematorium
Howdah	:	a throne put on an elephant made of silver
Jagir	:	estate

Jati	: caste or sub caste
Jodis	: duo
Kada	: bracelet
Kamaris	: waist band
Kanthas	: jewelled necklace
Kartik and Asod	: name of months in a Hindu calendar year
Kothi	: mansion
Kurta	: a loose collarless shirt
Mojdi	: footwear
Muhurat Puja	: religious rites at an auspicious moment
Munims	: cashier
Pagdi	: a turban
Parta	: costing and production system
Pedhis	: a shop or office
Sahib	: a polite title or form of address for a man
Sarpech	: a turban ornament worn by Hindu and Muslim princes
Satoriya	: a speculator
Satta	: speculation, forward/futures trading
Seth	: a rich merchant or banker
Sethani	: wife of a Seth
Shankhnaado	: blowing of a conch shell during a ritual
Shehnai	: an Indian traditional trumpet
Shraddha	: a Hindu ritual performed for one's ancestors who have left their physical body
Swadeshi	: a policy of nationalist self-sufficiency in India
Swaraj	: self-government or independence for India
Taalaab	: lake
Tauji	: father's older brother
Teerth Yatras	: pilgrimage
Teji Mandi	: call and put options

Index